WITH STRINGS ATTACHED

WITH STRINGS ATTACHED;

Reminiscences and Reflections by

JOSEPH SZIGETI

With 15 half-tone illustrations

CASSELL & CO. LTD.

LONDON · TORONTO · MELBOURNE · SYDNEY

WELLINGTON

First published 1949

ML
HI8
S9 A3

Printed in Great Britain by
Wyman & Sons, Limited, London, Fakenham and Reading
F.449

INTRODUCTION

—————·{◊}·—————

I HAVE always been partial to James Agate's inclusion
of musicians among manual workers. Physical fatigue,
healthy sweating, loose attire, the musician shares with the
manual worker. This mimicking of the complete lumberjack
may conceivably be an almost studied reaction against the
type of long-haired, velvet-jacketed, pallid æsthete prevalent
in my childhood. As G. B. Shaw told me during our long
walk on the promenade deck of the *Empress of Britain*, "You
fiddlers no longer look the part. The only one who does look
the part is—Einstein! In my music-critic days, which were
the days of Joachim, Ysaÿe, Remenyi, Ole Bull, it was very
different. . . ."

The element of pose enters into both conceptions of the
artist, I suspect; but if one must choose between them, the
"manual worker" picture is the less insincere and therefore
the less objectionable.

I always used to think of writing as the antithesis of manual
work, as the antithesis of all active, toxin-eliminating occupations: writing, the least matter-bound of all pursuits. No
canvas, no oils, no chisel, no wet clay—just the Word, with no
residual debris left from the work that has gone into the
product. I should have known better.

The seven or eight pounds of assorted notes that I have just
finished tying up and that I am at last getting out of my sight
are a reminder of how wrong I was in setting the writer apart

(5)

as an unencumbered spirit. As my writing progressed, I became gratefully aware of the advantages of the real job of my life—playing music in public to the best of my ability. No material reminders, not even memories, now survive of the countless revisions, rephrasings, reworkings that eventually produced the more or less "mature" and so-called definitive versions of my various musical undertakings. Of my labours on the Beethoven Concerto, for example, which have accompanied me now for four decades, no residual clutter remains. Every rehearsal, every performance of that work was like a rewrite job for me; yet every new approach to it was a first— with no strings attached from earlier commitments and performances.

What clean, model-factory conditions for Agate's manual worker! How loth we all are to be faced with material proof of our former musical statements! One hears stories about some of the greatest musicians of our time who are roused to frenzy when they listen to one or another of their recent test-records, roused to the extent of stamping the inert platters of shellac in fury under their heels; while some of their older recordings may excite even greater horror in them.

So it is, too, with editorial annotations of musical classics with which the editing musician is particularly identified. This probably explains the reluctance of the great Chopin players, the great Bach players, the great Beethoven players, to being nailed down in print to their own performing practice. One of these, in discussing his edition of a composer with whom he is especially linked, said to me: "Oh, that no longer holds good. I've gone 'way beyond that. *That* was in 1912. . . ."

Even the composer himself sometimes does not want to be bound by former versions of a given work of his. I have before me two editions of a suite for violin and piano of (I believe) lasting importance, by a living master. One is dated 1925, the other 1934. There are such appreciable differences between the two versions that when I perform the work I take the liberty of amalgamating the two, using some parts from one, some from the other. But when I recently told the composer of this procedure of mine, he pretended with the most disarming innocence in the world to have forgotten all about the earlier edition—of barely twenty years ago!—disclaiming all knowledge of it until I confronted him with that earlier version, now out of print.

But though the performing artist can improve his performance, and the composer amend his earlier conception, the amateur writer has no such power. You start to write a book like the one I am attempting, and you are given only that one chance. You cannot, as you could in the case of a Mozart sonata, benefit by the lessons inherent in every rehearsal and performance and consider each a stepping-stone toward the goal you have set yourself. There is no room for easy-going trial and error.

But in the field of music we are never, in the long run, judged on the basis of one movement, one work, one recital. Every musical statement of ours fulfils two functions: It embraces to some extent (for better or worse) the immediate job of communicating music to the people in front of us, and it also becomes a unit in those many performances—spread over the years—on the basis of which our "rating" is computed. We know that this rating of a player's stature is the resultant of the innumerable reactions of innumerable persons to innumerable performances.

When we hear, say, Casals, and tell ourselves, "To-night he has given the full measure of himself," we are in fact applauding not only to-night's performance but all the fragments of his performing past that we have been fortunate enough to glean. Our enthusiasm is also coloured by much of what fellow-enthusiasts have passed on to us. And a third factor may be the cumulative effect of being constantly reminded of the influence of style-formers, like Casals, in the playing of younger and lesser players, disciples of theirs, whether actual pupils or not.

Conditioned as we performers are to statements that are not definitive, that can be endlessly modified, rephrased, it is the more laughable to me that in my amateur rashness I actually started jotting down these notes—in a language not my own—in a little leather-bound note-book—on pages five by seven inches—and in ink: believing that the process of writing a book was as simple as that. What colossal cheek! It is not that I did not know what writing involves. I had always enjoyed looking at facsimiles of the illegible manuscripts, the marked-up galley proofs of great writers; but somehow I had associated torment with the master, and ease with the novice.

The little black book presently gave way to professional-looking yellow second-sheets. Then the yellow were supplemented by unprofessional and just as serviceable pink sheets, and blue. Finally it was on the impersonal stationery of the *Super Chief*, the *Portland Rose*, the *Lark*, the *Twentieth Century*, and the *Commodore Vanderbilt* that I made my endless scribblings during endless tours.

Doctors' books, a card-wizard's autobiography, the highly coloured reminiscences of a circus virtuosa, the urbane memoirs of a British painter—these and many others passed through my hands at this time. More often than not they only added to my bewilderment. I could not but contrast with my own scrawlings their professional polish, their abundance of good stories, the self-assurance that spoke from them (there's an air of finality about the printed page anyway). The several alternatives I habitually write one above the other, the crossed-out sentences, the French and German and Hungarian jottings in the margin—these showed up my indecision and insecurity all too well and often came near to wrecking my writing *élan* completely. On the other hand, it would be ungrateful of me not to acknowledge the many benefits I derived from such browsing and reading.

None of these stimuli, however, was so potent in keeping me at the self-imposed job, and in preventing me from

throwing up the sponge, as was the unexpected find of a book
of delightfully frothy memoirs in a second-hand bookshop.
Or perhaps I should rather say that the tonic effect was
produced by the motto on the title page:

Mémoires de Mlle Flore
Artiste du Théâtre des Variétés

*"Pourquoi n'écrirais-je pas mes
Mémoires? Ma blanchisseuse écrit bien
les siens!"*

Paris, 1845

Indeed, Pourquoi pas?

ILLUSTRATIONS

————··ʒʒ✦ʒʒ··————

CHAPTER I

WHENEVER I seek to recall my earliest years in the small Carpathian town by the name of Mára-maros-Sziget—unpronounceable to any but a Hungarian—the picture that comes most readily is that of myself climbing up the perilously long legs of my six-foot-four uncle, the double-bass player, the better to kick his shins at regular intervals while he tussled with his younger and shorter fiddler-brother. Knowing the double-bass player uncle's propensities, I always assumed that it was he who had started the fight and—innocent that I was—took the side of the weaker, for no other reason than that he *was* the weaker!

In our little world the choice of instruments seems to have been dictated by expediency or by corporeal dimensions rather than by talent or æsthetic considerations. Thus the double bass was a natural for the uncle who was oftener called "the long 'un" than by his name. Incidentally, his height often let him in for exquisite torture, since our band of assorted uncles usually played under ceilings so low that he had to bend over double to bow his bass, and no pauses for rest were allowed at these "rustic weddings"; any unauthorized break in the din of fiddles, clarinets, and bass made the musicians the target for empty Schnapps bottles and glasses!

Another incident that comes back is one in which my role was both more passive and more pitiable. It happened while I was living with my grandparents in the Carpathians, my mother having died when I was still a baby, in Budapest where I was born. I was aimlessly wandering alongside a brook when a cobbler's apprentice loomed up out of nowhere, to indulge himself in the sudden whim of smearing my hair all over with cobbler's glue, than which there is nothing more tenacious on God's earth. What heartbroken sobs while my grandmother tried to repair the damage! What horror at the senselessness of the thing! For—and it must have been this that chiefly stunned my infant mind—the cruel caprice had no meaning: there had been no provocation, no fight, the other boy and I had never even seen each other before.

My reaction to the family tussle mentioned above was quite in character with *our* little branch of the family—my father, my brother, and I, who during my earliest childhood lived together in Budapest. I always thought of the three of us as a separate unit. Father, leading café bands and teaching, was considered the rebel of the family, the one who swam against the current, who read Heine and Schiller in German, who—notable accomplishment in our little world—even knew a bit of English; he was an assiduous reader of Bellamy's *Looking Backward*, which was then comparatively new, having been published in 1888. Father would spin fantasies or debate warmly about brave new worlds whenever he could find a worthy partner, or—lacking this—a patient listener. He would fight for open windows, for cold sponge baths, for hot nettle baths (for the sores on my spindly legs)—this in a community where the arrival of winter meant the pasting up of all windows until spring.

The lessons with my father's brother Bernat in Máramaros-Sziget stand out as interludes of substance in the shadowy, day-dreaming existence of a naturally lazy boy. My uncle Dezsö, their younger brother, was the first "classical violinist" to emerge from our "band," and was a frequent subject of conversation, naturally held up to me as a shining example to follow. Dezsö, a pupil of Hubay in the 'nineties, was by then already living in Paris (a name that spelt enchantment to me), concertizing and playing in the Colonne Orchestra.* And his achievements in far-off Paris were not the only inducements to industrious study held out to me, for at the end of

* This uncle is now a member of many years' standing of the Metropolitan Opera House Orchestra.

each lesson Uncle Bernat would hand me his purse, from which I was to extract my reward for the work accomplished. Theoretically, I could have picked some of the untold riches of this leathern pouch with its pleasantly greasy smell of sheepskin; but I considered the shiny nickel and silver coins taboo and respected what came to crystallize itself into a gentlemen's agreement between us: I invariably took just one copper coin, of the smallest denomination. This penny would buy a handful of morello cherries, or a piece of *krumpli cukor*, a crude confection made of potato into a kind of sugar; it had a pungency that was both astringent and mouth-watering.

This same uncle used to take me places—to the salt mines near by, and to a mineral-water bottling plant where the primitive label-sticking and metal-foil-capping machine filled me with greater wonder than have any of the industrial showplaces I have seen since, like Lever Brothers' "Port Sunlight" near Liverpool, or the gold-flotation processes I have watched in Australia.

Uncle Bernat's daughter had married a minor police functionary, and it may have been this circumstance that gave him the notion one day of taking me along with him on a visit to the local jail. Here, accompanied by a lusty fellow of a warden, we dropped in on the various prison workshops. What impressed me above all was the easygoing absence of censoriousness with which Uncle called to some of the inmates, whom he evidently knew from the market place or some other haunts of theirs (where they would doubtless reappear soon, their short terms served). This tossing over one's shoulder of a "Well, good-for-nothing —at it again?" did not make rhyme or reason to the small seven-year-old boy who was being dragged along by the hand and for whom the idea of prison and punishment had dreadful implications.

If one is to avoid synthetic memories of childhood, one might as well admit defeat straight away and confess that the residues of whole years sometimes amount to no more than meaningless and disconnected shreds. In my own case, when I try to recall concrete incidents—the visits of my father from Budapest, or the sicknesses or the joys of childhood—the object that invariably comes at once to the forefront of my mind (with almost the attributes of a living protagonist) is the old apple tree in our courtyard. Everything I did or experienced seems to have had that tree as a witness, as a background, or as a rallying point. Our living quarters being cramped, most of the daily doings had their locale in the courtyard: the scrubbing of necks, applying of homemade arnica tincture to cuts or bruises, cleaning of muddy topboots (with well water—not with saddle soap), the smoking and talking sessions of my elders, my own munching of apples or gooseberries (there was a hedge whose berries had bursting skins that turned from green to wine-red in sheer overripeness)—every such memory seems to centre even now on this apple tree. In later years it was this tree that helped me to identify the house I had lived in as "the apple-tree house" (to distinguish it from my eldest uncle's house and other one-room premises that seemed to mushroom from it near by) when certain fantastically complicated housing, building, and rental deals between my father and this eldest brother of his had to be explained to me.

I was always reluctant to listen to the explanations of these labyrinthine deals, which involved now half a house, now one-third of a house; now the building by this brother on that brother's lot; the sharing of resulting rents (microscopic by to-day's standards) in such-and-such proportions; the paying of mortgages and building costs; the receiving of rents first in florins, then in crowns, then—worst of all—in inflated crowns during World War I, and still later, after the occupation of Máramaros-Sziget by Rumania, in *lei*.

It was only after my father had passed away, soon after the war, that I was finally rid of these recurrent legal and fiscal complications—rid of them in the following simple and painless manner: At the height of the frenzy of inflation in the early 'twenties, my old uncle came up to one of my Budapest concerts, handed me various documents, accounts, tax receipts (going back several years and involving florins, crowns, and lei), began an endless tale of mortgages, back taxes, and forced transfers from one currency to another, explained how lucky he was to have been able to get hold of some American money on the black market instead of paying me off in practically worthless inflated money, and—after these head-whirling preliminaries—proudly handed me eighteen American dollars! The day was well timed for what was almost literally a liquidation, and I gladly gave my signature without questioning anything, if only to free myself of the whole inextricable tangle; for I wanted to get away to a rehearsal—or it may have been a visit with Bartók or Hubay for all I know now: objectives so much more reasonable and immediate than the vague concept "real estate," which in those mad days of inflation and expropriations (especially on the Hungarian-Rumanian border) had ceased to have anything "real" about it.

The apple tree, then, and the moss-grown well—with the lure of the watercress growing inside it—were the setting of the few things I remember from those years. The well, by the way, was an ever-present temptation and menace to us little boys. Many were the warnings of the horrible end we should come to at the bottom of the well if we persisted in our wicked way of bending over (or, still worse, climbing over) the edge in quest of the cool, tart-tasting green. The first place that harried parents searched when an enterprising youngster failed to answer their call was, of course, the well.

The arrival of the inexplicable wonder of the first croaking, cylinder-playing phonograph, set up in our courtyard by the itinerant market-place showman; the "carpet baggers" and the "trainers"—men with monkeys or parrots trained to pick out paper slips with predictions printed on them; the fortune-telling gipsies who used to pass from house to house—all these were set between the apple tree and the old well.

An occasional bathe in the Tisza River, with blown-up ox bladders bound round my chest for safety; the young uncles and their gang, menacing the privacy of the womenfolk who were bathing in another stretch of the river, separated from us and dipping and splashing in their long homespun chemises and shrieking at the faunlike irruptions of the boy-gang—this summery vision in my memory is dominated somehow by woolly dark greens and glistening blackish greens. (Is it the glistening water patches of the rapid Tisza, seen from the approaches above, that still colour the scene for me?)

Still another memory is of hikes up to the outlying pasturages to buy pungent, smoky *brinza* goat cheese from the Ruthenian shepherds with their long black hair all smeared up with melted butter—*brinza* cheese, which gave that incomparable flavour to corn-mush polenta and supplied that missing element of play to the tedious chore of small boys—eating! What fun to watch the unpredictable and changing patterns of the cheese strands, which could be manipulated into hair-fine, elastic threads! And those shepherds—how timeless and changeless they are, how independent of the where and when! Whether I saw them in the Carpathians at the turn of the century, or in the Soviet Georgia of the late 'twenties, the unchanging occupation of tending sheep seemed to make them run together in my mind.

When driving up the Georgian military highway from Vladikavkas to Tiflis (one of the greatest scenic experiences of my two trips round the world), was it not the same shepherd of my childhood that I saw, enveloped in that dust cloud raised by his immense flock, the last-born of that flock draped round his neck like a boa! My wife's salutary corrective to the sentimentality of this pastorale was: "Come, Joska—the little lamb of this morning will to-night be the shepherd's *shashlik!*"

It was good to perceive the unifying thread that runs through one's experiences: Here was I, already a much-travelled virtuoso, married, on one of the most exhilarating concert tours of my career—yet at the same moment I felt myself once more the small seven-year-old in Máramaros-Sziget.

CHAPTER II

WHAT prompted and then ripened my father's decision to transplant me to Budapest for serious study I cannot now recall, but that it was part of a master plan is undeniable. Anyway, this meant the end of those first years spent with my grandfather and my foster grandmother, and set me on the threshold of that "other life" of which my father's annual visits from the city had given me a foretaste. For ever since I could remember I had identified "father" with "the future" and, in some subtle way, with "youth," in contradistinction to "the present," which was personified by grandparents, age, comfortable *laisser aller*. Everything in Máramaros-Sziget seemed but a token of things to come—particularly my uncle's fiddle lessons, with their playful connotations.

The significance of this identification of "father" with "future" and "youth" struck me with great force when, some twenty-one years later, I myself was at the other end of the relationship. When I in turn became a father—and a young one at that—one of the earliest games I played with my tiny daughter centred in this concept of youth as synonymous with "achievement." Whatever we singled out for admiring comment was called "*jeune*" rather than "lovely" or "wonderful" or "*épatant*." For "*jeune*" embraced all of these, became a positive and blanket endorsement of anything we chose to honour.

When the little girl offered me her plaudits for some particularly resplendent parental performance—a crude drawing, or the invention of some game or story built to her specifications—she would clap her hands and exclaim admiringly: "Oh, how *many* things you can do! How *young* you are!" Her almost clairvoyant linking of "youth" with "achievement"—instead of the more orthodox association of ideas: achievement, age, respect—kept puzzling me until I asked her one day, without anything having led up to the question: "Which do you think is younger, Mummy or Daddy?" This evoked the reply, given with condescending haughtiness (as if to say: What a ridiculous question!): "Daddy, of course—*because he can draw. . . .*" I sometimes indulge in the fancy of imagining parents who would teach children to respect their "youngers and betters," who would reminisce about "the good young times," who would eschew the habit of prefacing the word "master" by "old."

Speeding toward Budapest with my Bellamy-reading, cold-rub-down practising, open-window-advocating father, I was thrilled by the consciousness that I was privileged to travel in what was called by awestruck country folk a Blitz Train, which to me meant something that had quite literally the frightening attributes of lightning. I suppose the onomatopoeic magic of the word "Blitz" had as much as anything to do with our being overawed by the rapidity of this no more than average fast train. (Just as I suspect that in the push-over days of the 1939 Blitzkrieg this same hissing sound and connotation of swiftness in striking added considerably to the very real horror of the blows themselves.) Anyway, this train and the varnish-smelling wooden benches of our third-class carriage, lit by old-time gas lamps with their glowing Welsbach mantles, seemed a combination of what Superman and Buck Rogers represent to the boy of to-day.

The steady shower of sparks in the black night sky, given off by the cheap coal fuel of those trains, kept me up long after hours, fascinated, my nose pressed to the window. This "Nocturne in Black and Gold," as Whistler would have called it, was—so to say—a last fling at the careless daydreaming of my childhood.

Next morning—Budapest: crowds, horse-drawn trolleys,

and beyond these tempting distractions the menacing immediacies of the Conservatory. Why my father did not enroll me right away in the preparatory classes at the Music Academy, where Hubay headed the violin department, I cannot figure out. The fact remains that I took the long way around via enrolment in one of the second-string private conservatories, where I was put in the charge of a kindly enough (but I fear hopelessly inadequate) pedagogue, who was an obscure member of the opera orchestra.

What this estimable mediocrity lacked in pedagogic ability, he tried to make up for with gifts of baskets of fruit and wine from his little property in the near-by hills, thereby trying to stave off that inevitable day of parting when his star pupil would leave him for the rarefied atmosphere of the official state academy and—Hubay. The standing of my first music school and the level of the instruction I must have received there can best be conveyed by a few words about the owner-director, a rotund Swabian with the German name of Schoeller or Schnoeller. This purveyor of music instruction, a somewhat grotesque combination of crank and charlatan, fancied himself in the role of inventor of newfangled mechanical musical instruments. The monstrosity he demonstrated one evening at a pupils' concert, where he was assured of a docile and long-suffering audience made up of parents, aunts, and governesses, was typical of him: a frightening contraption of steel, horsehair, and rubber—a cross between a Swiss music-box, a hurdy-gurdy, and a violin-playing robot called the Violonola which Leipzig tried to inflict on the pre-radio and pre-juke-box world. The weird, whining sounds it gave out still haunt me.

That these first months of instruction at least did not harm me was evident when, soon after, I was presented at the Music Academy for admission into one of the classes preparatory to Hubay's. Great was our astonishment when Hubay, who presided over the jury, chose to admit me to his own class, dispensing with the usual steps. Now that I look back on it, this was all the more surprising since the instruction I received at Herr Schoeller's institution was of the kind nowadays ironically called the "book-under-the-arm" method.

(21)

(The pianists of those days were sometimes blessed with the counterpart of these pedagogic tortures—I am referring to the "coin-on-the-wrist" school!)

The streets of the big city probably gave that wide-eyed lad about as much as the regular elementary school did, if not more. It was inevitable that schooling should take a secondary place in an environment in which it was possible to make real progress in one's chosen craft within two or three years, and where this progress held out such glamorous promises: the career of a 'teen-age prodigy, with its opportunities for travel, its hope of escape from the sordidness of a life where each small silver coin counted. For in this life it was not unusual to buy for supper the fat of succulent smoked Prague hams, leaving the pink flesh to the more affluent customers. Our corner grocer was quite unperturbed if one of us came in to buy one-fifth of a half-pound chocolate bar; he would break up a dime's worth into five portions without blinking an eye. And it was the accepted thing among the schoolboys of our neighbourhood to cut up every pencil into three or four parts, thus making one of those handsome, yellow-lacquered, cedar-smelling symbols of schoolboy affluence, a pencil, serve three or four boys instead of one. Nowadays a pencil is carelessly left lying about, with no more proprietorship attached to it than to a match or a sipping straw. But among us it was an object of real substance, carrying within its slim body unlimited potentialities for barter: for multicoloured marbles, for stamps from far-off, exotic lands, for all sorts of edible delights. Thus the glamorous career of a prodigy viewed from the schoolboy point of view epitomized not only the satisfaction of Wanderlust but real affluence as well. Moreover, the imminent prospect of such a career for me also promised— and this must have been a potent if unconscious motive in my child's brain—my father's escape from a second marriage that had turned out none too well.

The walks to the Music Academy were adventures, voyages of discovery that meant a great deal to a boy who had no library of children's books, into whose home no newspapers came in a regular way, who owned no toys beyond hoop and marbles and no hobbies but the swapping of postage stamps. (It was years later, when I had already outgrown the normal age for such a plaything, that I received my first toy steam-engine. Though I was then living and concertizing in England, I developed an enthusiasm for it quite unbecoming in an adolescent of some fifteen or sixteen years with many public appearances in Berlin, Dresden, and London to his credit.)

On the way to my lessons I window-shopped at all the second-hand bookstores, and tried to pierce (not through logic but through imaginings) the meanings of the titles of the illustrated paper-backs and the probable nature of their contents. What I saw in one show window I linked with what was displayed in the next one, noticed titles that kept confronting me now in this bookstore, now in that—these titles forming themselves gradually into my intended future reading schedule (how much of it still only intended!).

At street corners the circular wrought-iron bill-posting pillars were another source of varied information, a sort of peep into a world into which I had not yet earned my entrée, the world of opera, of ballet, of the theatre; for every day the pillars displayed the bill of each theatre, with the full cast. There were also crude lithographed posters announcing unattainable luxuries, and sometimes election posters on which candidates fought each other with innuendo, often even with calumny.

One April day I came across some unfamiliar terminology on a blood-red poster rallying all proletarians (an unknown word to me then) to make a worthy showing on May Day, a poster full of exclamation marks, of figures of speech brimming with pathos, about the clanging chains of slavery, and so on. All of which—confused though the issues were to me as I walked on to the Conservatory—I forthwith proceeded to adapt to the opening recitativo bars of some romantic-virtuoso that I had lately heard in class for the first time: Vieuxtemps's D Minor Concerto. I have to smile nowadays when I think how perfectly expressive of the socialist May Day poster this romantic-pathetic Victorian music seemed to my childish imagination. I thought I could see "the awakening of the driven slaves" in that long opening crescendo "D"; in the recitativo eighth-notes that follow I sensed their tentative stumbling efforts at straightening up, at tensing their abused backs and limbs; I thought I heard the "clanging of chains" in the boldly-mounting chords that climax these first few bars!

Though quite aware now of the puerility of such arbitrary programmatic interpretation, I still, whenever I hear this concerto, see that little boy, fiddle case in hand, reading the poster during long minutes—reading most of it uncomprehendingly and yet setting it to what seemed to him appropriate music.

As I passed the small tobacco shops, the daily papers exposed on wire racks outside the doors brought me divers headlines, dispatches, and war news (in the Boer War then going on, most of us boys were pro-Boer); while the delicatessen stores' display of exotic delicacies like dried Smyrna figs and dates and tangerines, unknown to me when I came to Budapest, tantalized me daily—either with the very recent memory of my first revelation of these luscious goodies or with the imagined future indulgence in them.

The first automotive vehicle I saw on the street was a delivery tricycle of the Torley champagne vineyard. Its puffing and frequent stalling created a commotion among us little boys every time it puffed its way through our neighbourhood; whenever it had to be cranked up we were always on hand, standing around gaping. Another vehicle, the one and only hansom cab in the city, driven just for the pleasure of it by an Anglophile banker, an eccentric bachelor in a short, buff-coloured overcoat, brought me glimpses of that other and only vaguely divined world of unknown foibles, undreamed-of luxuries.

As I progressed rapidly under my master Hubay I began to penetrate into these (to me) foreign milieus. Being taken to play at some of the industrialists' houses, I was awestruck when the fully laden tea-table with cups of chocolate and whipped cream and petits fours from the fashionable confectioner rose from the nether regions—via the dumb waiter!—and was wheeled to where we were sitting. And again I was astonished by still another custom of the *haut monde* when, having been invited to dinner (as I frequently was) at the home of some music patrons, an old Court councillor and his wife who lived on our most fashionable avenue, I saw finger bowls passed around—and not finger bowls only, but also tumblerfuls of rose water with which to rinse one's mouth into the said finger bowls. . . .

My father's munificent gift of ten tickets to the covered swimming pool, giving me at the same time the right to swimming instruction of a sort; occasional visits to the circus where an exponent of the Loie Fuller style of dancing manipulated veils which the projection of changing coloured lights transformed into fantastic butterfly patterns—such were some of the pleasures that emerged in this new life of mine.

On our Sunday excursions to the "People's Park," several sideshows competed with this "Loie Fuller" dance act for my favour. There was one booth that never failed to enchant me—not any of the sideshows (for which one would have had to pay the three- or fivepenny admission price), but one that surpassed most of these in entertainment value. It was the so-called "Turk," the red-fezzed nougat seller with his virtuoso gibberish and double-talk, which clearly betrayed the flimsiness of his claims to a glamorous Levantine origin and placed it much much nearer to us in the Galician or Bukovinian regions of the Austro-Hungarian monarchy. To see this born showman manipulate the hatchet with which he chopped off chunks of nougat of varying and unpredictable size (this was precisely the point: "unpredictable!"); to watch him choose his sales victim, declare his sudden and unmotivated sympathy for him or her, a sympathy which he said irresistibly made him throw in a handful of pennies on top of the nougat mound— all this had the seemingly never diminishing crowd around him in stitches.

To this day I relish every authentically improvised manifestation of the art of swaying a crowd: whether exemplified by Charles "Chic" Sale, by an evangelist's "revival meeting," by a phoney auctioneer on some seaside boardwalk, or by Ed Wynn. My eternal regret is that I missed the typically American medicine-shows by some years—or is it decades?

Occasional appearances at benefits, school concerts, and the like now began to punctuate my existence, often causing me discomfiture intolerable to my shy nature. I was dragged and exhibited to influential committee members, as all prodigies are. Such practices—the bane of every prodigy's life—generate in a child a resistance, a feeling of outraged *pudeur,* which in my case showed itself in an invincible shame at being seen on the streets in my concert clothes: white alpaca sailor blouse with blue collar, topped off (and this seemed to me the worst of all) with shiny patent-leather shoes. I recall being taken in this outfit to a photographer on a sunny afternoon, and can still feel the torture of having my skin go all prickly from blushing, for I was convinced that every passer-by was staring scornfully at the unnormal, unboyish apparition that I judged myself to be.

CHAPTER III

OF my schooling, I retain hardly any memories except of the likeable personality of one of my teachers, whose features and kindly manner and name—Bellagh it was—I still recall; whereas, characteristically enough, I cannot for the life of me say what subject he taught. On the other hand, the appearance in the school courtyard, during some of our recesses, of probably one of the last of the ambulant versifiers is more vivid than most of the other school memories put together. The tubby poet with the waxed moustache and a merry twinkle in his eyes (his name was Janos Hazafi-Verai) would not only sell his poems for mere pennies —printed on single sheets of paper the way the chansonniers of Paris used to peddle theirs—but besides reciting and selling them would be ready to make a deal with the boys swarming round him and would improvise jingles on any subject they requested.

That these jingles were mostly at the expense of some particularly disliked pedagogue can easily be guessed. These teachers' most unpleasant qualities could be summed up in a very few words by the boys, and we had no more than expressed our little resentments piecemeal when we heard them, from the versifier's lips, transmuted into satirical doggerel. Thus, long before psycho-analysis became a household word, these last representatives of the wandering minstrels gave us boys a healthy release from the inevitable accumulations of the classroom with its frictions, fancied or real injustices, humiliations, setbacks.

Around this time, I got to know one of my father's pupils, a young man by the name of Milan Füst, a very indifferent player, even considering his frankly amateur status. There was something in his eyes, in their bold intelligent light, in the unexpected and critical thrust of his clipped speech, and in his generally supersensitive and nervous manner that somehow marked him as a budding creative personality; and we both, my father with his healthy judgment and I with a child's divining instinct, set him apart from all the nondescript boys and girls who frequented our modest living-room that served father as a studio (while I practised mostly in the kitchen).

He was the only child of a widowed mother (her livelihood was a small tobacco shop) who spoke the Magyar equivalent of East Side Yiddish-American, to the æsthetic horror of Milan, who was—as it turned out—destined to become one of Hungary's two or three most illustrious poets and one of the honoured guardians of her language.

Whether it was my intellectual curiosity or receptivity, or the fact that he in his adolescent *élan* needed an audience for his literary and æsthetic pronouncements, and that an obviously inadequate sounding-board seemed to him better than none at all . . . whatever the reason was, I became his diminutive "Eckermann." Starting out with some innocuous small talk, he would suddenly change the subject, vehemently throw definitions of "art" at his uncomprehending "disciple," or correct angrily and with a zeal worthy of a more mature companion some slovenly turn of phrase of mine, giving me grammatical and stylistic reasons for his censure. He improvised in words brilliantly, showing me the difference between description that is full of clichés and banalities and that which uses language with respect and economy and art. I still vaguely remember an improvisation of his about snowflakes melting against the window-pane. He was standing by the window, in the dusk of a spring afternoon, winter and snow in reality long forgotten, but he—to make his stylistic point clear—went on, rhythmically joining word to word, making me feel and see what he wanted me to feel and see.

One of his quirks was never to use or to let me use the word "writer" or "novelist"—it always had to be "artist."

In our language the word *iro* (writer) when joined to the word *ujsag* (newspaper) means journalist, and I suppose he was anxious to avoid confusion of the two concepts.

I owe my first contact with Shakespeare to him, for I soon learned to rummage in the stacks of papers and books he always left in the entry along with his hat and coat while he was having his lesson inside, and I promptly acquired the habit of browsing among them. It was thus that I encountered, in *King Lear* (Act I, Scene I), some of those "dark facts" that boys forever gather surreptitiously, and it was a bracing shock for me—tonic, and somehow reassuring—to learn such things through Shakespeare instead of from whispering schoolboys.

This fanatic man of letters later became one of the pillars of the vanguard review *Nyugat*, which made literary history in our language and with which I became familiar, through him, almost from its inception during my 'teens.

Not so many years after, he was already a poet attracting much attention in literary circles, and he made me feel proud when, around 1909 or 1910 on my return from London for some concerts in Hungary, he devoted half a column or so to me, in this same *Nyugat*, where an aloof, ivory-tower policy reigned, comparable to that of the *Nouvelle Revue Française* in Jean Rivière's days. To have him give me the accolade in deep-probing words that had none of the gushing, none of the journalistic frills, which I had by then begun to know; to have him tell me in such austere surroundings, among other things, that I should always seek out the never-ending challenge of Bach's solo sonatas—this probably meant more to me than all the professional music criticism I had come into contact with up to then.

Though subsequently, on my flying visits to Budapest, I put off from year to year the project of seeking him out in his monastic seclusion in Buda, I still kept in touch with his writing. I almost preferred this to sandwiching between the distracting necessities of a travelling virtuoso's daily schedule a hurried visit to this great artist in his solitude.

So our last contact too, in 1939, just after the present war had started, remained a token one: I asked him to a concert I gave and he reciprocated by sending me a volume of poems dated 28th November, 1939.

The circumstance that rooms in my paternal lodgings were let out to other persons provided me with a rich fund of information and impressions. To me, an observant youngster, there thus came a series of faces, hopes, professions, life histories, experiences of a kind from which he would have been shielded in a more bourgeois environment—in, say, the "aseptic" atmosphere of the governess- or tutor-directed nursery.*

One of our boarders, a student by the name of Juhasz, I recall less in his own right than in that of his father, a small-town postmaster who often came to visit his son. This soft-spoken gentleman with the visionary eyes that certain "screwballs" have, spent his leisure and spare money on nothing less than "perpetual motion." He always brought along toy-size models, delicate spider-limbed wooden contraptions with wheels, levers, and whatnots, whose functioning naturally delighted me while I listened (somewhat absent-mindedly, I fear) to his earnest explanations and deductions. One of his "theses" has stuck in my memory all these decades: something or other about the "power" that the trillions of *footsteps* of the billions of human beings represent, a power that is "lost to the world" because it has not *as yet* been harnessed. "Not yet—but just you wait, my boy!"

Since then how many harmless cranks have I listened to, patiently, and with even a certain sympathy and unavowed envy! And in such diverse places as Minneapolis, Paris, Szeged, and Brisbane. Listened to world-unity dreamers, or (more in my line) to propounders of infallible and incredibly speeded-up systems of "violin mastery." To hear these latter, all of whom seem to have discovered the one and only royal road to virtuosity, one begins to wonder how the art of violin-playing has managed to survive so long without their trail-blazing!

* A dietitian once told me how wide of the mark certain over-anxious parents shoot when they give their children only mineral water that is "bacteriologically pure"; how vulnerable to infection this makes them in later life.

Some of these illuminati—or their prophets or disciples—proclaim that "technique is speed." Some (how many of them!) have discovered that Paganini's secret was his particular way of holding the violin. Others talk about "finger magic" and increasing the stretching capacity of the hand by racklike instruments of torture or exercise. Still another prescribes "resistance exercises" with the help of "rubber bands, finger-tips, and wristbands" that may be purchased from their inventor. (One cannot but recall the tragic experience of Robert Schumann, whose hope of becoming a piano virtuoso was blasted when he permanently incapacitated a finger by experimenting with such a device.)

This obsession of our tribe with the stretching capacity of hands and muscles is aptly epitomized in a story told by Paderewski to Isidore Philipp, to whom I am indebted for passing it on to me.

It appears that a charming old compatriot of Paderewski's, a certain Michalowski, who deemed himself a Chopin specialist—in fact, a repository of the only true Chopin tradition—had lost his equally old and charming wife after a long and happy marriage. Friends, pupils, relatives, making their visits of condolence, found the old gentleman inconsolable. Tears were streaming down his face as he stood there in the Old World parlour surrounded by his sympathizers. His hands were gripping the lapels of his black frock coat, and the sympathizers noticed certain nervous movements of the fingers on the lapels. It took Paderewski's practised eye to detect that these finger movements were nothing but involuntary automatic stretching exercises. The bereaved pianist's obsession triumphed even in his hour of sorrow.

Then there are those who expound theories on the stance of the player, and hold that the way he disposes the weight of his body is the "key to the mystery." I remember seeing with amazement in one such oracular book reproductions of so-called historical paintings of Frederick the Great and Napoleon, which showed that this particular stance has been common to *all* great men, whether conquerors of continents or conquerors of Sarasate's *Caprice Basque* and of Paganini's *Moïse* Variations.

These prophets of "new" playing techniques are in a sense brothers under the skin of the inventors of the lost and secret varnish formulæ of Stradivarius and Guarnerius. Amateur fiddle-makers will tell you, with a visionary gleam in their eyes, that their calculations of the relative thickness of the "table" and "belly" of the fiddle and the *attuning* of the two parts to each other and so on have brought their violins within an inch of superseding Strads and Guarnerii etc. One high-ranking army officer (according to a United Press dispatch of 1943) "dismantled a rare Amati violin and minutely measured the vibrations of all areas of the wood, to correlate resonance with thickness of the wood, depth of the instrument and similar points," and used a "special ultra-violet ray process for aging wood."

I have seen many of these rhapsodists and listened to their talk, but I don't recall ever hearing that any one of them actually played the violin—which would be the kind of proof of violin theories that eating is of the pudding. For the procession of such visionaries has been unending in my life, from those early years in my father's house up to the present time.

Those "new" techniques, those Stradivarius-superseding formulæ, were not the only gospels preached to me there. I encountered many other unorthodox thinkers, among them the "world unity" dreamers. In about 1910 Emil Pirchan, famed scenic designer and painter (I came across some of his work lately in the *Encyclopædia Britannica* plates on stage design), with whom I had struck up a friendship after my Munich début, told me about Professor Wilhelm Ostwald's world-reforming idea. Although on a higher level than the naïve imaginings of the violin "illuminati," Ostwald's plan also struck me as eccentric. His organization had some such name as "Die Brücke" (The Bridge) and it was the epitome of German thoroughness if anything ever was.

Having won a Nobel prize in 1909, Ostwald devoted the whole of the prize-money to an effort to standardize the format of all printed matter—of books, stationery, envelopes, files, catalogues, and posters, of engravings and photographs, of the canvas of paintings, and even of packagings, I believe.

SZIGETI AS A BOY

SZIGETI WITH HIS TEACHER, JENÖ HUBAY, 1910

Everything was to be multiplied from a basic unit, thus retaining the relative proportions, whatever the size. The plan had a certain success: some Leipzig or Munich publishers adopted the *Welt Format,* and some business houses did too.

Ostwald's propagandistic activities also embraced several peace movements, the international languages Esperanto and Ido, the "Organization of the Organizers," and then the "Pyramid of the Sciences." At the time the more playful aspects of this *Welt Format* scheme (such as the colourful labels painted by my friend Pirchan), the divers plans for putting it over on a worldwide scale, rather amused me, and little did I then realize the typically Teutonic earmarks of the concept. It was not until recently, when I happened to be glancing through Ostwald's *Lebenswege,* that I took in this fact.

In such peaceful utopian plans the positive German virtues of thoroughness, methodicalness, the desire to avoid waste, are inherent; it is only when we encounter these same virtues diabolically distorted—as in some of the German schemes that have shaken the world since then—that we see things in their true light. As the American correspondent exclaimed, after commenting on the fiendish efficiency, the absence of waste, the "total" quality of everything in an extermination camp that he had visited: "Here it was demonstrated that it is perfectly possible to co-ordinate the utmost scientific order and means with the utmost barbarism of ends."

This German worship of methodicalness, of thoroughness, of "completeness" (I think Ostwald uses the word *Restlosigkeit* in describing one of his efforts in methodology) came to my mind lately in a macabre association of ideas. I had been reading about the death factory in Maidanek and about the meticulous book-keeping in the warehouses filled with the belongings of which the victims had been stripped (down to gold-filled teeth). When the writer deplored the fact that the German genius for organization and method should have been applied to *such* ends, I had a flash of "recognition" and some of Emil Pirchan's preachings of Ostwald's gospel of *Restlosigkeit* came back to me. The word *Restlosigkeit* means "total" . . . total war, total extermination, total domination, the "next thousand years." Such phrases were illuminated for me by this flash of recognition.

This sense of total orderliness in the conservation of *things*, which has its counterpart in a similarly total orderliness in the destruction of *human beings* and of the human spirit, was symbolized for me in a package I received from the music section of the OWI* on a November day in 1944: a photostat of the manuscript of a violin sonata found in the "warehouse" of the Maidanek concentration camp near Lublin, Poland, on August 27th, 1944, by John Evans of Reuters. The work which had been microfilmed and flown over to the OWI, was written by a Czech composer, Ernst Weil, who was undoubtedly killed at the camp. These manuscript sheets picked up in the ghastly warehouse by a newspaper correspondent remain probably the only physical traces of the living and the dying of a man.

* Office of War Information.

CHAPTER IV

·⟨◇⟩·

A T one of the parties I was dragged to during my
prodigy days, my hostess-sponsor tried to interest
some of her guests in providing me with an adequate
fiddle. That she was successful was due largely to the infec-
tiously enthusiastic buttonholing of the right people by the
glamorous young actor Oscar Beregi who at the time was our
"Great Profile" and who apparently was irresistible to all
whom he approached. Readers of Isadora Duncan's *My Life*
will find his picture in that book—but not his name. The
caption of the portrait reads merely "Romeo," this being the
role in which Isadora first saw him.

Isadora's first decisive successes (like Kubelik's about the
same time) seem to have branched out from the comparatively
small capital, Budapest. This propitiousness of our terrain
for budding international careers was all the more remarkable
because the dissemination of Press notices to other centres was
naturally impeded by our language—a language that is still not
"effective" beyond our borders. (There were only two
German-language dailies in Budapest, as against some fifteen
or twenty Hungarian.) One would think that this role of
incubator for international stars would have been taken more
logically by such a city as Geneva or Vienna: the first with its
French-language press that penetrated both to France and
Belgium, and Vienna with its prestige insuring any successful
performer there an entrée to all Germany and the German-
speaking territories.

But Budapest, with its typical cigar-chewing, furcoatsporting impresarios, was at that period and for some time afterward, a favourite place for discovering international talent. Only a few years before, our Opera had boasted a conductor of the stature of Gustav Mahler* (1888–91), to be followed soon after (1893–95) by Artur Nikisch, whom Koussevitzky reveres still as the prototype of the modern conductor and an unequalled genius of the baton. Concert-going was always in the blood of that Budapest intellectual bourgeoisie which before World War I was so typical, too, of Vienna, Prague, Zagreb, and other centres of the old Austro-Hungarian monarchy. This is illustrated in a remark made by one of the greatest musical artists of all time, who enjoyed a quite spectacular vogue in Budapest around 1910–12; having boosted his fees in Budapest each time he came, quite beyond the usual European level, and almost incredulously seeing them accepted without protest, he exclaimed: "I had to come to little Budapest to find my real 'suckers'!"

I still vaguely remember Kubelik's impresario, the legendary Norbert Dunkl, and sensational little Vecsey's Alexander Gross, for they were in the habit of getting photographed with their "wards," often in the act of sitting in the corner of the picture supposedly listening to "their" prodigy or long-haired young virtuoso, with the vague pictorial implication that they, Svengali-like, had a considerable share in the almost occult hair-raising accomplishments of those they promoted. It was a period piece right out of the 1860s.

My awareness of the stir that Duncan created at this time was heightened by the many pictures of her I saw in the lobby of the Urania Scientific Theater. On my way to the Academy I often stopped at this unique little show-place, the only theatre specializing in primitive motion pictures and projected stills, accompanied by commentaries somewhat in the style of those of our travelogues. The Urania was also the scene of Duncan's first successes.

It was only natural that all these fabulous triumphs— Kubelik's, Vecsey's, Isadora Duncan's—should have fanned the

---

* Brahms's oft-quoted remark—that it was well worth making the trip from Vienna to Budapest just to see *Don Giovanni* under Mahler—belongs here.

impatience of the youngsters studying at the time. That is why—in my case, too—it is difficult to say that my formal début took place in such and such a year. One's conservatory years were studded with tentative appearances of which—whether they were charity benefits or select semi-public concerts like those of the Casino of the Leopoldstadt—the Press took just as much notice as of formal recitals nowadays. The first "substantial" fee I remember receiving was precisely at one of these Casino affairs where the co-artist of "my" evening was the leonine young piano virtuoso Mark Hambourg. I received ten gold coins worth 10 kronen each, mounted on a cardboard with ten slits, equivalent to some twenty dollars.

Another remembered, if not memorable, appearance was at a charity performance at the Royal Opera which consisted of a game of chess—the living pawns impersonated by society girls and young men. (I wonder who impersonated the knights' horses?) I cannot, for the life of me, imagine how the directors of this fantastically slow-moving Victorian divertissement contrived to insert solo numbers into the framework, but apparently they did, my contribution to the evening's proceedings being a Hungarian Rhapsody accompanied by the orchestra in the pit. I always thought this one of the summits of the "corny" in the so-called entertainment field and relegated it to the dim and forgotten past until, on settling in California in 1940, I saw something similarly depressing described in the "Art Section" of our daily: a benefit performance with débutantes and young matrons impersonating (to the sound of soft music) famous portraits and genre pictures that hang in a near-by museum. It was a case for sighing: "*Plus ça change, plus c'est la même chose!*"

One thing that stands out in my mind while I am thus digging through these years is my intense shyness. I was very bashful in public places, my cheeks often flushed by conflicting reflexes of outraged shyness and little stirrings of vanity whenever, on entering a café with my father, I heard the gipsy "primas," Pali Racz XXXII (32nd son of his famous gipsy-band-leader father), salute me with the first two bars of Bach's Prelude in E, interjected into whatever the band

was playing—csardas, operetta medleys, and the like. A
fraternal greeting and a sort of accolade—from one fiddler to
another!

There were also concerts given at summer resorts in Hungary and Bohemia, the latter promoted by an amateur
impresario whose profession was that of ambulant jeweller,
doing business mostly in coffee houses, his numerous pockets
housing his wares packed neatly in tissue paper and unfolded
to the accompaniment of an impressive line of chatter calculated to "condition" the prospect.

This, my first concert trip across our borders, gave me my
first contact with the "foreign" Press and with a typically
Victorian moralizing attitude of music criticism. The reviews
of my concerts constantly brought up the name of Maurice
Dangrement, violin virtuoso born in 1867 in Rio, who died
an early death in Buenos Aires in 1893 at the age of twenty-
six: an early death that should be a lesson to aspiring young
virtuosi and their guardians, said the critics sententiously in
reviewing these early concerts of mine. For they claimed (or
rather declaimed) that his death had been hastened by tuberculosis, brought on by a dissolute life of gambling, drinking,
and other vices. In short, a terrifying end that they—old
hands at the game who had witnessed the astounding successes
of Dangrement in Vienna—would spare "the blond boy
whose frail appearance and whose style of playing last night
strangely reminded" them of this other virtuoso . . . and so
they went on, admonishing and cautioning my "guardians"
in melodramatic style. For those who like stories with a
moral, I may add that I have never learned to play cards and
have never indulged in any form of gambling. However,
the tuberculosis part of the Dangrement forecast almost came
true: in 1913 I had to undergo a cure at Davos, Switzerland,
on the "Magic Mountain" that is the locale of Thomas
Mann's great book.

Had these gloomy prognosticators known the atmosphere
my other summer concerts led me into, they would have
been justified in predicting for me a still more lurid end than
Dangrement's. For, participating as I did in some shows at

a summer theatre in a small resort in Hungary, I had free access to all performances, out in front or behind the footlights as the spirit moved me, and I plunged into this new world with gusto, picking up, incidentally, quite a little extracurricular information about Life in general, and drinking in plenty of back-stage lore. Thus the subtle influences that emanated from the relations of the somewhat tarnished prima donna with the reputed "angel" of the company (a typical spendthrift offspring of some prosperous, hard-working, small-town manufacturer) did not escape my attention—all boys are wideawake to news of this kind. Soon I learned how intimately the fortunes of this barnstorming troupe were bound in with the ups and downs of this duet between prima donna and backer.

Perhaps these bits of worldly wisdom, prematurely acquired, helped me over many a perplexing hump in later years when my career brought me in contact with art patrons, orchestra sponsors, and impresarios who itched for a Svengali role. Perhaps, too, these first insights into the mechanism of the relationship "sponsor and sponsored" were the reason I kept my subsequent career singularly free of sponsors, promoters, and boosters generally.

It was here that I first had my fill of the stage, seeing *Rip Van Winkle, The Chimes of Normandy*, and some operettas with Hungarian folk background; and here it was that I had to play with a seven- or eight-piece orchestra and like it. It was swim or sink. My piece had to be reorchestrated down to the numbers of this little band by its pianist-conductor. Looking back, I do not think that roughing it so early in life does one any harm; even in later life, when one has "arrived," a real trouper often has to adapt himself to exigencies, has to make the best of adverse circumstances.

Even in comparatively recent years—I am speaking of Europe—there were times when I had to play the Beethoven Concerto with a military band; then, on another occasion, with an amateur orchestra composed entirely of stockbrokers and bankers; in Moscow with that wonderful conductorless orchestra—which, splendid though it was, did make rather special demands on the soloist's presence of mind and communicativeness; and there was also that experience of playing the Mendelssohn Concerto for a television broadcast with orchestra and conductor several feet away and with the television cameras propelled on little rubber-wheeled trucks darting about, shooting the soloist from all angles, while he sweated under the pitiless Klieg lights, his fear lest the varnish of his Guarnerius might blister only increasing his already considerable discomfort.

My unorthodox beginnings were probably good schooling for all this.

Parallel with the somewhat stuffy atmosphere of the Academy classrooms some exhilarating experiences came my way: hearing some of young Béla Bartók's music played by him together with Hubay; the revelation of the until then unsuspected harmonies and orchestral colouring of Dukas's *Sorcerer's Apprentice* as early as 1903,* and so on. In addition, my first visit to Hubay's home brought me my first awareness of Italian primitives, of the Barbizon School, and of Monticelli whose unorthodox brush stroke intrigued me.

Hubay, who was quite out of sympathy with Bartók's and Kodály's work, was somewhat surprised when he heard me express in disjointed fashion some timid but favourable comments on this Bartók work instead of joining in the chorus of ironic rejection which was *de rigueur* in our circle then. Bartók in those days sported the so-called "Festive-Magyar" costume, even on the concert stage, in contrast with Hubay's formal white tie and tails. This costume included a short black jacket decorated with passementerie and closing uniform-like right under the collar. It was in the days of the intensely nationalistic "Tulip" movement—a propitious moment for all such picturesque and anachronistic gestures.

It was at this concert that I first saw Bartók, whose friendship and musical associations with me have become some of my most treasured assets. Though still in his twenties he was prematurely grey; and from that figure, with its luminous eyes, I must have breathed in something then and there which has permitted me ever since to follow his musical path with

* Barely six years after its première in Paris on May 18th, 1897.

perhaps greater ease and sympathy than would probably have been the case otherwise.

Soon afterward, as I was walking home from the Academy with a fellow-student much my senior, we met him; impressed as I was by what I had heard and by that self-protective aloofness which even then was so much a part of his being, I stepped aside while my elders conversed. It was not until the 'twenties that his Second Sonata and some transcriptions I had made of piano pieces of his, as well as his Rhapsody No. 1 (which he dedicated to me as a token of friendship), brought us into an ever-deepening contact.

I suppose it was the discrepancy between the normal students' ages and the ages of those I am tempted to call the "prodigy elects," not yet in their 'teens, that accounts for the lack of give-and-take, the lack of that healthy musical rubbing of shoulders that one generally associates with conservatory years. The younger group was automatically set apart—even by our more mature fellow-students—as *sui generis*, a genus vaguely freakish; and it is not surprising that this unfortunate aura prevented spontaneous groupings into quartet or trio or sonata teams with our musical elders and "betters."

There were no improvised sonata sessions with our "opposite numbers" from the piano classes, sessions that could have supplemented so beneficially the outstanding but essentially instrumental training we were receiving from our master Hubay. We knew some of these pianistic "opposite numbers" of ours, of course, but we never seemed to come together musically. They must have pursued their pianistic-virtuoso aims with the same regrettable exclusiveness and dogged perseverance we applied to ours, and it was not until years later that one of them, the phenomenally gifted boy pianist Ernst von Lengyel, who had a brief but sensationally successful career, became my sonata partner in a series of recitals in England around 1912. This mere boy—who died of tuberculosis during World War I—made his London début under the most exacting auspices, playing Liszt's E flat Major Concerto under no less a conductor than Hans Richter, at the regular London Symphony Orchestra series; for years afterward, musical London recalled how the orchestra men, listening amazed to the sovereign mastery of the boy's playing, failed to respond to Richter's cue at the end of the cadenza.

The musical contacts I had during these last months before my trip to Berlin, which already loomed on the horizon, were not the kind one would imagine preceding a momentous move like the one we contemplated. I was still surrounded by quaint personalities like one Schreier, who billed himself on the windows of the cafés where he appeared as "King of Harmonics," this being a specialty that he exploited to great effect in fantasias depicting the twittering of birds and which invariably produced a considerable increase of nickels and silver coins on his collection plate.

My cimbalom-playing aunt—from whom incidentally I had a few lessons on that percussive instrument before deciding on the fiddle—had meanwhile married a violinist who, after being the "star" of the military band in which he served his "buck private" days (these lasted three years in the Austro-Hungarian monarchy), became leader of our premier Operetta Theatre from which almost all the Viennese-Hungarian operettas of Lehar, Leo Fall, Oskar Straus, Emmerich Kálmán, and Paul Abraham started out on their world conquest. With an uncle leading the theatre band, it was inevitable that I should become a comparatively assiduous operetta-goer, so that I was far removed from the traditional picture of the earnest "white hope" of his conservatory who saves his pennies in order to buy scores and to frequent the gallery seats of the Opera and of Symphony Hall. No, the facts were quite otherwise: operettas, gipsy bands, "King of Harmonics," and the little childish rivalries of the classroom where *Carmen* Fantasias fired us with a passion worthy of better causes! The phenomenally successful Kubelik, emerging at about that time, represented the triumph of Ševčik's school in Prague; and somehow we succeeded in getting hold of a "bootleg" copy of Ševčik's technical exercises and clandestinely passed it around to each other, Ševčik's studies being taboo in the Hubay set.

CHAPTER V

A MEMORY I cherish of those days is David Popper's concert in 1905 in celebration of his fortieth jubilee on the concert stage as one of the all-time great figures in 'cello-playing. I cherish it not only for the obvious reason of hero-worship: Popper was the greatest pre-Casals exponent of his instrument and was my teacher in quartet playing. Unfortunately these quartet lessons were more or less "token lessons," for I do not remember having frequented them so assiduously as I should have done. After I had "performed" a Haydn quartet that David Popper had monitored for a school concert, my attendance at the Popper quartet classes seems to have become more and more irregular. What was responsible for these regrettable lapses was the obsession for exhibitionistic virtuosity that guided us "prodigies-elect" in the Hubay classes—an obsession that I have already described.

I cherish this memory mostly, however, for the one and only glimpse it afforded me of the vanished heroic days of virtuosity when the lionized player actually and authentically improvised his cadenzas in front of his rapt listeners. I know for certain that on this occasion the old master, white strands of hair crowning his boldly handsome features and his compelling eyes flashing, elaborated and extended a cadenza for the *Konzertstück* of his own composition (whose framework I admit was preorganized) during several breathless minutes catching fire from his own fire, piling those chromatic sequences of tremolo-chains (in sixth and intermediary thirds) one on top of the other, creating a suspenseful excitement that one was almost painfully aware of and that gave way to a sense of release as he reached the dominant chord that led back to the piece proper. It was a moment the like of which I have never since experienced in a concert hall.*

Such must have been the magic that legendary virtuosi like Paganini and Liszt wrought when they kindled their listeners to a quivering sensitivity and were in turn kindled by them to wondrous playing! This must have been what lent glamour to those operatic *Fantasias* we see listed on Paganini's or Liszt's programmes in the 1840s, whose titles we now read with lifted eyebrows and superior smile: *Grande Fantasie sur* this or that opera of Bellini or Rossini, *Farmyard Imitations* by Signor Paganini, and so on. We read the titles, but we cannot visualize the scene or imagine the bewitchment that radiated from the stage!

In the one relic surviving from those far-off days—my first autograph album—I find the following punning and therefore untranslatable lines, the pun on my name being shown here in capital letters:

Spielt Joska Szigeti
SIEGET DIE Kunst
und das herrliche Talent!
Ihr alter Schulmeister
DAVID POPPER

19 April, 1908

This Popper Jubilee brings to mind another celebration, this time in honour of my master Hubay's fiftieth birthday in 1908. During the preceding few years I had been extensively concertizing in England, making many trips to the Continent between my English tours; and now I came home specially to bring my tribute to the master whose worth had been revealed to me in ever-increasing degree during those years, paralleling my generally maturing outlook.

This concert—like the one given in honour of Leopold

---

* A similar magical moment is reported to me by a pupil of Dohnányi's who witnessed his improvising of a cadenza to Mozart's A Major Concerto; on being asked by his class the day after the concert where they could get hold of a copy, to their amazement Dohnányi told them that it had all been improvised on a mere preconceived skeleton structure of his.

Auer in the 'twenties at Carnegie Hall—was one of those once-in-a-lifetime occasions at which all concerned, public and players alike, are ready and even eager for the unusual and unorthodox. The programme listed all four of the Hubay concerti: one played by Hubay himself, and the three others by the three then most widely travelled virtuosi from his school—Franz von Vecsey, who ever since 1904 had been covering himself with glory; Steffy Geyer, an outstanding woman violinist who now lives and teaches in Switzerland; and myself. Vecsey's choice was the Concerto in G minor, No. 3, which Efrem Zimbalist has played in America to Hubay's often-voiced delight; Steffy Geyer's, the *Concerto all'antica*; and mine, the E Major Concerto, No. 2, the first performance of which I had heard Hubay give some years previously. Hubay showed his youthful mettle in the first concerto, sub-titled *Concerto Romantique*. To my barely sixteen years, his fifty seemed almost Methusalean and his performance correspondingly astonishingly youthful.

Since the "family tree" of concertizing violinists is something that the public is only vaguely conscious of, and as the memory of audiences is notoriously short, I might mention a few representatives of Hubay's school with the majority of whom America has become familiar. Besides Franz von Vecsey, who toured there at different periods of his career, there were Emil Telmányi, whose musicianship and unusual programmes have been appreciated by American audiences in the 'twenties; Erna Rubinstein, one of Mengelberg's importations during his New York Philharmonic tenure, and an especial favourite in Holland; and Edouard de Zathurecky, who was introduced by the Wolfsohn Bureau and who had been Hubay's assistant at the time when Robert Virovai was being coached in preparation for Hubay's classes. Virovai's American successes in 1939 and the following one or two seasons are still well remembered. Another Hubay pupil was Duci von Kerékjarto, who made several successive coast-to-coast tours in the United States. And there was that picturesque personality, Yelly d'Aranyi, who went to America several seasons in succession, also making some joint appearances with Myra Hess. D'Aranyi's sister, Adila d'Aranyi Fachiri, is also a Hubay disciple, who plays mainly in England. About the phenomenally gifted young Stephan Partos who died in his 'teens during—or just after—World War I, I know only by hearsay, but opinion seems to be unanimous among all those who heard him during his brief but sensationally successful career that he was touched with something like genius.

Virtuosi like János Koncz or Szentgyörgyi (the latter distinguished by an outstanding recording of the Paganini concerto); a composer-violinist like Zoltán Székely (who commissioned Bartók's Violin Concerto); quartet players like the founders or members of the old "Hungarian Quartet" (Waldbauer); Géza de Kresz, founder of the Hart House String Quartet and other ensembles; violinists active in many fields like Eddy Brown, Kalman Reve, Serge Kotlarsky, Helen Ware, and others too numerous to mention—all these have come under the Hubay influence. Even Adolf Busch's teacher, Bram Eldering, whose death during an Allied bombing of Cologne was reported in 1943, belongs here: Eldering was a member of the Hubay-Popper Quartet during the 'nineties and studied with Hubay before going to Joachim.

I leave to the last what is perhaps the most spectacular career from the Hubay fold: Eugene Ormandy's. After a brilliant beginning on the recital stage, he abandoned our instrument for the baton. His phenomenal rise from the pit of the Capitol Theatre on Broadway to the Philadelphia Orchestra (via the Minneapolis) needs no detailed chronicling. That he still retains a redoubtable mastery of our instrument he has proven to me repeatedly in improvised quartet sessions. This despite the fact that he never touches a violin nowadays.

It was a letter from Hubay to the famous old firm of Hermann Wolff (managers of Hans von Bülow and Artur Nikisch) that made possible my Berlin début. The first of *how* many? A virtuoso's life seems an endless succession of débuts. Isn't every recital in the "big town"—whether it is New York or London or Paris or Berlin or Vienna—a début? So I promised myself that in mentioning mine I would try to avoid the ever-present pitfall that besets any chronicler of our brood: "Next morning he awoke to find himself hailed by the entire Press of Thingumabob as the . . ." *ad nauseam*.

My Berlin début, then, took place in the small Bechstein Saal on an autumn morning in 1905. I was just thirteen. My programme was to my mind ill-chosen, a succession of *tour de force* numbers—the Bach *Chaconne* framed by the technical stunts of Ernst's F sharp Minor Concerto and Paganini's *Witches' Dance*. The recital was given to me free of costs and was a morning affair simply because there was no outsider to foot the bill for an evening gala. It was cheaper for the firm to give it as a semi-public affair, for the Press and invited guests only.

Thanks to the wholly unexpected gift of the Sunday pictorial supplement of the *Berliner Tageblatt* of December 10, 1905, which I received lately from a former resident of Berlin, I can fix the approximate date of this affair and place it in its context—at least according to the Sunday supplement's editor's ideas of the newsworthiness of that week's happenings. On this picture page, my photograph with the caption:

A Musical Prodigy—Josef Szigeti

is flanked by four other pictures captioned as follows:

Sir Campbell-Bannerman [*sic*], the New British Premier, Formerly Leader of the Liberal Party in the House of Commons.

The New Balloon of Count Zeppelin Being Towed Out of Its Hanger: The newest vehicle has a form that no longer derives anything from that of the old balloon [Luftballon]. The cigar-shaped vehicle is being towed by specially constructed ships on to Lake Constance, whence it is to ascend completely by its own power.
The New Monumental Arch in Brussels: King Leopold II made a present of this magnificent monument to the City of Brussels, to celebrate the 75th Anniversary of the political independence of Belgium.

Then a picture of a lady "looping the loop":

Mlle de Thiers of New York shows this feat currently in the Zirkus Schumann at which she is starring.

So much for my Berlin début. . . .

(47)

Of the weeks and months that followed my Berlin début I remember little; there was a concert in Dresden given by the Merchants' Club or Casino of that city at which I played the Mendelssohn Concerto with orchestra, and which must have come off to the satisfaction of all concerned, for it resulted in a re-engagement some years later, when my career had already passed this first groping phase. It was at this return engagement under the same auspices around 1910 or so that I shared the programme with a statuesque, dark-haired young singer of remarkable attainments (I am of course recording the general consensus rather than my own impressions). Her name was Lily Hoffmann and she was accompanied on the piano by a considerably older man of diminutive stature and delicate, one would say inbred, features; he was her husband, a Baron Onegin from the Baltic provinces, and songs by him made up one of her groups. She was none other than the great singer known later under the name of Sigrid Onegin, whose passing away in 1943 brought forth many a fine tribute to her art in the American press.

It was during that winter in Berlin that I got my first copy of the Brahms Concerto, and I plunged into the formidable and forbidding work without any guidance and with all the more recklessness and gusto. The thirteen-year-old was—at long last, so it seemed to him!—on his own, faced with a man-sized task, and he forthwith began to shed the diffidence that the classrooms of those days generated to an infinitely greater degree than they do in our pedagogically more enlightened times.

The "pension" where we stayed was managed, or rather regimented, by a very Prussian lady whose imperious posture was accented by those stiff net collars held up by tiny invisible whalebones which gave the blouses of the period their distinctive mark. It was there that I met the first American of my childhood, Rudolph Ganz's wife Mary, with their baby son Roy. It was she who first initiated me into the niceties of American superhygiene (or so they seemed to the boy I was), such as nailbrushes, and the brushing of teeth at odd hours—as before parties, for instance; she also supervised my manners at that long boarding-house table. From her I learned a little about the fabulous America her husband was touring annually, saw his programmes, was shown pictures of Carnegie and other halls, and generally drank in American lore.

She took me along to parties at which I sometimes played (accompanied by her at the piano), earning some modest semi-professional fees in the process. I suppose that these "sorties" were engineered by the kindhearted American lady, a singer herself, in the hope that she would be able to take back to my father the glad tidings, from one of these parties, that "the sponsor"—that fabulous and nebulous figment of every "wunderkind" parent's imagination—had at last been found.

This apparently never quite came off, though results of *some* sort were always forthcoming after these musicales. It was one of these that brought about an episode that I am reserving for my next chapter.

Besides Mary Ganz, I had another kindhearted "pilot" during those first Berlin days. I was often taken out to play at musicales by Dr. Bernhard Pollack, a distinguished ophthalmic surgeon and one of the finest chamber-music pianists I have ever met; he was a great friend of Fritz Kreisler's, whom by the way he once companioned and accompanied on one of Kreisler's early tours of the United States (I gathered that this must have been in the 'nineties).

That during this period of my being handed around, as it were, my father and I chanced on some queer birds was, of course, inevitable. One of the queerest was a morose bachelor with the characteristically clipped speech of the true Berliner; he made me play for hours in his gloomy baroque "interior" and presented me with—a pineapple. That it was the *first* pineapple we had ever laid eyes upon or sniffed at did little to alleviate my father's disappointment—he naturally had to be on the alert with regard to our finances. But I who wasn't too conscious about such worries eventually had *my* share of disappointment too : I did not know how to attack the fragrant and prickly fruit of my labours.

CHAPTER VI

WHEN in the twenties I used to take my little
daughter regularly to the circus, she—with that
sure instinct of a child—felt that I was not only a
kindred spirit in my relishing of the ring but that the comments
and explanations I passed on to her had a certain additional
inside knowledge that surpassed even the all-knowingness she
flatteringly endowed me with. Why I didn't blurt out to her
the probably incredible fact that I myself had been for a brief
few weeks a colleague of similar lion-tamers, clowns, and
trapeze virtuosi, I still do not quite understand.

For this disclosure would no doubt have added in this
young lady's eyes immeasurable glamour and prestige to her
"more than life-size" parent.

It all started in 1906 in a Berlin drawing-room. After I
had played some soli, one of the guests walked up to my father
and stupefied him by suggesting that I take a trial engagement
of a week in Germany's then most "splendiferous" music
hall. To my father's indignant remarks, he retorted with
some lines which I suppose to be Goethe's: "*Wo Du die
Musen rufst, da ist ihr Tempel*"—or something to that effect.

This gentleman, who happened to be legal adviser to the
recently erected Zirkus Albert Schumann Theatre in Frankfurt-
am-Main, further placated us by suggesting that I could take
this fling into an unknown world under an assumed name of
our own choice. This and the casual mention of a figure of
appealing dimensions gradually changed the picture, and soon

we were deep in ways and means of clinching the deal, with me contributing, with a child's love of make-believe, the assumed name (or let us say "alias") Szulagi—a rhythmical paraphrase on my name: a concocted name that made "any resemblance between" the fiddler who was soon to appear on a music-hall stage and myself "purely coincidental," as the legal phrase has it.

The director of this sumptuous establishment was the famous retired lion-tamer Julius Seeth (who I believe had been performing even in the far-off Americas of the 'nineties) and I suspect that he did not much relish the imposition on his honest-to-goodness music-hall bill of my legal friend's new-fangled ideas, such as adolescent virtuosi and assorted classic concerti. I can still feel the weight of his lion-tamer hands on my frail shoulders as we paused in our rehearsal the morning of my début. I was working away at the Mendelssohn Concerto with the piano-playing Kapellmeister of the outfit. Covering up a good deal of anxiety and confusion, the Herr Direktor, who had listened to me with bewildered and discouraged mien, boomed in a broad Bavarian accent the equivalent of: "Well, boys, go at it with a will . . . we can't have flops 'round 'ere!"

These grave doubts in our lion-tamer's mind were soon allayed by facts that spoke his language: applause, new faces, gate receipts. The newfangled ideas had evidently stood the test.

My competitors for the audiences' favours were a famous trained-dog act in which the dogs played firemen and put out a fire on the stage; the popular comedian of the day, Otto Kruger (not to be confused with the Hollywood star); a troupe of bicycle acrobats; a male impersonator of various famous ballerinas of the time. The headliner of them all was Abbie Mitchell and her "Tennessee Students." She was an enchanting Negro singer, a forerunner of Florence Mills of the *Blackbirds of 1925*, with a troupe of shuffle-dancing, banjo-playing, Spiritual-singing young Negroes. It was my first contact with this rich vein of American folk lore, and it awoke an interest that has persisted through all the intervening years. The line of my contacts with Negro performers goes through Florence Mills, Ethel Waters, the various Negro revues that created such a furore in Parisian avantgarde circles, *Green Pastures, Porgy and Bess*, the Hall-Johnson Choir, right up to my present associations with Duke Ellington, Count Basie, and Lionel Hampton.

My predilection for them and their return in kind, as well as my musical connections with such other jazz luminaries as Benny Goodman and Spike Hughes, has brought me a mention in Hugues Panassié's definitive volume *Hot Jazz*. Panassié singles out Spike Hughes's *Arabesque* (dedicated to me) as a piece "which certainly ranks among the most original works that jazz has inspired." With his customary solemnity, Panassié continues: "Hughes dedicated it to . . . Joseph Szigeti, probably because of Szigeti's great interest in swing performances. In *The Melody Maker* John Hammond tells how he once met at the Stork Club in New York 'Szigeti, the Hungarian violinist, listening avidly to the music of Peewee Russell, Frank Froeba, Eddir Condon, McKenzie and the others.'"

To come back to Abbie Mitchell, just as Monsieur Jourdain did not realize that he "had been talking prose all along," so I—naturally—did not suspect that I was "in" on an historic phase of the ever-growing dissemination of Negro music.

While I was collecting material for the present page, Abbie Mitchell—who is living and teaching in New York (in 1944) after her recent and well-remembered transcontinental tour in *The Little Foxes* and *Porgy and Bess*—contributed the following details:

Her group of twenty-two men and women were known originally as Memphis Students and later, on the European Continent, called themselves Tennessee Students. They were all good musicians; four of the 'cellists had studied with Leo Schultz. They were, in a sense, pioneering for Negro folk music, introducing to Europeans the Negro Spirituals and jazz as arranged by Will Marion Cook, who had studied violin under Joachim for many years, later working at composition with Dvořák.

Again and again Abbie Mitchell, in recalling her first impressions of young "Szulagi," spoke of his "intense seriousness." She and her Tennessee Students never missed a Szulagi performance. They would stand in the wings and watch the young boy, who never smiled, whose name they couldn't pronounce, "with a sort of idolatrous yearning and a feeling that we would like to know him better. . . . I remember his serious, interested young face in the wings watching the Tennessee Students go through their performance. It was only when he played that his face lit up and a complete metamorphosis took place. I always wanted to talk to him —he seemed so isolated—but I never did. His father always watched him from the wings and hovered over him at all times 'like a mothering hen.'"

My doubting Thomas of a lion-tamer came around to prolonging my engagement by another week and even built one of the Saturday matinée programmes around the entire Mendelssohn Concerto—an unprecedented concession from him, since each of its three movements entailed his cutting out a full-sized circus act. But he went in for striking contrasts in his variety bill: in Berlin there had been a leopard-tamer and a ballet of 500 girls; in Frankfurt there had been a lion-tamer, the excellent bareback rider, and Szulagi!

These weeks in Frankfurt were happy ones, and this strange interlude in my career was quite a wholesome experience for the adolescent that I was. It was wonderful to have those long sunny days free for some long-range practising (in prevision of the anticipated trip to London), to be allowed to stroll into the mysterious precincts of the huge darkened stage whenever I wanted to, to watch the practice sessions of the various performers and groups, to realize what dogged perseverance and patience were necessary to keep those ten or twelve minutes of their nightly appearance at par, and to feel their bonhomie toward me whom they must have considered an interloper from another world.

With the intentness of my years I took in everything as if I were destined to continue working on that plane; I even went so far as to read their trade magazine, Das Programm, with its fascinating descriptions of acts and its naïvely and transparently bombastic advertisements. By the way, when I compare their tone with that of the so much less wholesome

publicity current in *our* more "exalted" station in the world
of public performers, the comparison turns out to their
advantage. One would read about how this or that acrobatic
stunt or *salto mortale* originated at the Colosseum Variété of
—— on a certain date, how the originator of the act warns
against any infringement of his "rights," and so on.

My general impression was that in their world progress
was slow, based on solid achievement, that with them claims
had to be substantiated; whereas in our world "flash-in-the-
pan" performers often enjoy considerable public success for
a while—though in the end, of course, their careers are likely
to be short.

I was impressively reminded, some years later during
World War I, of this rugged honest approach that mountebanks, circus folk, and so on have toward their work and
their worth. I was staying at the sanatorium in Davos that
I mentioned before, and one day a little band of tightrope
walkers announced that a performance would be held at a
specified hour in front of our terrace. Tickets were so much
and were to be bought in advance at the concierge's desk.

The head of the family, in pink tights, sneakers, brown-
checked topcoat, and black bowler, proceeded to set up his
equipment, helped by his wife and youngsters. It was quite a
job to accomplish on our gravel path; when it was done, they
stood around and waited. The appointed hour approached,
went by, and still there were only a handful of us patients,
who had been tempted to watch the show by the little hand-
written poster and by the preparations.

We tried to recruit more spectators, but in vain; a handful
we remained. Another short wait and the head of the troupe,
without a word, signalled to the youngsters to help him
dismantle the paraphernalia. Off they went, without condescending to perform to an unworthily small audience,
their workers' pride hurt, disdainful but perfectly polite in
their dignified withdrawal.

If I speak of us public performers in the same breath with
—well—these others, it is with the consciousness that I am
not the only one to lump them together! When I first gave
a concert in Berne, I was vastly amused to see on my manager's

expense sheet the item : "*Kunst-und-Hausiererschein*—10 francs."
Now, *Hausiererschein* means "a permit to solicit trade or peddle
from house to house"; as I was not aware of having embarked
upon this perfectly legitimate means of livelihood, I asked the
reason for this permit. He told me that in the eighteenth
century the municipality had imposed this permit fee indiscriminately on all vendors, market-place performers, mountebanks, medicine shows, and the like and that the archaic
wording had never been changed!

No less a figure than Stravinsky thought along the same
lines—that music should come out of its "exclusive" habitat
right to the people, to the tents of the market place. It was
during his years in Switzerland that he said this, and the
conception of *L'Histoire du Soldat* owes a good deal to this
thought. But I am anticipating a later story.

CHAPTER VII

THIS first winter (1905–1906) in Germany was rich for me in experiences and far-reaching impressions of all kinds; it brought me the outlandish assignment at the Zirkus Albert Schumann Theatre, gave me my first début in a foreign land, and my first Ysaÿe, Kreisler, and Elman concerts, as well as auditions with two great men, Joachim and Busoni.

Of the last-named whose presence and influence were and still remain a constant reality to me, more later. Of Joachim, who was to pass away so soon, I have a less vivid recollection since, unlike the meetings with Busoni that stretched over almost a quarter of a century, the one with Joachim stayed isolated.

When Joachim's letter according me this private audition came, the big question that my father and I argued back and forth from then until the great day was: What should I play? We went through my meagre repertory time and again, trying to choose something that would answer every one of the conflicting purposes inherent in such auditions. At last I had my way: we decided on the Beethoven Concerto. Whippersnapper that I was, I had no compunction about playing precisely this "concerto of all concerti" (as Joachim—who was responsible for its renaissance—called it) for Joachim himself.

I can't reconstruct an exact picture of that meeting. What a boy who was less of a daydreamer would have savoured consciously as a fateful, long-to-be-remembered milestone on his path left me only with a vague sense of impact by the truly great. This was inescapable, daydreaming notwithstanding! Even the servant who admitted my father and me into the brown penumbra of Joachim's studio, which I seem to remember as being furnished in the massive pseudo-Renaissance style of that period, conveyed to us by her hushed, almost ritualistic air the extreme veneration in which Joachim was held.

Childlike, I had imagined the man universally called at the time "The King of Violinists" as taller than he was. However, just as to-day Helen Hayes appears to us inches taller than she is through some magical projection of her inner self, so Joachim's personality contradicted feet and inches. He accompanied me in the Beethoven Concerto on the piano, from memory, and later had me play some Paganini, during which—the atmosphere gradually lost its initial note of austerity—he now began stopping me, interpolating shop talk, questioning me, testing the artisan in me. (He knew only too well the tricks of the pedagogical trade—how teachers taking advantage of the child's innate imitativeness can palm off a counterfeit for the real thing!) The words of praise and prophecies for my future that he wrote in my autograph book he backed up with something more substantial at the end of my audition: a proposal that I should stay on in Berlin, finish my repertoire studies under him, and accept his good offices with regard to a patron who would relieve us of material worries. He mentioned the banker and amateur 'cellist Franz von Mendelssohn.

I fear nothing more than the bathos of the traditional account of this or that great man's "giving the accolade to the youngster destined for great things," with its enumeration of the attendant chunks of sententious wisdom that inevitably seem to accompany these fateful meetings and which, from then on, mould the life of the aforesaid youngster for ever and a day!

The plain fact is that I listened with only half an ear. Nevertheless, bits of Joachim's talk emerging from my memory many years afterward, without context, without order, were potent enough to have been father to thought and action that I at first—with the vanity of youth—attributed to myself. Stray sentences about the pride an artist should feel in resisting the prevailing winds of public fancy.

Sentences that might have been operative without my being conscious of them—when I resisted "expert" advice on how to shape my programmes (and how often since then!), on how to find the short cut to success in America when I first went there in 1925. And who knows but that my predilection for solving musical problems the hard way (technically speaking) —a tendency that some of my colleagues often make good-natured fun of—can be traced to that afternoon!

My resistance against many a prevailing prejudice, my insistence on what I felt to be right (perhaps the words *resistance* and *insistence* are simply euphemisms for plain pigheadedness and quixotism), often had to be smoothed over. This was done in particularly brilliant fashion once by Bob Simon, who was in charge of the press department of my management at that time. He wrote a little brochure entitled *Let Bach Do It,* which in that often imitated prose of his (now so much a part of the *New Yorker*) described the way I fought for a place in the sun, or rather for a place in programmes, for the formidable Bach solo sonatas with the (to some) interminable Fugues. He described not only the fights with local programme committees but also the unexpectedly happy reactions when my thesis was tested on the battleground: when these more venerated than loved works were at last heard in towns that had studiously avoided them or had been deprived of them by the over-cautiousness of the performer. Into this same pattern of stubbornness fit some of my excursions into contemporary music—but of this, more later.

To come back to the audition with the great man, it must have been some premonition of his impending death—he died in 1907—that somehow prevented my father from accepting his offer that I remain in Berlin under Joachim's guidance, an offer seemingly so full of potentialities. My father, with that fine instinct which compensated for so many blanks in his educational background, felt it would be a mistake to link my perplexed immaturity to the greatness that was already so much a part of the past. I find an unexpected corroboration of the rightness of his instinct in the memoirs of Sam Franko: "I have a letter from him [writes Franko of Joachim, whose pupil he had been in the 'seventies] in which he acknowledges himself to be a poor pedagogue. Of all his hundreds of pupils not one has become world-famous. They became skilled musicians, excellent chamber-music players, filled the position of concertmaster with credit, but none of them really made a career as a solo violinist."

There were other reasons, too. Prime among them was consideration for my master Hubay, especially as there was an understanding that I would coach with him during his summer holidays in Ostend on the Belgian coast. And, like all self-made and self-educated men, my father must have put a great deal of faith in the lessons that life would bring me and in the incentive that the virtuosi I would be listening to would inevitably give me. He must have reasoned along the lines that an unreflecting youngster could not expect from Joachim's master hands, by then disfigured by gout, the physic-ally exhilarating stimuli that he craves—in preference to mellow wisdom and stylistic guidance. At Joachim's invita-tion I attended one of his lessons at the Hochschule, saw the master seated alone on a little platform in the middle of the room, no violin in his hands, listening, criticizing—but not demonstrating. This lack of interplay, this lack of kindling the pupil's enthusiasm through actual example, made for a certain remoteness in their relationship, or so I thought. It was as if the little platform symbolized the absence of flow between the two.

After I had attended this lesson the Master invited me to his Quartet evening scheduled for the following week at the Singakademie, one of those "Joachim Quartet Evenings" which for decades had been making musical history—a privilege I quite unforgivably failed to seize upon. There must have been a reason, but seen in retrospect *what* reason could be valid for such an omission?

This Joachim episode could perhaps be considered a great opportunity missed, but I personally take leave to doubt it. I have always proceeded by trial and error and, in spite of the attendant waste of time and energy, I still think that to drift for a few years and work one's way through the mediocre and superannuated to the fine and lasting values probably serves one best in the long run.

CHAPTER VIII

AFTER the strange interlude in Frankfurt-am-Main, there followed one more vaudeville adventure, this time at the Odeon Theatre in the lovely Bavarian baroque city of Wurzburg, a name that will mean a good deal to thirsty habitués of Luchow's on Fourteenth Street in New York City. The couple of weeks I spent on this engagement were to be the last of their kind, as far as I was concerned. For this shabby, old-time "Variété," which seemed to exude the smell of stale beer (in contrast with the ornate showplace in Frankfort, where no liquid refreshment was served during performances), had about it a great deal of the atmosphere of Marlene Dietrich's *Blue Angel* film. The fact that its "artists" were expected to have their meals in the "canteen," run by the management, brought me into an off-working-hours contact with my colleagues that must have been considerably less than welcome to my father and must have hastened his decision that this vaudeville episode should be my last.

Soon we were to embark upon a trip to London, my first across the Channel and the first into English-speaking territory. To us—inhabitants of a Hungary where German was then spoken along with the native Hungarian more than it is nowadays—England meant "abroad," to an incomparably greater degree than Germany did, naturally. The barrier of language was sufficient in itself to make this essential difference, for I spoke no English at all. Everything—hansom-cabs, the meals at the long table-d'hôte at our Bloomsbury Square boarding-house, the queer assortment of humanity peopling it, the fact that only inhabitants of our square had access to the fenced-in bit of green that gave its name to our locale (only houses on the square had the use of keys to this little oasis)—took on added characteristics of the foreign, the exotic, the puzzling; especially since my father's English, acquired on the oil fields of Austria, turned out to be less than adequate, and since the Hungarian "go-between" who found the London managers for my début was not always available to my eager questionings.

This go-between, Joseph Teleki by name, a self-made man who was then in the last stages of tuberculosis (of which he died soon after), was quite a character. He used to tell me of his early struggles—of how he plunged into English simply by learning by heart practically the whole Hungarian-English Dictionary, of how he had worked himself up into what was to become his profession of dramatic agent, with a mastery of English equal even to the task of translating (or at least supervising) the adaptations of some of his "wares" from English into Hungarian and vice versa. He was—if I remember rightly—an agent for Ferenc Molnár, Melchior Lengyel, James M. Barrie, Israel Zangwill, and other playwrights. What he thought of my fiddle-playing I remember much less than I do an overheard stray remark of his to my father, a remark that made me flush: "Make no mistake! Had Joska been destined to become a cobbler he would have turned out to be a rather *extraordinarily* good cobbler!"

On my at first timid exploring walks in the neighbourhood I was often embarrassed by the stares that my somewhat outlandish get-up provoked. I wore a short overcoat with "Persian lamb" collar and cap (made of wool, *bien entendu*) and a sailor blouse, above which—incongruously enough— a starched stand-up collar peeped out, this whole outfit emphasizing how little I "belonged" on that London sidewalk of 1906, still very Victorian in all essentials and where oleographs and statuettes of Sir John Millais's cloyingly sweet "Bubbles," advertising Pears' Soap, looked down at me from shop-windows, reminding me that here I was, washed ashore in a very strange land.

My impending début, however, in Bechstein Hall in

Wigmore Street (since renamed Wigmore Hall) soon changed all this. I was equipped according to the boys' fashion prevailing in the London of the time and taken to the old photographic studio of Elliott & Fry's to be photographed against the backdrop of a studious-looking manorial library, my head held in its place by the concealed neck-clamps that every self-respecting photographer considered an essential in those days.

I was taken to call on Victorian celebrities, like Francis Korbay, the composer of the then often-sung *Hungarian Puszta Songs*, Paolo Tosti, composer of best-selling ballads like *Goodbye*, and Sir Laurence Alma-Tadema whose pseudo-Greek idealized Victorian paintings still commanded absurdly high prices. Visits like these, rehearsals, and auditions with "prominent" personalities familiarized me gradually with parts of London very different from the Bloomsbury and New Oxford Street district to which I had limited myself on my early strolls.

The management under which I made my début was as unorthodox as might be expected from the efforts of a Hungarian dramatic agent on behalf of a boy-violinist. Thus it happened that I was managed by two "outsiders": one, a former music critic, or it may have been singing teacher, of German origin, a flashy dresser and glib talker, offspring of respectable Rhine-wine importers; the other, a backer of stage plays and touring stock-companies who had never before ventured into the concert field. This unconventional managerial set-up brought about an equally unconventionally framed début: it was a hybrid orchestral plus piano-accompanied-recital affair. I played—I believe—two concerti, the Ernst and the Mendelssohn, in the smallish recital hall where even an orchestra of reduced numbers was somewhat out of place, following them by virtuoso and salon pieces accompanied on the piano.

This somewhat unorthodox début opened the way to the barnstorming more usual in those days than it is now when the launching of a career follows certain almost scientifically worked-out patterns and minutely planned publicity campaigns.

Summer concerts with small symphony orchestras in seaside places like Bournemouth, Eastbourne and Brighton followed many London appearances—mostly with orchestra—under the auspices of the National Sunday League which had then only recently started its campaign against the dismal Victorian Sunday. Even in this more enlightened period Sunday concerts had to be camouflaged as "Sacred Concerts" and include a specified minimum of songs and ballads of religious or semi-religious character. The courageous campaigning of the National Sunday League took the concerts also—or perhaps principally—to the under-privileged working-class districts of London, more in need of relief from the Sunday gloom than the more affluent West End. At one of these—I can't recall whether it was at a Whitechapel or an Ealing theatre—the Salvation Army tried to dissuade our audience from entering the theatre and thus jeopardizing their salvation by breaking the Sabbath. They staged a countershow on the sidewalks, plumb opposite the entrance to the theatre, exhorting the passers-by and blasting away on harmonium, trombones, cornets, and drums—yes, above all, drums! They kept up this infernal din almost to the middle of our programme—I could hear it from the stage throughout my Wieniawski!— and then they apparently withdrew to more promising fields of proselytizing.

There were also sundry other appearances, after ceremonial Guild or Masonic dinners in the City, in impressive old City Halls like Drapers' Hall, when I was told to withdraw during the after-dinner speech-makings and esoteric ceremonies— for I had, of course, peeped in on the glitter and lavishness, on the almost medieval pomp of these affairs staged by the "Worshipful Company" whose first charter had been granted in the fourteenth century. As the members' ladies did not take part at these dinners, each guest was given a five-pound box of chocolates to take home. I, too, was given one, the opulence of which, of course, overwhelmed me who still remembered the not-so-distant days of the chocolate bar costing a fifth of a dime.

However, I began to get accustomed to other notes of luxury, too—rides in hansom-cabs, suède-topped boots with mother-of-pearl buttons, and visits to theatres, music-halls, to Buszard's funereal-looking black-and-white confectioner's shop and restaurant on Oxford Street where one dropped in for cakes baked on the premises and for a glass of lemon squash made the old and hard way: peel and juice and water boiled all together, then cooled and served from a jug. It was at this venerable restaurant that I met my first (and, I hope, last!) culinary Waterloo. A patroness who had invited me to lunch ordered real turtle soup with old sherry, whose velvety unctuousness my untutored palate interpreted as plain goo; after a spoonful or so, I begged to be excused from finishing it.

This culinary reminiscence brings to my mind another, whose locale was not far away. I see Caruso presiding over a long table at Pagani's Restaurant just behind Queen's Hall, supervising the seasoning of huge mounds of something-or-other "Bolognese" in the chafing dish in front of him. In those days I was a "rubberneck" eager to have the various celebrities frequenting Pagani's pointed out to me. Later on, my signature was to join the innumerable autographs which covered the walls of one of the upstairs rooms and which were covered with sheets of glass as time went on and that particular square got to be swarming with signatures. In those days the signatory felt he was "perpetuating" his name and fame on that indestructible wall, under that solid slab of glass. To-day Pagani's is only a memory, bombed out of existence, together with Queen's Hall.

CHAPTER IX

————————·{◆}·————————

A CHANCE meeting with a music-loving couple,
living in the pleasantest part of Surrey, brought me an
invitation for a stay of indefinite length and gave me
my first experience of the amenities of cultured living, of
books and playthings shared with the two children of the
house, of a beautifully tended garden, of parlour-maid in
starched apron and cap answering to her surname of "Prit-
chard" or "Standish" or something similar, whose butlerlike
functions were clearly set apart and above those of the rest of
the household staff. The bulky Panhard, one of the finest
automobiles of French make in those pioneer days, was soon
accepted as a matter of course by the boy who only recently
had regarded his first meal in a dining car or his first ascent in
one of the then rare Budapest elevators as a thrilling and—
in the latter case—somewhat scary experience.

However, I felt no trace of snobbish elation at having
reached this level of comparatively high living. I knew that
it was merely a happy interlude, a fluke, and that I hadn't as
yet "reached" anything. I just took it all in my stride while
it lasted, with boyish thoughtlessness, knowing well that soon
enough I would revert again to my former modest estate—
and revert to it *easily*. Meanwhile I aided and abetted my
host's hobby-horse riding, recording for his sapphire-needle
phonograph innumerable cylinders on the hand-assembled
recording outfit; playing the Bach *Chaconne* and several concerti, most of them even without any accompaniment, for in
those heroic days of the phonograph the recording fan, who

C

was a rare bird indeed around 1906, was less concerned with musical values than with the mechanics of the thing and with "progress"! Sometimes in my host's absence in the City I would sneak into the library-laboratory and do some experimental self-recording on my own, for no other reason, I suppose, than that it was clandestine and therefore desirable. Those were the days of the belated toys, hoops, spinning tops, and steam-engines, of Andersen's *Tales,* and of *Treasure Island,* of my first copies of the Beethoven sonatas and of the three Brahms and the César Franck sonatas. (No, I had not even possessed the music of these works up to then.) Altogether, it seems to have been a time for repairing past omissions— omissions not only of work left undone, but of childish games that were never played.

I just mentioned Andersen's *Tales* and Stevenson's *Treasure Island.* Omissions of unplayed games could hardly be repaired; those of sonata-playing and of reading could be. My reading had always been haphazard. Leaving school just before my Berlin début in 1905, I carried away only the most sketchy rudiments of education. Even the Hungarian classics, prescribed at grade school, were closed books to me.

So it happened that I started to read pell-mell the vanguard Hungarian moderns, many of them incomprehensible to my ten or eleven years; Maupassant and Wilde; Barbey d'Aurevilly in luridly illustrated German or Hungarian paper-backs; *Tom Sawyer, The Last of the Mohicans, King Lear,* and Jules Verne. Later in England I started out with the equivalent of our present-day pulp literature; then I stumbled on *Tristram Shandy,* on Andersen's *Fairy Tales* and *Treasure Island,* which my nurseryless childhood had made me miss; on Tolstoy and Gorky, on *Three Men in a Boat,* Hazlitt's essays, *Peter Pan,* Stevenson's *Virginibus Puerisque, Idle Thoughts of an Idle Fellow,* Zangwill, George Eliot's *Adam Bede,* Dickens, some Chesterton, and so on—intermingled with (say) *Faust* in English, or perhaps *La Dame au Camélias* in Hungarian!

As for my French reading, I began during World War I with a cheap edition of *Manon Lescaut,* on which I scribbled my rough translation, with an occasional copy of the *Journal de Genève* and a dictionary to help me translate and laboriously gather vocabulary.

Before I could even stutter in French, I was offered the post of Professor of the Classes de Virtuosité in the Geneva Conservatory—plunging into this somewhat prematurely attained dignity with my gibberish concocted out of German, French, and English.

It would not be exactly true to say that during these years in England I was oblivious of the times in which I lived. I did read newspapers after a fashion (or perhaps I should say after *my* fashion, of which I may have something to say later), but I did not try to make up my mind about anything, nor did I itch to have opinions on everything as do most lads in their 'teens. Whether it was an upper middle-class Englishman explaining to me the current thesis of backing up British foreign trade with dreadnoughts, or my lovable old friend Felix Moscheles telling me about Mazzini, whose portrait, by Moscheles, looked down on us during our frequent Sunday suppers, I did more listening than precocious talking.

To hear Moscheles reminisce under that portrait that was dominated by the look of Mazzini's fearless, uncompromising eyes, eyes that seemed to hold the onlooker in their power, was an experience that left its mark upon me. It was not only the more picturesque aspects of Mazzini's revolutionary and conspiratory activities that fascinated me during these Sunday suppers, the accounts of his clandestine visits to countries in which a price had been set upon his head, and tales of the detectives who were constantly shadowing him during his London exile. What impressed me most during those formative years was to hear about Mazzini's almost utopian ideas concerning compulsory insurance that should prevent any man from becoming a pauper in his old age. These ideas were expounded by Mazzini in 1862 while my mentor Felix Moscheles, then a young man, was painting his portrait, and in the light of modern sociology they do not seem so far removed from the compulsory-insurance concepts of the Beveridge Plan. With a few verbal touches Felix Moscheles would humanize for me this portrait of the incorruptible fighter and conspirator. He would repeat the standing joke between them. Moscheles would ask: "Well, how are things? What are you doing?"—to which Mazzini would invariably reply with a smile: "*Je conspire*." He would tell me about Mazzini's death in Pisa under the assumed name of "Mr. Francis Braun"; of the recognition of his worth long afterward as "The Apostle of Italian Unity." Such were some of the gleanings of my visits to the Moscheles studio.

The only tangible trace of this friendship that remains with me is a page in my boyhood autograph album—a rhyme written in German by the venerable host of these Sunday suppers. After some lines on the aspirations that should guide his young friend toward "Olymphic heights," on the never-ending toil that is the lot of the true artist, he concluded with:

> Von Deinem Bogen lassen wir uns führen,
> Von Deinen Saiten uns begeistern, rühren.
> Nun, lieber Joska, sammle Lorbeer-Zweige
> Und stürm die Welt mit Deiner Wunder-Geige!*
> FELIX MOSCHELES

1 Juli 1906

When in about 1909 I got to know the daughter of "Pasha" von der Goltz in a German university town—Goltz later served as field marshal in Turkey during World War I —and when her young son demonstrated to me the muscle-building virtues of the Prussian goose-step (and no doubt lectured me on the character-building virtues of the Junker code as well), I had memories of the peace-loving internationalist Felix Moscheles to fall back upon. Godson of Mendelssohn, he was the son of the pianist and composer Ignaz Moscheles. The elder man, a younger contemporary of Beethoven, had had the honour of transcribing *Fidelio* into a *Klavierauszug* under the supervision of the Master himself for Beethoven's publisher Artaria. In 1824 he had taught

---

* Freely translated as:
> By your bow let us be led,
> By your strings inspire and move us.
> And so, dear Joska, collect laurels
> And take the world by storm with
> your wonder-fiddle.

Felix Mendelssohn, then aged fifteen, and thereafter was his good friend until Mendelssohn's death in 1847.

In Felix Moscheles's studio home in St. John's Wood, I handled not only Bach, Beethoven, and Mendelssohn manuscripts but also such revered relics as medallions containing Goethe's and Mendelssohn's hair. In the presence of a living link with this heroic past, I also had some glimpses into the future. Prince Peter Kropotkin, the exiled Russian revolutionary, lived near by and was a frequent visitor. I will not pretend to conversations with the author of *Memoirs of a Revolutionist*, but I do remember the Slavic charm and beauty of his daughter, some years my senior, I think, whom I can still visualize, radiant, in a red voile dress at one of the Moscheles gatherings. Though I did not presume to speak to Kropotkin, I did pick up notions of what he stood for, did read various pamphlets that were lying about. One of them condemned the pernicious practice of giving children "militaristic" toys: guns, dreadnoughts, tin soldiers. I also heard a lot about Esperanto in this studio. Here also originated the idea of my appearing at that Queen's Hall concert at which all the songs —even *God Save the King*—were sung in Esperanto, and at which my fiddle-pieces were the only non-Esperanto contributions to the programme.

Even though I did not speak to Maxim Gorky, who was among those present, on another Sunday, beyond asking (with a mute gesture) for his autograph, which he gave me on an unused penny postcard I happened to have in my pocket, still I was conscious of an unwonted solemnity, an urgency in the air that afternoon. It made me a hushed and thoughtful Sunday-supper companion for old Felix Moscheles for the rest of that evening!

There was a platform in the studio on which I had often stood, playing the light-hearted virtuoso stuff to which I was partial in those days, and sometimes also the Mendelssohn Concerto that godson Felix, then probably around seventy years old, often requested.* On the Sunday when I saw

* Whenever, in my boyish exuberance, I would play the first movement in an exaggeratedly fast tempo, Moscheles would gently chide me, saying: "Joska, it's marked '*Allegro comma molto appassionato*'—not '*Allegro molto comma appassionato*'!"

Gorky, there stood on that platform three or four solemn, emaciated men with high-cheek bones, in black sack suits, Gorky in the centre and Lenin among them. It was not long after the abortive 1905 revolution. (Gorky's friendship with Lenin dated from the time of this their first meeting in London at the Fifth Congress of the Russian Social Democratic Labour Party in 1907.) The men spoke, each in turn, in Russian, in calm, factual tones. Someone gave us a partial translation, and subscription blanks were passed around for contributions; my contribution was the meagre silver cash I happened to have on me.

I am not much of a collector of relics, especially since the time when the wife of a world-famous pianist unwittingly made me see the full horror of this addiction. She told me of the hardships of their wandering life, encumbered by huge cabin trunks, reconditioned with shelves on which stood, upright, as in a library, scrapbook upon scrapbook, snapshot albums, bulky collections of programmes, files with the accounts of many concert tours, even collections of multicoloured ribbons from "defunct" laurel wreaths, all stamped in gold letters with those "unforgettable" and now equally defunct dates. . . . Still, when on my third or fourth trip to Soviet Russia, shortly after Lenin's death, I made some records there on their completely obsolete recording equipment (dating from 1912 or 1913), I insisted at the laboratory that I be given one of Lenin's recorded speeches as a souvenir. Transporting such a record across the Swiss border was something of a risk in those days, Switzerland not having yet recognized the Soviet Union. My wife, with the innate feminine instinct for smuggling, solved this problem by pasting a handwritten label over the original one. Her label read:

Test Record
Slavonic Dance by Dvořák
Played by Joseph Szigeti

It was a record we often played to Russian friends when we moved to Paris. Unfortunately I only got the general

(70)

outline of its meaning, in sketchy translation, while the record was being played. It was a plea for unity and a warning against anti-Semitism, with its insidious, disintegrating poison. This prophetic record must have been spoken in 1921 or 1923, some ten years before the Nazis started propagating their monstrous creed with the demoniac drive and results we have come to know since.

When I think of those totally inadequate "acoustical" records I made in Moscow for a State Music Organization called *Muspred,* and when I remember the almost childlike pleasure and pride they gave to all concerned, my hindsight makes me see something symbolic in all this—something symbolic of the pride of those who in the middle twenties were heroically building up their world out of ruins, in an isolation that was imposed on them; who were surrounded by hostility and nonrecognition; and to whom every "first" achievement, however inadequate it may have been compared with the *Zagranitchni* product ("foreign" or, literally, "beyond the border"), meant something infinitely precious and inspiring.

There were "flash-backs" to the *past,* too, during those Sunday suppers with Felix Moscheles. The strange coincidence that I should in my early 'teens have come in close touch with this contemporary of Mendelssohn, Richard Wagner, Robert Browning, and Rossini made me the recipient of a number of treasurable first-hand stories. There is, for example, this expression of Rossini's adoration of Mozart as the master of them all: "Beethoven," Rossini told Moscheles, "I take twice a week, Haydn four times, but Mozart I take every day of the week." Moscheles also often gave us graphic descriptions of some incidents of his early years in Paris. He told of Richard Wagner standing at the piano by the side of Mme Pauline Viardot, who was reading *Tristan und Isolde* at sight. Wagner was turning the pages and occasionally broke in with a few words when he could no longer contain his enthusiasm before the grandeur of his own creation. "*N'est-ce pas, Matame,*" he would exclaim, "*N'est-ce pas, Matame, que c'est suplime?*"

He often repeated and enlarged upon the story of how

Queen Victoria, after having Mendelssohn play to her one afternoon, asked him what *she* could now do in return for the enchanting hour of music. (We hardly need a Winterhalter or a Laurence Housman to help us conjure up the "Conversation Piece.") Mendelssohn, after some hesitation, and prefacing his unusual request with the appropriate apologies, asked the young Queen whether Her Majesty would allow him an inside glimpse of the running of the Royal Household. Whereupon she herself accompanied him on a tour of the royal apartments and nurseries, including in this tour even such intimate domestic details as linen closets, giving Mendelssohn an insight into royal domesticity such as very few mere mortals at the time were privileged to have. They made this tour in the roles of the experienced materfamilias and enlightened pater-familias that they were, comparing notes and giving one another points on the management of their respective children. It was a privilege that Mendelssohn apparently prized so greatly that he never tired of telling it to his little godson with many added picturesque details.

The unsuspected domestic simplicity of royalty was brought home to me, too, when I played for Queen Elizabeth of Belgium in 1923. (I had played for her for the first time in 1910.) It was at the Château of Laeken that the informal musicale took place. There was only one guest present, a young man who, like Queen Elizabeth herself, was an amateur violinist. For some reason I was directed, on my way to the small family drawing-room, through the dining-room and, on passing through it, I saw there, lying neatly all in a row on the sideboard, the family napkins, rolled up in their silver napkin rings.

For *really* regal living, however, give me a prima donna any time! Or, rather, a "Queen of Song" like Melba. Her concert party—or shall we say retinue?—on that tour of England in 1909 boasted no less an "assisting pianist" than Busoni in some cases, Wilhelm Backhaus in most others. I believe John McCormack, then barely twenty-five, was also with us most of the time. There was a bass singer, too, in accordance with the time-honoured formula of the English "ballad concert," which meant operatic arias and ballads by soprano, tenor, and bass, in succession, without end: songs like "I Hear You Calling Me," ballads by Liza Lehmann, Teresa Del Riego, and so on, with a few instrumental numbers thrown in. Philippe Gaubert, the famous French flutist who later became conductor of the venerable Société des Concerts du Conservatoire of Paris was with us, also, playing obbligato to some of Melba's coloratura cadenzas. Everybody seemed to have carried his own accompanist with him; and Melba's pianist, who also functioned as a coach, had his wife with him as well. All these, added to Melba's inner circle consisting of maid, secretary, and manager, made up quite a sizable party. Hence, when Melba one night had the whim to return to London after a concert in the Midlands, and found that there was no convenient late evening train, she chartered a special consisting of a single diner and an armchair car. Our numbers and our appetites and our chatter must have gratified her queenly penchants considerably and made this expenditure, considered most eccentric in those climes and times, seem to her quite worth while. At the end of a tour she would distribute among her loyal subjects tiepins and brooches each in the form of an "M" in diamonds or rubies, or lesser stones, as the case might be, all in the authentic royal manner. Once, when I was afflicted with a cold in the head and a running nose, she herself supervised the sprinkling and atomizing with eucalyptus oil of the floor back-stage and of the stairs leading to the platform, keeping me, with imperious "exorcising" gestures, as far from her person as was possible. Somehow her gestures lifted this "ordinary or common cold" above the plane of the million other ordinary or common colds. Ordinary or common indeed! She worried constantly about anything that might endanger *her* larynx and *her* vocal cords— or, as American present radio advertising jargon would phrase it, the world's most honoured . . . larynx. Anyway, all this grotesquerie seemed somehow in keeping with the whole anachronistic set-up and build-up.

With what relish would she tell us the oft-written story of the birth of "Peach Melba"—a story seemingly inseparable from the very name of Melba—while her entourage would listen dutifully with the appropriately courtier-like attention due the recital of an historic event by the protagonist of that event. The story ran somewhat as follows: the Chef of the Savoy in London where Melba was staying during the Covent Garden season, none other than the great Escoffier, declared himself heartbroken at not being able to get tickets for the completely sold-out Melba gala performance that night. Whereupon she set in motion the machinery that somehow always manages to yield that extra pair of seats for any supposedly sold-out gala. Next day at lunch there gleamed on her table the delectable silver cupful, covered with chopped burnt almonds, accompanied by a courtly note of thanks from the *maître*, announcing that he had named his "creation" after her. At such moments, or when she held forth on the very special merits of Canadian whisky as against the what she termed undrinkable product of Scotland which, said she, was not fit . . . and so on and so forth, there was something likeable and refreshing in her very unpredictableness.

From a strictly musical point of view I owe her few lasting memories, but the girlish freshness of that voice and the indolent languorous grace with which she sang some things remain unforgettable to me to this day. Recently, when arranging for publication some short pieces for violin, I decided to include Lalo's "Aubade" from *Le Roi d'Ys* in the series, probably to give substance to my memory of her singing of this song. A small thing, to be sure, but her own; and ineffably beautiful this small thing must have been to have retained its hold on me through all these years.

CHAPTER X

ANOTHER song associated with this period, which for some three decades lay dormant in my memory only to emerge suddenly for no reason at all that I can tell, is *Snow*, by the Norwegian composer Sigurd Lie. It also found its way into my series of transcriptions. This delightfully atmospheric song, which never leaves the ground bass of D, remains linked in my memory with Blanche Marchesi, with whom I also toured the English provinces at about this time. Here was a singer with a very different musical and cultural background from that prevalent at the time among "ballad singers"; cosmopolitan in outlook, with the authentic grand manner. Small wonder, since her formative years had been spent in the studio-home of her mother, the great Mathilde Marchesi, who treated singers like Melba, Sembrich, and Etelka Gerster like just so many pupils, and pretty imperious the manner of the Maestra must have been, according to hearsay.

However, it is not only the "grand manner" that I remember when I think of Blanche Marchesi. She, too, was an imperious lady, who carried her bulk, compressed into the lines of the period, with a dignity that did not exclude self-persiflage about her steel-and-whalebone "build-up." There was a maternal warmth in her manner toward me, and obvious interest in my development. Her worldly-wise and theatre-wise humour was to me another of her memorable attributes; a sense of humour which, however, completely deserted her whenever her professional vanity was involved, as in the always perilous question of "billing." The quite disproportionate passion with which she held forth on the moral wrong caused her by the top-billing of Busoni, her learned legal dissertations on what was and what was not sanctified by usage, her threats of holding out for moral reparations—all opened up to me entirely unsuspected vistas of professional ambition, of tooth-and-nail fighting for what one deems to be one's place in the sun. It all seemed Greek to my somewhat indolent adolescence. I was an "assisting artist," paid by the week, I had the least propitious placings on the programme (the opening number and perhaps the one after the intermission), and that was all there was to it. When some provincial paper came out unexpectedly with the headline "Madame Marchesi and Szigeti score," or "Backhaus and Szigeti at So-and-so Hall," this rise in my status did not unduly excite or elate me, though I cannot vouch for my father in this respect. . . .

It must have been Blanche Marchesi who gave me seats for the concert performance of Ethel Smyth's opera *The Wreckers*, conducted by Nikisch at Queen's Hall. Dame Ethel Smyth in her delectable memoirs which will, I think, withstand the ravages of time infinitely better than will her music, speaks fervently of Blanche Marchesi's singing in this opera, and of her selfless spirit of co-operation.* The indomitable and very British fighting spirit of Dame Ethel, a woman composer who challenged all sorts of Victorian and Edwardian conventions in her private life as well as in her music, probably made a deeper impression on me than I realized then, or even years afterwards. Those polemical "Letters to the Editor" of hers, the courage and promotional skill that went into her efforts to win a place for her music and also for that of her British fellow composers, were quite an eye-opener for me.

My natural laziness and the unwonted amenities of my mode of living at the time—in that garden-home in Surrey —combined to create a pleasantly drowsy, slightly confused, static frame of mind, and kept from me all disturbing thoughts of self-development, of self-criticism. The indolence of the

* Dame Ethel Smyth in her *What happened next* (1908) calls Blanche Marchesi "one of the largest-souled artists I have known."

so-called awkward age, *l'age ingrat* (with more than its share of puppy loves), was, I suppose, aggravated in my case by the many regressive factors in a "boy-violinist's" life. The constant grinding out of the same obsolete salon pieces by Sarasate, Hubay, and Wieniawski, which seemed to serve their purpose well at these Ballad Concerts and Park Lane musicales and on provincial tours, was a significant regressive factor, and so was the desirability—expressed tacitly all around me—of "retarding" the moment of passing from the status of "boy-violinist" to the unglamorous one of adult musician. This holding at bay of manhood is generally aided and abetted in every way by the "prodigy's" entourage and impresarios, and it is not surprising that I acquiesced, with the shrewdness of the lazy adolescent, in this game of not allowing myself to grow up too soon.

Just as I had been sent on to the platform in a white alpaca sailor blouse and shorts (necessitating some depilation!) for an overprolonged period, so my entourage now devised for me an "artistic" accoutrement of black velvet jacket, flowing white "Lavallière" tie, and (thank Heaven for this at least!) long black trousers. Apparently I showed none of the normal impatience of the young man to attain to the dignity of conventional evening clothes.

Though I wore them in the daytime and not on the platform, my grey suède-topped shoes with their mother-of-pearl buttons evidenced the foppish attitudes of this 'teen-age phase, from which apparently I emerged unscathed. It was with an amused shock, with the shock of the *déjà vu*, that I saw the counterpart of the shoes of that long-forgotten boyhood on my friend Hamilton Harty in the fall of 1939, when I last saw him in London. For it was only then that the subtle relationship dawned on me: Harty, the composer of the first concerto dedicated to me, his rehearsal-visits to my Surrey home, his dandyism which I boyishly copied. . . .

Foppish, too, were parts of the musical pattern of my life at this time. What but the most saccharine salon music would have been appropriate to that musicale which to me is indissolubly linked with the first hothouse nectarine I ever tasted, and with my first orchid! The musicale was given by a bachelor neighbour of the Duchess of Albany at Esher in Surrey, in her honour. (I remember he had made his fortune with that bluish-grey, water-resisting paint so indispensable in the coating of battleships!) The uncritical audiences at such parties probably fostered in me that self-indulgence of which hothouse plants and luscious fruits and suède and velvet and mother-of-pearl seem to me now, in retrospect, almost symbolic.

Externals like these emphasize the indirection of these years that unduly prolonged the marking-time of 'teen years. It was the lack of guidance during this period that makes me stress everything that helped me overcome the torpor of these years. My long talks with Blanche Marchesi and with Busoni helped, as did my glimpses, through Ethel Smyth, Hamilton Harty, and Josef Holbrooke, into the struggles of composers. (Holbrooke was another of those chronic writers of protesting letters to the editor about the neglect suffered by indigenous music!) Looking back, I can barely understand how I did not find the road to quartet playing at this formative period, which would have been so timely for plunging into the treasures of quartet literature, nor how it is that no self-appointed mentor volunteered to show me the way to these treasures.

All this is probably traceable to the reluctance to grow up that seems to be inbred in prematurely exhibited virtuosi, especially those of my generation. It is a vicious circle: maturing influences pass the youngster by because he does not act his age, and his development is retarded precisely because they are absent. I remember a gay party at Myra Hess's home at which I felt strangely and painfully out of place surrounded by young British musicians and composers who were regaling themselves with pastiches of each other's works. The reasons for their roars of laughter were all but unintelligible to me, for, not knowing the models, I could not relish the caricatures.

My first public performance of a Beethoven sonata, the C minor, was with Myra Hess at a joint recital in Dundee, Scotland, when I was already in my middle 'teens. I was still groping my way in the (to me) new realm of Beethoven's language, whereas Myra Hess, though barely out of Tobias Matthay's school, moved in this world with the assurance and the stylistic conviction of a veteran. The word "veteran" may seem somewhat of an exaggeration in connection with the Myra Hess whom I had first heard at a pupils' concert at this school a year or two previous to our joint recital. But, although she was not yet sufficiently grown-up for a formal hair-do at that school concert, her playing already had a mellowness, an intimate graciousness (I am tempted to call it a "sweet reasonableness"), which I have never since encountered in any young virtuoso, unless it may have been in the eleven- or twelve-year-old Heifetz's touchingly beautiful performance of the Bruch G minor Concerto in Berlin, some years before World War I.

But in one thing Myra Hess stands alone: her playing seems never to have gone through those unfortunate phases that mark (and mar) the development of most other virtuosi. Eloquence born of understatement, a rare gift indeed—and, I suspect, a particularly British one—was hers even in that youthful time. And I can well imagine Myra Hess, Dame of the British Empire, in these recent war days, brushing aside the homage and gratitude due her for the incalculable good she wrought during the London "blitz" by her National Gallery lunch-hour concerts, with the same deprecating smile she used to have for us in those early days when we pointed out something particularly admirable and lovable in her playing of, say, the first statement of the theme of Beethoven's G Major Concerto. To many of us, the almost unique quality of her playing is her selfless humility in the presence of great music— her air of asking us: "Am I not privileged to be able to bring this to you?"—Never: "Am I not a wonderful pianist?"

When I came under the management of the London firm of Schulz-Curtius and Powell, Herr Schulz-Curtius, representative of the Bayreuth Festivals in London, asked me the embarrassing question whether I played any of the Mozart concerti, and upon hearing my negative answer suggested that I learn one of them. On the other hand, his partner, ebullient young Lionel Powell, founder of the Celebrity Tours which later in the 1920s introduced Galli-Curci, Heifetz, and

Horowitz to England, and an amateur fiddler of sorts himself, gave me his own copy of Sarasate's show-piece, *The Nightingale* (full of naïvely literal, imitative passages in harmonics), to incorporate into my repertory. Conflicting advice indeed from two partners of the same managerial firm!

Herr Schulz-Curtius's excellent advice about Mozart, which took some time to sink in but which eventually produced results, reminds me of another incident that proved similarly an eye-opener for me. I had to play for the great musician Vincent d'Indy in Paris and, as I then considered Carl Goldmark's Concerto a masterpiece (this epigonous composition paraded as such for several decades in the late nineteenth century!), I had made it the rather unfortunate choice for my audition with César Franck's greatest disciple. D'Indy accompanied me and everything went according to plan in spite of this stylistic *faux pas* of mine; he even volunteered to give me a letter of introduction to Edouard Colonne, all-powerful founder of the famed "Concerts Colonne." No doubt this must have been the unavowed purpose of the audition, as it always is in such cases; youngsters who are dragged by their managers to the musical great are seldom in quest of constructive advice and criticism, but rather seek letters of introduction, quotable "testimonials," and similar instruments that may bring immediate dividends. . . .

D'Indy, however, besides giving me this welcome letter of introduction, added something infinitely more valuable on parting: the advice to be more selective and critical in choosing my repertoire. He demolished with a few shattering remarks, I remember, the prestige the Goldmark piece then still had in my eyes, and he gave me a concrete example of what he meant—I still have the notation in d'Indy's handwriting on my copy of the Goldmark Concerto.

> 12 Sonates pour violon avec basse chiffrée
> par Jean-Marie Leclair

and the name of editor and publisher. Strange bedfellows indeed: Leclair and Carl Goldmark! Now that I come to think of it, it is rather understandable that the Goldmark Concerto should at that time have had an exaggerated prestige in the eyes of the stylistically unformed 'teen-age fiddler I was. Don't most of us tend to attribute a fictitious importance to events, interpretative vehicles, and connections that highlight our own egos? In 1910 Goldmark's eightieth birthday was being celebrated by the Hungarian state with gala concerts both at the Budapest Opera and at his birthplace, Keszthely, and I had been chosen to play the A Minor Concerto on both occasions. Reason enough to raise the (I'll admit even now) effective, lushly melodious period-piece several pegs higher in my biased boyish estimation! During these festive days the venerable old master with the sparse, flowing white locks and the singularly fiery eyes that belied his age used to indulge in his passion for water travel by getting on one of the little "propeller" boats that plied the Danube between the close-spaced landing stages on the Buda and the Pest sides of the river. One sunny afternoon he took me along with him. We stood on deck, bareheaded in the brisk breeze, talking for all we were worth, Goldmark paying our three or four cents' fare each time a new ticket had to be bought. The ticket collector, seeing us travel from terminal to terminal without ever getting off, looked on amazed after punching and repunching tickets for us time and again. And I, in turn, was amazed at the liberality with which the old master whose music so manifestly belonged to the gilt-and-plush era should speak of Paul Dukas's *Ariane et Barbe-Bleu*, which had recently been produced at the Vienna Opera and had naturally evoked a great deal of adverse comment among the more conservative elements. "I don't understand it," Goldmark told me. "It's a new language. But the thing that matters, and that determines my attitude, is that Dukas's music has its own physiognomy. That's what makes me sit up, listen, try to probe its meaning—hard though this is for my old ears. Yes—music that has its own physiognomy," he continued, as if talking to himself; "that's the thing that matters. . . ." When I visited him in Vienna in his modest bachelor lodgings I found him soaking unused postage stamps off the corners of envelopes in a washbowl. He joked: "This is my means of subsistence, you see: autograph-collectors' self-addressed envelopes. I soak them off. Quite a little income. . . ."

In other domains, too, there was this same lack of being monitored. Instead of making regular pilgrimages to the National Gallery, the Wallace Collection, and the like, I wasted beautiful spring afternoons on those ephemeral Royal Academy shows at Burlington House, with their anecdotal "problem pictures." The word "problem" in this connection did not by any means refer to pictorial or stylistic problems; it referred to such grave questions—threshed out at great length in the newspapers—as that of the exact nature of the disease that a solemn-faced doctor was revealing to the young man sitting in front of his desk. The canvas—I am recalling only one of many—was entitled *The Verdict*, or something equally cryptic and argument-provoking.

I wonder whether "problem pictures" did not have their parallel in music, too. As I look back on the somewhat exaggerated prestige enjoyed especially at that time by Sir Edward Elgar's *Enigma* Variations (what superb performances of this work have I heard by Nikisch!), I cannot help speculating on the possibility that it was partly due to these typically Edwardian elements of the cryptic and the argument-provoking—in short, due to the "Royal Academy problem picture" element—that this beautifully wrought work largely owes its popular appeal. I am sure that this is true at least in England, where learned discussions are still going on as to the identity of "Dorabella," "Nimrod" (who according to recent commentators was Mr. Jaeger, of Novello's), and others.

My reading was most haphazard; the novels of Seton Merriman, Marion Crawford, and the Baroness Orczy were not exactly calculated to give my "picked-up" English a solid foundation. However, chance sometimes supplied the deficiencies of environment and put into my hands Hazlitt's Essays, *Tristram Shandy*, volumes of Robert Louis Stevenson's correspondence, and the like.

Transplanted almost entirely unschooled from my native Hungary to a country whose language I was picking up casually, I found it easy to camouflage—aided by an appropriate accent—my lack of the basic elements of education and of discipline which regular schooling gives one. The blunt fact is that these lacks could not have been so successfully concealed in my native land! (On second thought, this may also be the reason for the assiduous conservation of the assorted but equally "cute" accents that adult virtuosi and prima donnas over here dish up after decades of residence in Anglo-Saxon countries!)

My narrow, purely vocational interest in the great violin performances of these years—Ysaÿe's, Kreisler's, Elman's, Thibaud's—led me often to Queen's Hall and, fortunately for me, they brought me many rewards as a by-product of these expeditions in quest, primarily, of violinistic thrills and experiences; they brought me, for instance, familiarity with symphonic literature conducted by Henry Wood, Artur Nikisch, and Hans Richter.

A natural penchant for the theatre helped to give some little substance to these aimless, happy-go-lucky years. But here, too, Beerbohm Tree productions of Shakespeare would be followed by some ephemeral "season" success: with Bernard Shaw's *Man and Superman* (largely unintelligible to me then) followed by his *Fanny's First Play*, and Barrie's *Peter Pan* perhaps by the staged patriotic "pamphlet," *An Englishman's Home*, my theatre-going was somewhat of a jumble too. . . .

One of these tours in the provinces brought me into renewed contact with Busoni, just at a time when I most needed the impact of such a personality. I had played for him in Berlin some two or three years before, and the inscription in my autograph album gives a glimpse of the born pedagogue Busoni could not help being, even at such a casual auditioning. (How many of these must have been crowded into his days?) He wrote:

Ich wünsche Dir, dass Deine Kunst Dich
befriedige—dann wird sie Andere erfreuen;
doch das Erste is wichtiger.
Herzlichst,
FERRUCCIO BUSONI
1906

Which may be loosely translated as, "My wish is: may your
art satisfy you—others will then rejoice in it; but the former
is the more important." It is significant that he should have
given a boy, at the very first meeting, in just a few words—
especially in that pregnant last line—a musical ideology so
comprehensive that it could, if followed in the right spirit,
suffice for an artistic lifetime.

What worlds Busoni opened up for me! Listening to him
—sometimes four or five times in one week; talking to him:
What a contrasting atmosphere after futile prima-donnas'
tantrums and tenors' chalking up of the "count": "Triple
encore to-night as against double encore last night!" He was
playing his transcription of the Bach *Chaconne* at every concert,
and never one of these many performances but that I stood in
the wings, taking it all in, again and again, until he, with that
unique blend of Olympian aloofness and intensely human
generosity characteristic of him, one night, quite unexpectedly,
asked me to play the *Chaconne* to him in his hotel room the
following afternoon. How unforgettable that hour! I
recall his elucidation of the large pattern that the grouping of
several related variations into variation-clusters, one might
say, brings into the vast structure, and his insistence on mono-
chrome treatment of some of the variations instead of the
violinistically traditional "glamourizing" of each and every
one of them. A few bars on the piano to make his meaning
clear, a juxtaposition of Bach's original phrasing with the
pernicious (as he called it) "traditional" phrasing (stemming
from the redoubtable Prof. Riemann's theories)—and scales
seemed to fall away from my eyes; the edifice stood there in
all its architectonic harmony.

Another day—we were in York—as I was passing his table
with my father, he stopped me. "Have you visited the
Minster?" he asked. Upon my shamefaced "No," I saw the
familiar censoriously raised eyebrows, immediately mitigated
by the kindly smile of the true pedagogue. Whereupon
followed a short exposé of what this particular "document" of
true Gothic meant to him, what a necessary antidote it was
to the overrated cathedrals in Cologne and Milan with their
spurious Gothic. The pedagogic faculty in him (a faculty

much rarer than we think) had the magic power to transmute even such a little incident into something that became part and parcel of his disciples' behaviour-patterns. Many years afterward I was touring Spain, and when—playing in the cathedral towns of León, Avila, Burgos, and Valencia—I gave up my routine afternoon rest on concert days to visit their cathedrals, I was not consciously and dutifully remembering a pedagogue's precepts, but was responding to something that has organically grown within me since that shamefaced "No" in the dining-room of the Yorkshire cathedral town.

The weeks, on this tour of the provinces, spent under the influence of Busoni, the man and the musician, were the ones that shook me once and for all out of my adolescent complacency.

CHAPTER XI

THE stages of a fiddler's life, of any player's life, are easily mapped out in retrospect simply by determining his repertoire assets at any given period and recalling the times when additions were made—in fact, by indulging in a kind of stocktaking or inventory. But I have barely made this brash statement when I am reminded of one unchanging factor in the instrumentalist's life which wipes out the contours of the years and the clusters of years; which is a constant in the transitions from childhood to adolescence, to brave young years, to maturity, to the years of routine, to those of the shedding of skins and, finally, to the crystallization of one's style . . . I refer to the standard works that accompany us from cradle to grave. The great tasks which these masterworks represent remain ever challenging to the true artisan. This goes without saying.

Is it not terrifying to envisage the fiddler or pianist, curly-headed, lace collar on his little Victorian velvet jacket, manhandling the same Mendelssohn Concerto, or the Bach Chromatic Fantasy and Fugue, Schumann's *Carnaval*, or the Beethoven C-sharp Minor Piano Sonata (popularly called the "Moonlight"), using or abusing the same masterpieces through the course of a half-century, right up to the almost inevitable crumbling of his faculties—to the last bald-headed, paunchy, semi but not final farewell years!

What a paradox that we start a career in boyhood to the tune of ". . . miracle . . . young musical god . . . who draws his bow across the heartstrings of *all* humanity . . ." as a phenomenal, clairvoyant interpreter, and after decades of profound study and achievements at last reach the stage when we become the "always dependable X, who gave the usual creditable account of himself in the Y concerto." (Or, as Oscar Levant recently summed up similar phenomena: "If you're good, somebody's got to buy you a violin. Then someone else has to get you bookings. Others have to use their influence to get people to listen to you. After all this, if you're lucky you end up by playing at Roxy's.")

A similar grotesquerie, of an Alice in Wonderland topsy-turviness, is the paradox that while the curly-headed little genius, at the beginning of his concertizing, is teamed up with "decrepit old" conductors, concertmasters, and orchestral players—who are, in fact, young or middle-aged—he ends his career at sixty or so as a vigorous, forward-looking virtuoso, full of youthful magnetism, surrounded by conductors, concertmasters, and orchestral players of twenty-five to forty or so, whom he *now* of course considers his contemporaries!

At one time or another we all are faced with this situation, and the real test is how successfully we meet it. The failure to face facts often keeps us from accepting the musical responsibilities of our maturity. I remember Artur Schnabel telling me, after an admirable performance by his friend Carl Flesch of the Ernst F-sharp Minor Concerto (a superannuated work in the virtuoso style of the mid-nineteenth century, bristling with "wunderkind" difficulties): "To think that Flesch, great master that he is, at his age, with his paunch, should be sweating over a piece like *this*!" Almost fifteen years after Schnabel made this remark to me I find it restated in his book *Music and the Line of Most Resistance*: "Old actors play the parts of old persons. Sportsmen at a certain age stop their attempts to break records . . . one could easily define what kind of musical performance is not quite appropriate for people in full maturity (for instance, mere bravura)."

To come back to this retrospective stocktaking, I am amazed at the lack of solid musical foundation and outlook in those all-important and very brief years of my studies. It may have been the latent desire to duplicate (and duplicate quickly) a sensational pedagogical success: Hubay had just presented to the world Franz von Vecsey, then aged ten or eleven. Vecsey made his Carnegie Hall début on January 10th, 1905, after having in 1904 given a dozen concerts in three weeks in Berlin and repeated the same feat in St. Petersburg. It may also have been the unavowed wish to meet the challenge—still pedagogically speaking—of the flow of miracle-products coming from Leopold Auer's camp. The fact remains that when I set out to make my Berlin début, in 1905, my repertoire consisted of only the Wieniawski, Ernst, Mendelssohn, and Viotti concerti, the Bach *Chaconne* and the solitary Prelude movement of the E Major Partita, Paganini's *Witches' Dance*, Tartini's "Devil's Trill" sonata, sundry Spanish dances by Sarasate, Saint-Saëns' *Rondo Capriccioso*, salon pieces by Hubay, and last (and definitely least) Fantasias on *Carmen* and *Faust* and on Russian and Hungarian airs, strung together by Wieniawski and Hubay respectively in the prevailing potpourri style of the 'eighties.

This is less astonishing than it may seem when one sees that Leopold Auer in his *Violin playing as I teach it*, published in 1921, speaks of Bach's Concerti in this condescending way: "With regard to J. S. Bach's two Concertos for violin, I have never given them to my pupils to study because, from my point of view, only the two slow movements in them are musically valuable and really worthy of their composer; while the first and last movements of each Concerto are not very interesting, either musically or technically. This, of course, is my own humble opinion".

Joachim, too, wrote about gems like the Mozart Concerti in D major (K. 218) and A major (K. 219) in a half-patronizing, though affectionate manner as having a *kleinen Zopf* (a little pigtail) "though a most charming one."

I don't remember ever hearing in class a Bach concerto or the Brahms Concerto or César Franck's Sonata or Chausson's *Poème* or a Handel or Mozart or Beethoven sonata. I did play the Beethoven Concerto, but without awareness of its place in the microcosm that Beethoven's scores represent for us. The quartets, piano concerti, the piano sonatas, and even the symphonies (except for the Seventh, which the school orchestra had played) remained *terra incognita* for me.

In our classroom in Budapest there prevailed an atmosphere

of such puerile technical rivalry, we were so completely absorbed by the externals of our craft, that I have difficulty in conveying this satisfactorily, still more in explaining it. Hubay was not only a great virtuoso but also an excellent musician who had come under Joachim's spell, and under that impulsion had formed a quartet which became famous and with which Brahms and other great musicians often appeared. He was by no means the shallow *fin-de-siècle* virtuoso that one might suspect him of being from these remarks of mine. I am afraid they do not quite reflect the enchantment that distance is said to lend to most things.

One should, in justice to Hubay, ascribe this unfortunate state of affairs in the classroom not to him but primarily to us so-called prodigies and, above all, to our parents who generated such an unhealthy impatience. Naturally this impatience led to shortened periods of study and to a more and more sketchy curriculum from which everything but the "useful" war-horses was eliminated. It was quickened by the coincidental meteorlike ascent of Vecsey, the sensational success—as a violinistic technical wonder—of Sevčik's disciple Kubelik, and the rumours about a violinist from Auer's school —more glamorous and emotionally exciting than either of these—Mischa Elman.

When I came to Berlin in 1905 thus inadequately equipped, I heard for the first time not only this phenomenal young violinist but also Kreisler and Ysaÿe. To make clear the impact of their playing on me—a playing of a fire, an elegance, a rhythmic incisiveness which I had never even imagined—I should have to be able to convey the style of playing of the only virtuosos I had heard during my conservatory days: Burmester, Kubelik, Marteau, Hugo Heermann. It is obviously impossible to do this. These first impressions were too amorphous, too lacking in critical perception, too biased by schoolroom prejudices. In Berlin I was on my own, and I was bowled over by Ysaÿe, Kreisler, and Elman.

I lump them together because that was how, in my childish unpreparedness, I felt their individual revelations merge into one collective impact on me. This was not so childish as it would seem on the face of it. I sensed a dividing line between the violin-playing I had heard during my Budapest days and what I was hearing now. One I associated with the past, the other with the future. It was not until some years later that I was to hear Thibaud, Enesco, Huberman, and Casals—greatest of all string players, as Kreisler calls him; and Heifetz, of course, had not yet been revealed to the world.

In thus instinctively drawing a dividing line, I was making a no more arbitrary distinction than grown-ups do when they refer to styles of art in terms of centuries without taking into account the finer shadings caused by overlappings. But even as I see it now my instinct in roughly grouping my listening experiences into two camps was justified. I remember rehearing Willy Burmester in Berlin in 1905. In the previous Budapest years I had, along with the rest of the city, applauded him with childish enthusiasm. My still vivid disappointment at his Berlin performance, the let-down I felt, clearly showed me that I had passed a turning point in my æsthetic awareness when I abandoned myself wholeheartedly to the impact of Ysaÿe, Kreisler, and Elman.

I know now, with critical hindsight, how different they were; their nationalities (Belgian, Austrian, Russian), their roots in three distinct schools, their ages alone, were enough to make them so. But together they formed in my mind an entity—the opening of a door.

Let any concert-goer of the 1920s who heard Burmester, Kubelik, and Marteau (still playing in public at that time, Burmester having died in 1933, Kubelik in 1940, and Marteau in 1934) compare his impressions of these players with those of Kreisler, Elman, Heifetz, and Thibaud. He would certainly find that these two groups of players were unmistakably on opposite sides of this imaginary line. In spite of the disparity in the ages of Ysaÿe, Kreisler, Elman, Heifetz, and other contemporary players, and in spite of their stylistic individualities, there *is* a common denominator in their playing, something that proclaims it as of our time.

The fact that players of the first decade of our century, like Marteau, Juan Manén, Felix Berber, César Thompson, Arrigo Serato, and no doubt others, could not take roots in the United States, could not build up a following that would have enabled them to resume—after World War I—where they had left off, bears out, I think, my observation that a new ideal of beauty in violin-playing was being formulated around that time and that those whose style did not develop toward this new trend had little chance of maintaining their hold.

Generalizations or composite pictures are nowhere more perilous than in such a fluid, changing medium as the art of fiddle-playing. But that is no reason for persistently avoiding them; it has always struck me as odd that those who comment on violin-playing so seldom seem to approach the subject the way literary or art critics do theirs. There one finds no hesitation to pin down certain years as the birth of this or that trend, to attribute some far-reaching influence to one chosen work, or to one exhibition, or even to a single painting. All these things are perilous too, but still not deterrent. Because our instrument is one of the very few unchanged things in our time, must the conception of the style of playing it remain unchanged too? After all, it is a commonplace that styles in all arts change; that, being fluid, they move not only forward to new fields but backward to proven ground as well.

In the spring of 1945 Ferruccio Bonavia, the London critic whose background (he was a pupil of Joachim) gives his words added weight, referred to this cycle. He pointed out the *apparent* novelty of the style of a young player that "vindicated theories to which all the great players of the last generation—Joachim, Sarasate, Ysaÿe—would have subscribed." He credits her sensational success to a reversion to a former style, to "the classical styles of older schools which did not know the graces and elegances of a later age," and goes on to say that "it is a lamentable but undeniable fact that the raising of the average technical standard has been accompanied by a curious reduction of other values.

"Tone especially," he continues, "in other days so true an index of character, has lost both power and variety since it came to be an accepted rule that vibrato is more important than bowing in the production of a warm, pleasing sound. No doubt the new systems led to easy successes, but now Mlle Neveu has won greater success by ignoring them."

In a report on the 1937 Concours International Eugene Ysaÿe at Brussels, Carl Flesch (who with Thibaud and myself was one of the judges) remarked that technique has taken the place of spirituality. "Although the material, mechanical work is unsurpassed," he pointed out, the warmth and the mystery of music have departed. Speaking of the deadening effect of "grim, joyless, technically flawless playing which makes a Mozart concerto sound like a Kreutzer study," he quoted Chesterton's comment that the age that discovered the microphone is an age that has nothing to say. (Which is remarkably like E. B. White's devastating comment on television: "I attended a television demonstration at which it was shown beyond reasonable doubt that a person sitting in one room could observe the nonsense in another.") Flesch continued: "Is it possible that the new schools have given a technical endowment to a generation of violinists who cannot use it to any purpose?"

The results of the contest were considered startling. Soviet players completely overshadowed those of the older, more famous schools. This is the order:

1. Oistrach—Soviet
2. Odnoposov—Argentine (Russian-born)
3. Liza Guillels—Soviet
4. Boussia Goldstein—Soviet
5. Kozolupova—Soviet
6. Fichtengolz—Soviet
7. Lola Bobesco—France [born in Transylvania, I think]
8. Paul Makanowitzky—Russian origin?
9. Robert Virovay—Hungarian
10. Angel Reyes—Cuban
11. Brenzola—French or Italian
12. Champeil

Belgium Vieuxtemps', Leonard's and Ysaÿe's country, where the contest was held, and which had the violinistic allegiance of Kreisler, Marteau, Kochanski, Thibaud, Enesco, and Flesch, did not reach the finals; nor did Germany—the Germany of Joachim and Auer. Looking into the reasons for the Soviet victory, Flesch concluded that while "other

Governments gave their candidates good wishes, the Russian team was granted support as generous as though the Olympic Games were in question. Moscow provided its children with superb instruments to play upon; it sent them to Brussels, together with trainers and accompanists, long before the competition opened so that they could accustom themselves to the atmosphere and come to the trial fresh. The player who obtained the second prize did not, though a Russian, belong to the U.S.S.R. team, and had been leading the orchestra at the Vienna Opera the night before he left for Brussels."

Flesch admitted the high degree of technical ability of the Russian team, but said that they, like all the others, concentrated too much on the material aspects of music. He believed, however, that the danger of machine-worship can be averted by closer contact of West with East. "Music," he wrote, "has been pre-eminently international in the past. Composers, performers, students have always wandered over the earth at will, learning and teaching, fertilizing, vivifying. It has been reserved for the present age to set up barriers and classify musicians according to their nationality or religion."

Although most of the great or near great at the turn of the century are no more than names to us, it is nonetheless possible to piece together from evidence gathered here and there a composite picture of players like Henri Petri, Adolf Brodsky, Arnold Rosé, César Thompson, Hugo Heermann, and Franz Ondříček, in which the sensuous beauty, colouristic finesse, and dramatic contrasts, the vibrant and scintillating quality and streamlined smoothness that we have come to expect from modern violin-playing would be conspicuously lacking. I had sensed that a new quality had been added to violin-playing ever since that first visit to Berlin in 1905. This feeling was intensified when during this same winter I heard Joachim's disciple Carl Halíř, the second violinist in his quartet, give a singularly heavy-handed performance of the Mendelssohn Concerto at one of the Nikisch concerts. This coming right upon the revelation brought by my first hearing of Eugene Ysaÿe, Mischa Elman, and, soon after, of Fritz Kreisler (in Viotti's A Minor Concerto under Nikisch) must also have had its share in our not deciding on the obvious course of studying under Joachim. Many years later this "new quality" in violin-playing was brought home to me with particular force by reports of fabulous fiddlistic doings in America, centring around the stellar figure of Jascha Heifetz, reports brought to me some time around 1919 by a Swiss pianist who was making annual tours in the United States. I was then teaching in Geneva and, as the interchange between European and American concert halls was not yet well under way after the First World War, I was naturally curious to hear as much as possible about these prodigious new players. When I pressed my pianist friend for some concrete descriptions instead of his vague generalizations, all he could do was to repeat over and over again and stutter: "I can't describe it ... but it's different. *C'est toute autre chose ... c'est ... c'est ... scintillant!*" That was the best he could do.

CHAPTER XII

BUT perhaps it is easier to judge of the new trend in fiddle-playing by observing the common or garden variety of players than by thinking always of the outstanding exponents of the art. Great achievements are necessarily less affected by environment, by the general climate, than run-of-the-mill playing is; for that reason it is pertinent to evaluate *any* kind of playing that comes our way. If we were to listen attentively for snatches of violin tunes in popular music recorded around 1906 or 1907, and compare these with violin-playing in the sound track of a present-day Hollywood musical or in one of the ultra-sophisticated commercial broadcasts with their glistening and lush fiddle tone, it would make this point clearer than any attempt at analysis. Or to give another example: we unfortunately do not know how a Strauss waltz was played by Johann Strauss and his band, but those of us who are as familiar with the playing of the Vienna Philharmonic as with the humble fiddlers in "Schraml" ensembles still have some sort of link with the playing style of those far-off days, and we can imagine how strangely unsophisticated and unglamorous the genuine article would sound after certain broadcasts of popular music.

Juxtapositions like these would also show us better than any words can the reverse side of the medal, what Lucien Capet, the great French quartet player and one of the most profound of Beethoven interpreters, meant when he spoke in his *Art de l'archet* of the "éternelle effervescence" of

present-day violinists. How well I remember that contest at
the Paris Conservatoire at which he, Thibaud, and I were
judges, and his mock-admiration every time an excellent, slick,
luscious-toned youngster came out and played still faster and
still more smoothly than the preceding one: "*Mon Dieu,
quels doigts épatants! Quel bon ébeniste!*" he would exclaim.
("Heavens, what dizzy fingers! What a whopping cabinet-
maker!") And does not Carl Flesch in his *Art of Violin Playing*
sigh over the levelling influence of our time and over the
monotony and the comparative sameness of our players that
is engendered by the ever-persistent vibrato?

How often, nowadays, one is tempted to apply Ernest
Newman's quip about the great Melba's singing. I was
touring with her and read this devastating Newmanism in the
Birmingham *Daily Post*: "Melba's singing was uninterestingly
perfect and perfectly uninteresting." In the same vein James
Agate called Melba's singing in *La Traviata* "faultily faultless."
This was in 1908, I believe; and thirty-five years later Sir
Thomas Beecham, in his recent autobiography, says something
very similar: ". . . we have reached a stage where we are
confronted with the paradoxical situation that, while never
before have there been so many musicians who are credited
with impeccable mechanical excellence, there have also never
been so many dull and uninspiring interpreters."

If there is anything that I am trying to avoid, it is the
tendency to take sides and to discount completely opposed
schools of thought; this may appear to be vacillation. But
then no amount of writing about a thing in which one is an
active participant can do the job of explaining one's point of
view half so well as one inevitably does by simply playing!
I have tried to conserve my faculty of browsing among
fiddle styles as one browses among books. Thus, I can
sample the flavour of the thing, enjoy this or that happy
phrase, without subscribing to its essence and without incorporating it into my "library."

I am not alone in ascribing to the first years of the century
a new approach to violin-playing—the addition of new
ingredients to our brew. Carl Flesch in his *Art of Violin
Playing* saw Fritz Kreisler as "the first who most nearly divined

SZIGETI PLAYING WITH THE PERSYMFANS (CONDUCTORLESS) ORCHESTRA, MOSCOW, DURING BEETHOVEN CENTENARY, 1927

BÉLA BARTÓK AND SZIGETI REHEARSING THEIR BERLIN PROGRAMME, *c.* 1929

in advance and satisfied the specific type of emotional expression demanded by our time. This is the reason why, in spite of his astounding violinistic precociousness, his actual participation was recognized and appreciated at a period comparatively so late. (As late as 1896, that is, at the age of twenty-two, he was not considered worthy of occupying the position of second violin in the Vienna Hofoper orchestra.)"

A rather nice parallel to this verdict of the estimable Hofoper board is the episode Sam Franko relates about young Eugène Ysaÿe's audition before the redoubtable but mediocre conductor Pasdeloup in 1888 or 1889. Franko, who was present at the audition, recalls that Vieuxtemps brought his protégé along, and that Ysaÿe played on the master's Amati "beautifully. Imagine Vieuxtemps's annoyance and anger when Pasdeloup said to him afterwards: '*Non, je ne peux pas le laisser jouer; il n'a pas de son*' (No, I cannot let him play it; he has no tone)."

My reservations concerning certain aspects of current trends are shared and even exceeded by Flesch. "The technical and tonal smoothness of to-day stand on a noticeably higher level, especially among the violinistic middle classes, than they did 50 years ago—while the number of outstanding personalities, on the other hand, has grown less." In another context, he speaks of "the blatantly sensuous, artificially inflated, rather than naturally matured, spirit of our time."

Virgil Thomson sustains this opinion in one of his recent columns by saying:

> One of the striking phenomena of our epoch is the large amount of absolutely first-class instrumental technique that is in the hands of lesser musical temperaments. . . . The violinists, almost to a man, are frigid, too. The pianists are a little warmer but not much. And 'cellists are practically funeral directors. Everywhere variety of musical expression is sacrificed to something that is thought to be impressive, commanding, irresistibly majestic, whereas majesty is merely a character part like any other and a not very vivacious one.
>
> What most artists believe to be majestic nowadays is the big round tone. They display this, if they have it, in every piece. And when they feel obliged, out of some minimum of loyalty to a composer's indications, to play less loud than forte, they play

with a small round tone. To the production of roundness they will sacrifice rhythm, dynamic proportion and even, in ensemble work, blending. To loudness they sacrifice, of necessity, the colour gamut.

In a tribute to Dr. Albert Schweizer I read this: "As Dr. Schweitzer abhors violence in human relationships, so does he abhor the modern violent organ tone of *stridency* and *blatant noise* (italics mine!) instead of sonorous power. There was a saying among his Alsatian friends, 'In Africa he saves Negroes; in Europe he saves old organs.'" He was interested in their reconditioning and rebuilding.

However, I suppose we must accept certain facts and lacks as inherent in our time. I would go so far as to suggest that such seemingly unrelated things as the cinema organ, the various electrical instruments for the home, the infinite possibilities of tone doctoring and amplifying (after all, it was the microphone that made crooning what it is), the prevalence of the saxophone tone in popular music—that all these have changed the general attitude toward violin-playing more than is generally realized. It would lead too far to investigate the changes in our playing style that the universal use of metal strings has effected. The overamplification of the solo parts in concerto recordings—obviously a distortion of musical values—is another of these negative influences.

When one imprudently ventures into controversy and on to shaky ground, it serves him right if—on re-reading his own dicta—he suddenly feels in need of corroboration. Help comes when and where one least expects it. While touring Canada in the 1940's, I chanced upon a six-weeks-old London *Sunday Times* in the club car. With the incorrigible nostalgia of Europeans, I pounced upon it avidly. With the equally incorrigible "*déformation professionnelle*" of the public performer, I turned to the music and drama section and found the following from the pen of James Agate, to whom I am particularly partial. In this article, Mr. Agate refutes the legend about Sarah Bernhardt's "famous *voix d'or*," or—to put it more exactly—he refutes Bernard Shaw's strictures about that "*voix céleste* stop which Madame Bernhardt . . . keeps always pulled out."

Mr. Agate bases his refutation on a gramophone record of Sarah Bernhardt's which he subjects to a minute analysis. He describes in detail how, in this twenty-nine-line speech from Racine's *Phèdre*, "Sarah pulls out the *voix céleste* stop for eight lines and pushes it in again, after which there is no hint of it until . . ." and here Mr. Agate specifies the exact point. Then he speaks of how and where "the full organ is turned on, and the speech is rushed to its frenzied, not golden conclusion." What the keen-eared critic then opposes to the "eternal" *voix céleste* stop, or the "eternal" *voix d'or*, is Sarah's "entire register," from which she could choose according to whether she was "tigress, snake, martyr, empress, coquette. . . ." In short, if I understand him rightly, his attitude is like the one that prompted Lucien Capet's already quoted remark deploring the *éternelle effervescence*, the lack of a variety always demanded by the musical context, in the playing of many of our present-day violinists.

Capet's judgment also seems to me to parallel Carl Flesch's distinction between the category of players who have "the tone beautiful in itself," the "beautiful tone as a component of their technical possessions" which is "always at their disposal," and the second category of players who "first have to achieve their personal tone quality by steeping the tone in feeling, by giving it a soul"; whose tone when they are playing "in the wrong psychic mood" tends to make "a dry and cold impression." Flesch then analyses "the tone beautiful in itself" as against "the inspired tone" and warns the possessors of the former against "a certain emotional indolence" and "routine" and against "the danger of surprising and captivating one's listeners during the first ten minutes only to bore them quite as intensely after a little time." It is this boring overallness of "the tone beautiful in itself" (in Carl Flesch's phrase) that Peter Yates* must have had in mind when, in *Art and Architecture*, he says of one of our most brilliant violinists: "The tone of X is like an interchangeable slip-cover patterned with large sleazy flowers which he slips over the original texture of any composition."

* The moving spirit behind those exemplary programmes given by the "Concerts on the Roof" group in Los Angeles.

Virgil Thomson in an article addressed to performers sounds a similar note of warning: "A 'beautiful' tone is not really beautiful. It is merely glamourized, monotonous, inexpressive. And it is about the least useful device in music for keeping an audience awake."

In reading critical reviews of one's own playing, one is naturally biased, while "disinterested" reading of reviews of others' playing, I find, brings many profitable gleanings. Within a few days two New York critics wrote about two different performances: "The tone was too often moist and one consequently missed the fine contrasts that may be obtained by a periodic application of a drier timbre"—and: "His rhythm was precise, his tonal textures dry, the expressivity complete. . . . How much added juiciness [Tchaikovsky] can stand is an unsettled problem of interpretation."

It is interesting to see the adjective "dry" used otherwise than in a disparaging sense: as a positive feature of a performance. Can this be a reaction against the eternal "Schmaltz" of our recent past? These seem healthy trends; they point to certain excesses of the opposing school of thought, exemplified by a criticism I came across lately (in 1944) in a New York paper. The critic speaks of a "tone so rich and luscious as to make you want to take it home and bake it in a cake," and goes on to say that "all the sounds produced both by the soloist and the orchestra were a joy." So there we have it in a nutshell—"tone" or "sound" worshipped as an end in itself, with no recognition of the fact that these are only, as Schnabel put it once in conversation: "transporting vehicles of musical substance" (*Beförderungsmittel*). Flesch, in the 'twenties, raised his warning voice against this tendency.

In a different context Albert Jay Nock plies with irony those "who had 'majored in English,' 'specialized in English,' or even, *Gott soll hüten,* taken a master's degree in English. After sampling a good fair taste of their quality, I got into the way of telling them I would take their word for all they knew about English, since obviously the one thing they did not know was what to do with it, and that was the only thing that interested me."

To revert to Mr. Agate, he turns his attention in another column to crooners and to the mike, which he calls that "interposing ironmongery," and here again he deplores "the sentimental stop" that "must be kept pulled out all the time, ceaselessly and relentlessly," pouring out "always the golden voice and never less than the golden voice, known to-day as 'Crooner's throb.' . . ."

This insidious danger, which is ever present in this mechanical age, was well illustrated, it seems to me, by a story Schnabel is fond of telling. It was in the 'twenties, in the declining days of the mechanical piano. He had refused to make Pianola rolls, and the spokesman for the company, eloquent in his desperate attempts to sway Schnabel, brought out as a supreme argument: "But, Mr. Schnabel, we have so perfected our reproducing technique that we now have sixteen nuances at our disposal!" Whereupon Schnabel, in his best tongue-in-the-cheek manner: "Yes, but . . . my playing has . . . seventeen!"

A recent newspaper story about the mike "techniques" in force on one of America's most highly Crossley-rated radio hours is revealing in this respect. It seems there was some trouble with a prominent woman violinist's fortissimi (apparently she was a stranger to crooning practices), and the maestro made these classic remarks to the reporter: "She has become accustomed to playing for large concert audiences. We must not disturb her. Many a fine soloist comes to us here *with that trouble*. We iron it out easily, though, *and they are none the wiser!*" (My italics.)

The unsuspecting millions are also none the wiser as to what is being done to their listening habits, how they are being conditioned by the mass—and mess—of sound that is aimed at them. They hear the cinema organ's wobble and probably they like it because it reminds them of the human voice or of the vibrato of a stringed instrument. But they don't realize something that came to me with a shock the other day when I was listening to a popular music broadcast: that the process is being reversed nowadays, that we seem to have reached the point where *the string orchestra is imitating the cinema organ*. Thus the vicious circle seems to be completed.

As Olin Downes recently wrote: "Sound transmission, thus far, has done harm rather than good to legitimate singing. The crooner or tooth-comb soprano can survive over the microphone who would never have a conspicuous success in concert hall or opera house. It is the men with the buttons and the pegs who shape that tone for the listening public."

With all the talk about tone in this chapter, its own tone is—I find—reticent because I was not able, or perhaps not willing, to "let wariness give place to complete frankness."

CHAPTER XIII

"IT is a moot point whether the coloratura singer or the fashionable fiddler is the bigger fool. To be compelled to decide between the broken melodies of Vieuxtemps and Wieniawski and the unbroken insipidity of Shadow Song and Mad Scena is like having to choose between the rescue of wife or mother. There *is* no choice."

And in this vein James Agate goes on. But let us stop right here. Aren't words like these, coming from an arbiter of taste of Agate's standing, sufficient to wither a fiddler's ego almost into non-existence? Vieuxtemps! . . . Wieniawski! . . . The worlds their Fantasias and Polonaises and Airs Russes meant to me, and that not so many years ago! And now, James Agate . . . *that* precisely is the thing that smarts; that this knocking of our fiddling brotherhood should come from *his* pen! But wait, there's worse to come, in this same book, *Playgoing*: ". . . you might say that musicians have less brain-power than any other type of manual worker."

Such then is the contumely that is being meted out to us violinists as a body! This is what comes from those infantile fixations of ours that originated in our conservatory and prodigy years, when we considered our Sarasate and Wieniawski and Vieuxtemps pieces and fantasias as the *ne plus ultra* of our tasks! And such knocks come from the most disconcertingly unlikely quarters: from the versatile Angna Enters, for instance, so clairvoyant in things æsthetic. She deplores* the fact that violinists have no repertoire numbers

* In *First Person Plural*, N. Y., Stackpole, 1937.

based upon the Spanish *cante jondo,* in which the violin is used as the voice, and the orchestra or piano as the guitar. She adds: "It would be a novelty after the Wieniawski concerto." There we have it again. And coming from an outsider and from a critic with such flair, this almost audible sniff hurts one's self-respect more than even Artur Schnabel's already-mentioned censure of our playing stuff like Ernst's Concerto. . . .

After this preamble let me try to reconstruct for myself the ways in which gradually, and none too soon, I freed myself from some of these fossilized repertoire-remnants of my 'teens.

I have said that parts of our repertoire are dropped in the natural course of events, as skins are shed. As I see it now, the recipe I followed during the long and wearisome process must have been simply not to regret time spent on any task if such a task compelled me to use some new set of tools—never to mind whether the yield justified the effort! You made up your mind not to regret even those cases when a quite disproportionate amount of time and energy and auto-suggestive imagination had been expended on tasks that just happened to come your way and which subsequently did not prove worthy of the expenditure. They had served to sharpen your tools in the same way that "unworthy" journalistic assignments sharpen literary workers' pens and heighten their faculties of observation and conciseness of expression; for did not André Gide "cover" the Cours d'Assises sessions as a self-appointed task, subsequently gleaning from these a volume, *Souvenirs de la Cours d'Assises?*

There were times when, for the sake of a single appearance, I did not shun the sometimes rather formidable job of mastering and memorizing a thirty-five-minute concerto, which I was never to play again! Early in my career there was that ambitious concerto of the estimable violin pedagogue, Josef Bloch. This sympathetic old bachelor, after turning out literally hundreds of "educational pieces" graded according to difficulty, let himself go to his heart's content, wrote a full-length concerto, published it this time at his own expense (his publishers disapproving of "ungraded" difficulties and unbridled length in their wares), had it produced by me at the Budapest Philharmonic, gained his brief moment of glory—and there the matter ended.

Then there was Dohnányi's Violin Concerto, a different story altogether, for Dohnányi's international status as a composer assured any of his works a respectful hearing anywhere. But it so happened that after that one performance in the 'twenties at the Berlin Philharmonic, conducted by Fritz Reiner and made memorable for me by the presence of Fritz Kreisler, I never had occasion to play this work again. Both Carl Flesch and Albert Spalding had played it some months before with several orchestras, and, the unfortunate attitude of conductors toward second and third performances being what it is, I never got around to incorporating it into my regular repertoire.

The vogue of Prokofiev's First Concerto, which started soon afterward, of course, had something to do with this. After my performance of this concerto—a work that to this day remains unique in the whole body of Prokofiev's output —at the festival of the International Society for Contemporary Music in Prague on June 1st, 1924, under Fritz Reiner (Reiner always was a glutton for new music), I was soon playing it everywhere in Europe: in Berlin under Bruno Walter; in London and Paris under Ansermet; in Amsterdam at the Mengelberg Concerts, and so on. All in all, I played it some two dozen times in one season.

There were other "occasional" performances—that is, performances of works taken up for some occasion. These, for some reason or other, never reached that stage of constant repetition, of being put to the test in different musical environments, which to me constitutes "incorporating"—a word that I use almost literally. One such is the Second Sonata of that moody, silent, pipe-smoking poet Arnold Bax (now Sir Arnold Bax—"Master of the King's Musick"), which I played with Harriet Cohen three or four times. Another is George Templeton Strong's Poem for violin and orchestra entitled *An Artist's Life*, written on a Berlioz-like autobiographical literary theme. Now ninety years old, this sturdy American pioneer of music, an expatriate of many decades,

D*   (105)

dedicated the Poem to me soon after I took over the "classes de virtuosité" at the Geneva Conservatory in 1917; besides its local première under Ansermet and at the Zürich Tonkünstler-fest in 1919, I have in all these years had occasion to play it only at one of the New York Philharmonic concerts in Mengelberg's day and with the Cleveland Orchestra under Nikolai Sokoloff.

Templeton Strong, a comrade-in-arms of MacDowell's, told me many a story of his Wiesbaden days in the 1880s when he roomed with his friend MacDowell; also of his visit to Liszt in Weimar, an occasion on which the great man accepted the dedication of one of the young American's symphonic attempts.

Many glimpses of New York's early musical life and of Anton Seidl's Philharmonic tenure around 1890* came my way through the picturesque reminiscing of this newly-won friend. The circumstances of the departure in 1878 of this young Manhattan patrician for Europe in quest of a life devoted to music, instead of accepting the career open to him as a member of the swanky New York law firm of Strong & Cadwalader, could not fail to kindle my imagination with their almost Goethean *Wanderjahre* overtones, and we soon became good friends.

He never regretted the decision he had taken in 1878 and often used to tell me that his comrade MacDowell might still have been among the living had he taken a similar decision —had he refused to re-enter what Strong termed the "arena of musical life in America with its strife and high tension." Once, speaking of one of the greatest masters of contemporary music idioms and "isms," he said: "Mon cher, you'll see— MacDowell's *To a Wild Rose* will attend the funeral of X's work and live thereafter!"

Strong's frugal tastes, his rugged simplicity which so admirably suits his present milieu, his sovereign contempt for all sham, made me deeply appreciate a word he used over and over again when commenting on my performance; it was the

* Anton Seidl, in spite of his German name, was of Hungarian origin, like those other famous musicians with German-sounding names—Hans Richter, Leopold Auer, Joseph Joachim, Artur Nikisch, and Carl Flesch.

word *probité*. "*C'est la probité de votre art, mon cher,*" he used to say, "that sets it apart." His sense of humour, too, endeared him to me. In 1940 when his *Ondine*, composed away back in 1882–83 in Leipzig and played at New York's old Steinway Hall in 1885, was produced by the Swiss Radio, he announced the resurrection of this nearly-sixty-year-old brain-child of his on printed postcards that carried the line at the bottom: *Prière de ne pas faire de visites, de n'envoyer ni condoléances, ni fleurs.*

Strong's speech, whether in English or in excellent French or German, was flavoured by an accent as pungently American as hickory smoke and was as autochthonous to his native country as chewing-gum and "Westerns." He received copious supplies of both these from back home and promptly, and vainly, tried to convert me to these Americanisms.

The last time I saw him was in the fall of 1939, during World War II, after the Geneva première of the Violin Concerto by our friend Ernest Bloch. When I left for the United States soon after, I carried with me Strong's photograph, gratefully inscribed to Toscanini, who had broadcast one of his early works in 1939, together with many friendly messages which I was to deliver orally both to Toscanini and to Bloch. I still see the wiry old man, at his old-time stand-up composing desk, looking more "American Gothic" than ever, embracing me and implying rather than saying what he felt at my departure for his country at such a time . . . and what *any* parting meant to a man of his age. However, from what I hear about him now (in 1946), the only thing that these long war years seem to have done to the sturdy nonagenarian is to have compelled him "to walk with a cane so as not to break the furniture !"—as he puts it.*

The earliest of my many associations with composers came before I was twenty, with the concerto which Hamilton Harty dedicated "To Joska Szigeti, in Friendship," and which I suspect set the pattern for my subsequent approach to other such tasks. For I think more and more that one's whole musical make-up is conditioned by some such early experience from which is evolved the "working method" that serves one

* Templeton Strong passed away in Geneva in the summer of 1948.

in the most diverse tasks and at different stages of development.
I believe that every man, however humble his work, evolves
his own "method," the blueprint that Paul Valéry speaks of
in his *La Méthode de Leonardo da Vinci*. Harty* was then—
around 1908—England's premier accompanist; and my
working at his manuscript concerto, with him at the piano
coaxing out of his instrument all the orchestral colour which
he had dreamed into his score, was probably decisive in
forming what a long-suffering and excellent pianistic partner
of mine later on termed my "expensive tastes" in accompanying.

This concerto, which I played a number of times in
London and elsewhere under Sir Henry Wood, Sir Landon
Ronald, and others, gradually found its way into the repertory
of other violinists too, mostly Anglo-Saxons. I had the
somewhat "paternal"—or, rather, "godfatherly"—satisfaction
of hearing the still disarmingly charming work, more than a
quarter of a century after my introducing it, in an excellent
broadcast performance by the BBC Symphony Orchestra
under Sir Adrian Boult, with Paul Beard as soloist. Some
years later, in January, 1944, to be precise, it had its first New
York performance—thirty-five years after I had premièred
it—at Mishel Piastro's recital, with piano accompaniment.

It was the first new work I carried across the Channel,
playing it in Budapest and also in Cologne under Fritz Steinbach, the famous Brahms interpreter. Steinbach, who was
then director of the Cologne Conservatory, told me after the
rehearsal about a young man of extraordinary musical and
violinistic attainments who had amazed a recent visitor to
his institution, the composer Max Reger, by playing to him
from memory the then much-discussed Reger Violin Concerto. This young man played in the Cologne Orchestra on
the occasion of my performance of the Harty Concerto, so
he himself told me in New York some thirty years later; he
was Adolf Busch.

Busoni, Albert Roussel, Prokofiev, Milhaud, Hindemith,

* Soon after World War I, Hamilton Harty was called to the helm of
England's most "mellow" orchestra, the Hallé Orchestra of Manchester,
Hans Richter having designated the young Irishman as a likely successor.

Stravinsky, Ravel, Ernest Bloch, Joseph Achron, Henry Cowell, Eugene Ysaÿe, Charles Ives, Szymanowski, Alban Berg, Bartók, Alexander Tansman, and others do not, of course, belong to these partly melancholy recollections, for their works are still *living* parts of my programmes. I am tempted to drag in at this point a perhaps far-fetched comparison. Haven't we all address books which, as we go along, seem to contain only "live" names, "live" addresses? Little by little names become pale, meaningless, drop out; the day comes when whole pages seem to us obsolete, relics of a past era. Not long ago, while handling my wife's address book of a few years back, I couldn't refrain from remarking: "*Un cimetière.*" It is then that we start a new book.

Busoni's Violin Concerto and his Second Sonata (the one with those transcendent Variations on the Bach Chorale "*Wie wohl ist mir, O Freund der Seele*"), on the other hand, is the exact antithesis of these vestiges of one's past which no longer retain their living connections with our present. His personality was too overpowering for that, and the imprint he left on anyone who had the privilege of coming into contact with him was too indelible. How vivid the memory of everything connected with him remains to this day! The talks during those first meetings in Berlin in 1906; that tour we made in England together in 1908 or 1909; the rehearsals for those orchestral concerts, just before World War I; the morning champagne libations at Huth's Weinstube in Berlin with Egon Petri, Michael Zadora, Theodore Szántó, and other disciples, when I drank in, too, the sparkle of his inimitable talk; then the after-concert sessions in some Italian wine-restaurant or at the famous Restaurant Foyot on the Left Bank in Paris, near the Senate; our walks and talks in Zurich and Geneva, during those war years—doubly unbearable to this "European" in the exact Goethean sense; the coffee palavers in the 'twenties, when he had returned to his home on the Viktoria Luisen-Platz in Berlin (it was at one of these that I first met Paul Hindemith and Ernst Křenek) and so on right up to that concert at the Berlin Philharmonic in 1922. After playing his Violin Concerto, I led Busoni by the hand down the steps of the platform to receive the homage of an audience that included practically every musician and conductor of note then in Germany—Klemperer, Hindemith, Scherchen, and many others. He was already marked by lingering illness; thin, wasted, his hands cool and waxlike in their sculptured beauty; chilly, as he must have been in those last months of his life, his wrists enclosed, in lieu of shirt-cuffs, in a brown, long-sleeved woollen sweater that contrasted strangely, ominously, with the long black silk-lapelled frock coat, like the one Liszt wore in his last pictures.

I was never to see Busoni again.

The circumstances that led to my intimate connection with Busoni's Concerto were somewhat unusual. It was the other way round in our case: it was the executant who was trying to convince the composer of the worth of his work!

Busoni in those days, mature, aloof, objective toward his own work as toward everything else, had already gone beyond that stage of development which had produced the Violin Concerto. One Sunday morning in (perhaps) 1912 I played it with him in Maud Allan's beautiful studio in Regent's Park, where he was staying at that time; and it was with a half-indulgent, half-proud, "paternal" smile that he welcomed back his own neglected brain-child with the words: "Well, I must admit it's a good work though unpretentious!"

Speaking of these "early" works of Busoni's, dating from the end of the nineteenth century, it seems to me possible to conjecture that Busoni's Second Sonata with its Variations on the Bach Chorale may have influenced Alban Berg whose Violin Concerto, composed in 1935, also climaxes in Variations on the Bach Chorale: *Es ist genug! so nimm, Herr, meinen Geist.*

This Sunday morning music-making with Busoni led to the three performances under his direction—in Berlin, Paris, and London—which are among my most cherished memories, and which in turn resulted in what Busoni's first biographer, Leichtentritt, termed a resurrection of this almost forgotten work. And what concerts those were! Brought about by the devotion of those who believed in him (as in Paris), or organized at his own expense (in Berlin), or sponsored by the gallant National Sunday League at the

Palladium, in London. There were no openings for comparatively unrecognized composers in those days as there are in our happier times of Contemporary Music Festivals, Broadcasting Corporations, and Maecenases who commission, publish, and record new works.

So it was in sometimes inadequate physical surroundings that the performances were presented. In Paris, for instance, at the now defunct Concerts Sechiari (in a suburban theatre) Busoni not only conducted his own works (the *raison d'être* of the concert!) but also a Mozart symphony, and Liszt's *Mazeppa*, besides playing the piano. But what did the setting of a concert matter when the audience included d'Annunzio and Rainer Maria Rilke, musicians of such varied types as Widor and Moszkowski, painters and journalists, all of whom made a Busoni concert the unique thing it came to mean!

In Berlin it was Sibelius who came to the artists' room to embrace him—Sibelius, to whom he had dedicated a movement of his *Geharnischte* Suite, composed at about the same time as the Violin Concerto.

Then there was the banquet in a private salon of the Café Henry, where these twenty or so, the wonderful inner nucleus of our audience (d'Annunzio among them), heard Busoni in his *Fantasia contrappuntistica* before settling at the round table.

I still see Busoni in the restaurant of the Gare du Nord, where Rainer Maria Rilke, the Polish pianist Turczynski, Egon Petri, myself, and a few others said good-bye to him. We were discussing the concert, the banquet, the lack of intuition of certain critics who accused him of incoherence, lack of form, proportion, "measure" (if I remember rightly); whereupon I pulled out an envelope on which I had scribbled the timing of the various sections of his *Indian Fantasy* (then in manuscript) and which proved—if such things *can* be "proved"— the inner proportion and shapeliness of his composition. And he, grasping the scrap of paper, thankful for even so unimportant a token, for so small a testimony, knew that justice would be done—later. Of this justice there have been telling signs: the London broadcast of his *Doktor Faust* a few years ago, the Liszt-Busoni evening at the London Promenade Concerts in 1937; the increasingly numerous recordings of his piano works; and the Busoni Memorial Concert of the New York Philharmonic-Symphony Orchestra in 1940, conducted by Mitropoulos and with Egon Petri and myself as soloists.

The leave-taking from Busoni, which I just mentioned, was referred to in a note from Rainer Maria Rilke which, though it cannot measure up to any of his published letters as to content, is so characteristic of his *courtoisie de coeur* that I cannot resist from giving it here in translation. I do this although I realize that it is more the externals than its contents that constitute the "message" of this simple courtesy note: the poet's exquisitely sensitive handwriting on the thin grey paper, the envelope with its grey seal affixed by his ring, and the gesture of having it conveyed by a messenger instead of through the mails.

As the translators of his letters, Jane Bannard Green and M. D. Hester Norton say: "He took pains with his letters, not only with their content but with their appearance as well. The pages are exquisitely neat, for he wrote naturally in a regular, elegant, calligraphic hand."

The note is dated October 28th, 1916, from Munich, Keferstrasse 11 and reads:

Your ever so kind remembrance arouses in me (like everything that has reference to the Paris that is lost) both joy and melancholy. That hour of ours at the Gare du Nord became for me actuality and presence again through your words.

At that time I wished ever so much to hear you play and now that you offer me such a handsome opportunity for so doing I am not free to accept: the Première of Strindberg's *Traumspiel* which is very important to me personally and for which I already have the seats since last week. Alas, alas.

Instead of returning to you the tickets I shall give myself the pleasure of presenting them to two young, extraordinarily gifted girls, the daughters of Gerhard Oukama Knoop, in the knowledge that I am giving you thus two most sensitive listeners.

They will substitute for me, listening and feeling doubly!

Please don't take my arbitrary disposing of your gift amiss and believe me how much I desire to be able to hear and meet you again some other time.

Yours very sincerely,

RAINER MARIA RILKE.

CHAPTER XIV

————— ·{✧}· —————

THIS commerce with works new to me, and with their composers, inevitably had a broadening and maturing influence upon a young man in his 'teens, growing out of his so-called "prodigy" years somewhat reluctantly. This reluctance to grow up is, by the way, the great pitfall in the development of most "prodigies." For few things can be so helpful in evolving an individual "working method," a method applicable to *all* tasks, than the proud realization that one is starting something from scratch, starting something in which imitativeness, whether conscious or unconscious, can have no part—the realization that the results of one's labours will soon be passed upon by the composer himself!

There is magic in this knowledge, especially after the unavoidable parrot-like imitativeness of a young instrumentalist's early years! And little does it matter—taking the long view of things—if some of these self-imposed tasks subsequently prove to have been less than worth while. Even if the majority of the composers called "moderns" turn out to be nothing but still-born "contemporaries," the good it will have done the young player to grope his way in uncharted territory is something that will have left a lasting mark upon him. (Thrice lucky the player who, in these gropings, finds himself in the bracing, rarefied air of the Highlands instead of —alas! so often—in the neighbourhood of some Main Street!) For every Debussy or Ravel sonata, for every Prokofiev or Stravinsky or Alban Berg concerto, for every Bartók *Rhapsody* or Bloch *Schelomo* or Szymanowski piece, how many "duds"! We know that Fritz Kreisler "made" the Elgar Concerto, but we forget that he has done more than his share for ephemeral works as well. And I was once proudly told by that amiable gentleman, Baron Frederic d'Erlanger, composer of the *Hundred Kisses* Ballet, that Kreisler had given the première of his Violin Concerto early in the century. I remember hearing Casals in Brussels in a 'cello concerto by the Dutch composer Julius Röntgen, lavishing upon it the witchery of what is probably the greatest art among all string players. For— though Casals did give to the world "definitive" performances of the Bach solo sonatas and of most of the 'cello classics (as "definitive" as anything *can* be in recreated music)—it did not prevent him from devoting himself to the Röntgens and the Emmanuel Moors. He often played Moor's 'Cello Concerto, as well as the Violin and 'Cello Double Concerto, with no less a fellow propagandist of Moor's than Eugène Ysaÿe! That typically Victorian, post-Mendelssohnian composer, Sir Alexander Mackenzie, under whose baton I played once or twice in my early London days, had none other than young Mischa Elman, then at the most glamorous stage of his career, play one of Mackenzie's extremely long works at a Hans Richter concert. All I remember of this is Elman's ravishing performance and the vague feeling that I was present at a belated première, belated by some four or five decades. What if neither Elman nor anyone else has ever played it since? There is that other Elman première to counterbalance it, that of Glazunov's Concerto, on which the ink was scarcely dry in 1905 when I heard him give it under Nikisch at the Berlin Philharmonic.

But there is another and less obvious factor in the development of an instrumentalist which may be worth going into: looking through manuscript works in the composer's presence —works for orchestra or piano, or chamber groups, or oratorios—with the composer pounding away at the piano, bellowing the different parts, satisfying his desperate need of communication with a sympathetic musical soul, sometimes *even* going so far as to invite criticism from his more or less willing victim. It is inevitable that a certain percentage of time given to these sessions is time lost, but to be able to look into a composer's workshop, to see "Work in Progress," to be privileged sometimes to offer disinterested suggestions—all this can be very rewarding to the virtuoso. For, in the very nature of his virtuoso career, he spends too much time in repetition, in an often egocentric, sometimes egomaniacal, contemplation of "Himself" as measured against "The Work." And in these sessions the listener, usually alone with the composer, is forced to take an almost active part; nothing less will satisfy the composer. The latter's keyed-up sensitivity will detect any let down in our alertness, and woe to us—we may then have to listen to a whole section all over again!

All flippancy aside, however, this is almost invariably a healthy intellectual exercise; we follow the composer in his *Schwärmerei* while keeping *our* critical faculties active. We identify ourselves with his dreams and enthusiasms to a greater extent than we would in a comfortable orchestra stall, where we can so easily shut out unwelcome sounds and abandon ourselves to random thoughts, and still we manage to keep a certain equilibrium between our objectivity and the composer's wish-fulfillment dreams. This is perhaps the nearest some of us will ever get to the joys and the birth pangs of the creative worker; I mean, those of us who—prevented perhaps by an overdeveloped critical sense—do not indulge in composition.

The knowledge that, as a direct result of one's pioneering, a work is beginning to take root in the repertories of fellow-players; the knowledge that as a result of this or that performance of some new work still in manuscript, publishers have "bitten" and that publication is on the way—these, too, are moments that compensate a little for the missed joys of creation.

This discipline of the presence of the composer . . . how irreverent and irrational of me that Mark Twain's jingle about the trolley conductor keeps intruding into my present task, which, like all hobby-horse riding, tends to make one somewhat self-consciously solemn and "dignified." You have guessed right—the jingle that I can't get rid of is:

"Punch, brother, punch with care,
Punch in the presence of the pas-sen-jare!"

which I can't resist paraphrasing thus:

"Listen, brother, listen with care,
For you're in the presence of the com-po-zare!
Make your face tense, and no non-sense,
For you're in the presence of the com-po-zare!"

After this undignified sortie, I almost hesitate to catalogue
some of these sessions: the jingle might drown out the quiet,
reminiscent mood that comes on me as soon as I start looking
back on some of these meetings, most of which I really
treasure.

Among these, my memories of Eugène Ysaÿe are particularly precious and come to me with the same kind of
vividness that the impact of his playing seems to have left
on all who had the elating experience of hearing him.

His Solo Sonatas, the first of which, the one in G minor,
he dedicated to me, probably are more important as a violinistic
testament than as a creative effort that can stand critical
evaluation in cold blood. What gives them significance is
that they are a repository of the ingredients of the playing
style of this incomparable interpreter.

In the middle twenties, after I had spent a day or two
playing quartets with Ysaÿe at his seaside home, Le Zoute,
on the Belgian coast, he called me to his bedroom and showed
me the green leather-bound music manuscript book that was
always at his bedside, a pencil stuck between its pages. When,
on opening it, I found my name inscribed above the first pencilled sketches of the G Minor Sonata, I had an almost juvenile
thrill such as infinitely greater music, composed for me since,
has failed to give me.

This statement is something that only those who have
come under his spell in his "great days," before 1914, can
fully appreciate. Here was perhaps the last representative of
the truly grand manner of violin-playing, the living link with
Vieuxtemps, the dedicatee of the César Franck Sonata and of
Chausson's *Poème*,* and the first interpreter of the Debussy

* There can be no doubt in the mind of any violinist who had the good
fortune to hear Ysaÿe in his great days that the solo exposition in Chausson's
Poème with those typically Ysaÿean sinuous double-stop passages across the

[*continued on page* 118

Quartet, showing me music he was composing *à mon intention*
—composing with my playing in mind! I am unashamed to
admit that any level-headed evaluation of musical content, of
architectonics, was out of the question for me at that moment,
just as it was—though to a lesser degree—when later I began
studying the extremely difficult work and when, still later, I
started playing it in most music capitals. This was one of
those cases I referred to in the preceding chapter, where
autosuggestion is the prime mover . . . one of those cases
where one is willing to throw overboard the critical yardstick
that tempers one's enthusiasms every so often.

There he was sitting on the edge of his bed, majestic in
his enormous bulk, not unlike a Rodin statue (perhaps I was
thinking of Rodin's "Balzac" on the Avenue Friedland).
That anachronism, the long nightshirt, its white folds draped
around the Jovian figure, seemed to lend the scene an added
aspect that for want of a better word I would call monumental.
He began talking of "my" sonata and of the others he was
planning, telling me what they would mean to him when
completed. He was well aware of the importance of his
intensely individual double-stop, chord, and "across-the-
strings sweep" techniques in the history of violin-playing.

A glance at some of the pages showed me that here indeed
was a work in the making that would permit later generations
to reconstruct a style of playing of which the inadequate
Ysaÿe recordings give us barely a hint. These recordings
were made when he was past his prime, the repertory he drew
upon was anything but representative, and the recording
techniques were, of course, still primitive.

I felt that these sonatas were more to Ysaÿe than yet another
work would be to a composer whose *prime* function was
creating. They were, perhaps, a subconscious attempt on his

---

strings could never have been written but for the inspiration—and probably
the collaboration—of Ysaÿe. I was confirmed in this feeling when by
chance I met David Holguin, a pupil of Ysaÿe's. He told me how, one
morning in class in Cincinnati, André de Ribeaupierre asked Ysaÿe about
the genesis of this particular passage, saying: "It sounds as if you had
written it yourself." To which Ysaÿe replied with a smile: *Mais oui,* that
is precisely what I did—on Chausson's framework."

part to perpetuate his own elusive *playing* style. (While writing this I wonder whether our "time-capsule" idea does not stem from a similar urge to perpetuate ourselves and our time in some of its everyday aspects.)

As I see it now, these sonatas of his were also in the nature of a bequest: three of them were dedicated to Kreisler, Thibaud, and Enesco. And when in 1937 Queen Elizabeth of Belgium—whose *maître de chapelle* Ysaÿe had become after his return from America—instituted the "Concours International Eugène Ysaÿe" it was fitting that the statutes of the competition should specify that each violin contestant must present one of these sonatas along with the regular violin classics. Thus Ysaÿe's dream did come true to a great extent: the youngsters whose playing we were judging at that 1937 "Concours" (Carl Flesch and Thibaud were co-judges) and who had never heard the master were yet, in the very nature of things, by the reproduction of those sinuous, baroque, nervous Ysaÿean passages, arabesques, and whimsical musical ideas, perpetuating something of his essence.

When I wrote to Ysaÿe about the response my playing of his G Minor Sonata had brought in London, Berlin, New York, and elsewhere, he answered in that typically *fin-de-siècle* manner one sometimes finds in Massenet's or Chausson's letters, telling me how my news had warmed the heart of the *vieux ménétrier*—the old village fiddler, as he called himself. The specially printed and signed Japan-paper copy of the sonatas, imprinted with my name, is still another indication of this somewhat *fin-de-siècle* attitude and also of the sentimental importance Ysaÿe accorded what I think was his last work.

To have to one's credit the dedication of works like the Chausson *Poème* and the César Franck Sonata—can there be greater proof of the impact of Ysaÿe's interpretative genius on his creative contemporaries? And to have been entrusted by Debussy with the first performance of his Quartet is not a negligible episode in *any* interpreter's life, even an Ysaÿe's. Less generally known is the fact that Debussy originally conceived his *Nocturnes* as a violin solo for his friend Ysaÿe. A parallel to this came to my knowledge the other day when

I was visiting Ernest Bloch in his telephoneless retreat at Agate Beach on the Oregon coast, and he played to me his symphonic pieces *Hiver-Printemps*, composed in 1905. Upon my remarking on the Ysaÿean turns and shapes of the string writing, Bloch exclaimed: "But of course! How could it be otherwise? I intended *Hiver* as a violin poem for Ysaÿe and only later turned it into its present symphonic form. You'll find the score in its original conception as a violin work among the papers, sketches, and scores I left to the Library of Congress."

Bloch, by the way, freely concedes to Ysaÿe's encouragement and sponsorship a major role in his development as a composer. The sixteen-year-old violinist had been taken to Brussels by his mother to play for Ysaÿe with a view to studying with him. The boy did play to the leonine master, and he did get occasional (I am afraid *too* occasional) lessons from him; but very early in their relationship Ysaÿe dissuaded young Ernest's mother from letting him follow the career of a "mere" violinist. The friend of César Franck, Chausson, Saint-Saëns, Fauré, and Debussy soon discovered the boy's creative gifts, did not disdain to play one of the adolescent's earliest attempts in his salon to the Brussels intellectual and artistic élite, and from the very beginning insisted upon Bloch's pursuing the thorny path of a composer instead of becoming just "another" violinist.

No wonder that Ysaÿe always remained contemptuous of the easy laurels of the virtuoso. He invariably drew up programmes of heroic proportions not only for himself but for his pupils as well. He was impatient with the vogue that the prettified, more or less authentic classical transcriptions had during the first decade of our century. One of his pupils of his last years, Josef Gingold, tells me that when he played to him one of these typical encore pieces by one of our great arrangers, Ysaÿe exclaimed: "*Je vous en prie*, don't play these *sucrettes* for me again. Don't you know I have diabetes?"

That Ysaÿe in his younger days did not bestow this almost exaggeratedly elaborate care on some of his friends' brainchildren was brought home to me when Charles Martin Loeffler wrote to me in 1933, apropos of my recording of Loeffler's transcription of the Chabrier *Scherzo Valse*, which

Ysaÿe had made so much his own, and in answer to my inquiry about his violin compositions, which I was eager to know:

> As to some of my unpublished works, there was a Divertissement in three movements and 'une machine russe' belonging to the series 'Veillées de l'Ukraine,' inspired by Gogol's volume, for violin and orchestra. All of which our great friend Eugène Ysaÿe managed to *lose*! I forgive him! Chausson's lovely 'Poème' was lost in the original score by him! *That*, fortunately, was found after a year or so.

From Ysaÿe it is an easy association of ideas that carries me to Ernest Bloch. For had not the master of *Schelomo* and of the Viola Suite sat at the feet of Ysaÿe, studying the violin with him in Brussels? Who, knowing both Ysaÿe's playing and Bloch's string writing, can fail to acknowledge the impress that the former's style, at least so it seems to me, left on Bloch? I am thinking of pages like the cadenza in the Violin Concerto, of the noble pathos of *Nigun*, of the bardic poetry of *Schelomo*.

When I saw Bloch, soon after the outbreak of World War II, at his hotel overlooking Central Park, he picked up his violin—he had started playing again at the time of the composition of the Violin Concerto (1936–38)—and showed me fragments of a projected "Symphony for Violin Alone." As late as May 13th, 1944, he wrote to me from Agate Beach, Oregon, announcing the completion of a new work for orchestra, a Suite in three movements: Overture, Passacaglia, and Finale, played in the fall of 1945 by the Philadelphia Orchestra under Monteux. He adds: "Completed after innumerable revisions, there still remains to be done: revision of the orchestration, nuances, bowings, copying . . . a few months' work."

In this letter he seems obsessed by the idea of time. He speaks of his sixty-four years and of his "remaining and also fading" energies and exclaims: "*Le temps presse!* . . . I must create as much as I can." This letter to me also includes a touching epitaph to Carl Engel who had recently died. Bloch writes how "it went to his heart" to receive a box of cigars from Engel—as it happened—two days after the latter's death;

he calls this present from his friend a posthumous greeting and speaks of Carl Engel's premonitions of death, expressed in his last letter to Bloch: "I live only for death, which seems to me the most logical thing in the world. But it is so tiresome! We have all eternity for death and still it pursues us during our few days of life." Bloch comments: "When will it be my turn?" But toward the end of his letter he recovers his affirmative mood saying: "I am still holding out! Age and a broken leg and bad knee have not kept me from chopping down, sawing, and transporting more than one hundred big trees and from preparing the ground for an immense truck garden. The very solitary life that my wife and I—and four kittens that I am nursing since the poor mother died six weeks ago, ten days after giving birth to them—lead here seems to agree with us. We have hills, ocean, flowers—the great works of music and literature, of thought, of those whose eternal light has made bearable for us the sad present."

How far away from "the sad present" that day in 1909, at Neuchâtel, that brought us together, not as composer and interpreter, but with Bloch in his capacity of fledgling-conductor and with me as his 'teen-age soloist in the Mendelssohn Concerto. Since then how many gaps of long years during which we wouldn't meet or even hear from each other, and still, what continuity in our friendship! How many milestones in these thirty-odd years: the Sonata, the Concerto, the *Baal Shem* Suite—which I recorded as early as 1926 and which was, I believe, the first work of his ever to be recorded. Then followed—"as a token of appreciation," so the accompanying letter said—*Nuit exotique*, which he wrote in Santa Fé in the fall of 1924. Dedicated to me, it represents a fusion of two of the dominant themes of Bloch's inspiration, the ideas of "night" and of the "exotic." An English critic, particularly well-versed in Bloch's *œuvre*, called *Nuit exotique* the equal of those two moving "night pieces": the slow movements of the Viola Suite and of the quintet. No doubt the material of this *Exotic Night* issued from that sketch-book of Bloch's which is devoted entirely to exotic fragments, a sketch-book often spoken of by his entourage, but never seen by any of us, which is as it should be. I believe the Indian and exotic elements in the Violin Concerto also could probably be traced to the same source.

While he was directing the San Francisco Conservatory in the middle 'twenties, long letters came from him, all in his swift expressive hand, trying to persuade me to leave Europe and come to San Francisco to head the violin department in the institution to which he was then devoting all his energies. This suggestion precedes by only a few years repeated offers during the Weimar Republic from the Berlin Hochschule at which Joachim had taught, and an offer made to me by Dr. Frank Damrosch in person in 1926.

On the very day he and Kreisler and the whole of musical New York carried the great musician Franz Kneisel to his last resting place, Dr. Damrosch came to me at the Hotel Ansonia unannounced, and asked me whether I would consider moving to New York from Paris and taking over Kneisel's classes—a flattering offer for one in his middle thirties and which by virtue of its timing had a considerably enhanced value for me.

Returning to these "atelier sessions" with composers—to use a blanket description that will fit all of them after a fashion —they were of the most diverse kinds. One of the less rewarding ones, to put it mildly, was that afternoon in Paris, in the late 'twenties after I had made my first tour of Soviet Russia. I was "visited upon" by a famous Russian musicologist, the author of important theoretical and critical volumes. I see myself sitting next to him on the piano bench while he relentlessly pursues his way through an interminable neo-Scriabinesque sonata he had composed, me squirming beside him on the bench as though it were the "hot seat"! The task of talking *around* the issue without hurting an obvious fanatic's feelings! The impossibility of making clear to such a fantast the impracticability of his endless sonata! Such were the occasional purgatories which one simply had to accept as part of the bargain.

But certainly in the long run I had the best of this bargain. I like to think of that summer day in idyllic Donaueschingen with George Antheil, playing and singing to his audience of one his manuscript symphony in the empty dining-room of the old hotel. It was during the second or third Donaueschingen Festival in the early nineteen-twenties, long before his *Ballet Mécanique* days. Antheil's brilliant talk was not the least of his attributes. Apparently Stravinsky thought so too, for the story went around that the two had spent an entire night talking, in a discussion of æsthetic principles and the like.

That memorable session at Blüthner's piano store in Leipzig with Stravinsky playing his Piano Sonata to an audience of three—a friend, the representative of the Koussevitzky Publishing House, and myself—stands in a niche of its own. It was in 1923, after a very prolonged and very Russian midday meal that followed the Furtwängler rehearsal for the Gewandhaus première of his Piano Concerto. I remember I had my violin along, as I had been asked by Stravinsky to play Bach's Solo Sonata in A minor for him afterwards. He played his Sonata twice in succession, then turned around and said simply to us, deeply-impressed little group: "*Tchistaya rabota!*" ("Clean work!") Needless to say he was referring not to his playing but to the intensely "worked out" contrapuntal texture of this piece of his neo-classical period.

Now, twenty years later, here we are, both living in Southern California, meeting at my home, and playing the Duo Concertant that stems from 1932 but belongs to the same phase of neoclassicism. It is like reliving a past experience to sense in the now sixty-two-year-old master essentially the same attitude, admirably compounded of equal parts of humility and pride. "*C'est extrèmement travaillé,*" he says of the first movement of that work which Virgil Thomson called "an achievement unique in history" in its "completely satisfactory balancing of sound and of musical interest." Simply "extremely worked out," as a Persian carpet weaver would say of his masterpiece, or as we imagine the anonymous cathedral builders or stained-glass masters spoke of their work. And Margaret Marshall has recently brought out the similar contact between craftsmanship and creative writing. "This joy of the writer [in his craft]," she says, "is embodied in the product, just as the joy of the craftsman, or so I've always felt, is embodied in the chair or table—and almost as palpable as the seasoned silky wood or the good design."

While playing, replaying, and discussing certain unorthodox devices of mine (to reinforce the G-string passage in the Gigue of this Duo), he professed with utter simplicity his love for the physical aspects of music realization. As if he needed to explain the roots of this attitude of his, he added: "*Vous comprenez*, my father was an interpreter, he was a singer. I grew up with the consciousness of the executant's essential part in bringing our written music to life." What a contrast with that growling remark of Hans Pfitzner's, reported to me: "I don't care a hang *who* plays my Sonata, as long as he has the indispensable minimum of technical equipment."

This feeling of intimacy for the "how it is done" is shown in markings like the one in the score of Stravinsky's *Histoire du Soldat*: "*Glissez sur le sol avec l'archet en toute sa longueur.*" It is as if he enjoyed in imagination the slim, silky sound of that long-drawn-out bow while he marks the instruction into his score! In the *Pulcinella* Suite I find: "*Très court et sec mais pas très fort.*" Doesn't this (except for the *très court*) sound like something out of a poetic wine list such as one encounters in a restaurant with exquisite cuisine and cellar? "Fruity, but mellow, with an inner glow," or "Fiery, but with a velvety unction." A remembrance of past enjoyment and a guiding toward future "degustation" of something delectable, whether of a vintage wine or of a particular kind of bowing, seems to be common to these heterogeneous things: score markings and poetic wine lists. . . .

It is this awareness of Stravinsky's of what the executants of his music do, his interest in the instrumental "know-how," that makes working with him so delightful, even if sometimes pretty strenuous. For, in Ernest Ansermet's words (as quoted in *The Real Jazz* by Hugues Panassié): "The importance of the writer in the creation of a work is well balanced by tradition as represented in the performer. Though the work is written, it is not *fixed*, and can only be completely realized in execution." Stravinsky, in order to make his intentions realistically clear, is quite willing to disregard and often contradict commentators' dicta that have been read into his music; sometimes he will even deviate quite considerably from his own pronouncements. Speaking about the genesis of the *Duo*

Concertant, he writes, beginning with a quotation from C. A. Cingria's *Petrarch*:

"Lyricism cannot exist without rules, and it is essential that they should be strict. Otherwise there is only a faculty for lyricism, and that exists everywhere. What does not exist everywhere is lyrical expression and composition. To achieve that, apprenticeship to a trade is necessary." These words of Cingria seemed to apply with the utmost appropriateness to the work I had in hand. My object was to create a lyrical composition, a work of musical versification, and I was more than ever experiencing the advantage of a rigorous descipline which gives a taste for the craft and the satisfaction of being able to apply it—and more particularly in work of a lyrical character.

However, while preparing the *Duo Concertant* for recording and for concert performance, Stravinsky used quite a heterogeneous set of interpretative guideposts. One movement he described as "monolithic," and a certain all-important motif as "Bach-like," while the Eclogue, No. 1 with its irresistible motoric drive he found like a *Kazatchok* (a Cossack dance), and so on. I, too, delivered myself of sundry remarks more fitting to a commentator than to an executant; for instance, I spoke of the Giorgione-like lyrical and chastely formal beauty of this or that thematic line. But the most unexpected—and still, I must admit, extremely apt—illustrative guidepost came when Stravinsky "interpreted" the first Trio of the Gigue. He jumped up from the piano and, with the humorous grace of an Oscar Karlweis, danced and hummed and mimed this refrain from Johann Strauss's *Gypsy Baron*, in impeccable German:

Glücklich ist
Wer vergisst
Was nicht mehr
Zu ändern ist.

So there we had it: the Bach-like and the monolithic and the Cossack elements, and the Viennese grace and lilt of a Johann Strauss operetta, plus the rigorous lyrical discipline of which Cingria's book spoke—all these ingredients co-existing in this masterpiece. Thus it was not for nothing that Stravinsky chose for it the title "Duo Concertant," which does not attempt to "interpret" its style. Titles like "Scènes pittoresques," "Suite italienne," "Visions fugitifs," "Danses fantastiques," and "Suggestions diaboliques" do commit the composer to a certain extent, whereas titles like "Duo Concertant," "Music for the Theatre," "Music for Orchestra," "Prelude," "Intermezzo," "Bagatelle," "Moment musical," and "Impromptu," of course, do not.

Béla Bartók shares with Stravinsky this ever-present consciousness of the role the player fulfils, of the part the physical properties of the instruments, too, have in the audible realization of his works. In Bartók's Second Piano Concerto he actually specifies which section of the tympani's taut skin he wants struck and exactly how; and this certainly after much preliminary experimentation, and by no means on the say-so of this or that tympanist.

I see Bartók in his villa in the hills of Buda—his tables, couch and piano littered with those hard-earned discs of folk-fiddlers, mostly unaccompanied, which he had recorded during many epic years of folk-lore exploration. He plays them to me while I follow the intricate, almost hieroglyphic signs on the literal transcriptions he has made of these, as he has of thousands of others. Putting me to the test: whether I would recognize the sometimes infinitesimally small rhythmic or melodic shreds that went into the Rhapsody, No. 1, which he dedicated to me in 1928; making the distinction, while discussing these themes, between the unimaginative, premeditated *incorporation* of folk-lore material into a composition, and that degree of *saturation* with the folk-lore of one's country which unconsciously and decisively affects the composer's melodic invention, his palette, his rhythmic imaginings.

I have never commissioned any work for my own exclusive use; I somehow always managed to have my hands full without that. The nearest I came to commissioning a work was when I had a brainwave about suggesting to Benny Goodman that he authorize me to ask Bartók to write a work for the three of us—Goodman, Bartók, and myself—to be underwritten financially by Benny. The result was *Contrasts*, which we repeatedly played and also recorded; about the rehearsing of this Benny has some interesting things to say in his autobiography, *The Kingdom of Swing*. There were all sorts of complications, chief among them Benny's hope—though not his proviso—that the work should be just the right length for a double-sided twelve-inch disc. This was not the case, and Bartók was somewhat apologetic about the "overweight" when giving me the timings of the work.

In his scores, by the way, Bartók sets down the timings to the split second, like this: "6 min., 22 seconds"; whereas Alban Berg in his Violin Concerto allows, apparently, a latitude of fully five minutes by noting on the fly-leaf of the work: "Duration 25–30 minutes." This difference in outlook on the part of two contemporary masters, both trail-blazers, always puzzled me. I asked Bartók for the reason. "It isn't as if I said: 'this *must* take six minutes, twenty-two seconds,'" he answered; "but I simply go on record that when *I* play it the duration is six minutes, twenty-two seconds." An essential distinction, this.

Bartók wrote, when sending the score to Benny and me: "Generally the salesman delivers less than he is supposed to. There are exceptions, however, as for example if you order a suit for a two-year-old baby and an adult's suit is sent instead—when the generosity is not particularly welcome!"

A good deal has been written about this work, but one angle has been neglected: that it was completed, according to the manuscript which is before me as I write, "in Budapest on September 24th, 1938"—the very day when Hitler's Sudeten demands had *almost* succeeded in setting flame to the Europe that was to give him another eleven months in which to arm. This date of September 24th is still present to me. At 2.15 a.m. on that day I was broadcasting from London through the British Broadcasting Corporation to Canada and the West Indies—hence the unusual hour; and on my way to Broadcasting House I saw the morning papers on the pavement with headlines screaming out the Czechoslovak general mobilization. Groups of the people who make up the nocturnal crowd of Regent Street and Oxford Circus were standing around the shouting news vendor, and at the B.B.C. bleary-eyed, overworked officials told me that Jan Masaryk had just broadcast his last plea to the United States.

SZIGETI WITH GYPSY URCHINS, BUDAPEST, 1932

EDWARD MacDOWELL AND GEORGE TEMPLETON STRONG AT WIESBADEN IN THE 1880's

The picture of the creative artist meticulously putting the finishing touches to a work—during days when the whole world was holding its breath—is consoling and inspiring. But this same Bartók, anti-Fascist that he has always been, did not hesitate to answer the summons from the new parliament in liberated Hungary, in the spring of 1945, with an unequivocal yes. He had been elected to parliament by the people along with three other Hungarian exiles: former President Count Michael Károlyi; Professor Rustem Vámbéry (president of the New Democratic Hungary movement); and George Boeloeny, writer, who had been active in the French underground.

Ever since the Berlin concert that I mentioned apropos of Busoni and at which the programme included (besides the Busoni Violin Concerto) the Berlin premières of Stravinsky's *Sacre du Printemps* and Roussel's *Pour une Fête de Printemps,* I had become Roussel-conscious. In the early 'thirties I frequently saw frail, bearded Albert Roussel, looking more and more the naval officer he used to be in his youth, despite the flowing "Lavallière" cravats to which he was partial; he came trudging up the four flights of stairs to our Paris apartment to go through his Second Sonata with me—a work I played in most important centres: London, Paris, Berlin, New York, and Moscow—and to discuss ways and means of adapting for the violin his *Segovia*, a little piece written and named for the great guitarist. This Second Sonata of Roussel's, which I propagandized wherever I could, became a symbolic weapon in my American management's well-meant, good-humoured crusade against my programme policies.

It came about this way: an out-of-town manager who was a prospective "buyer" was taken to my recital at Carnegie Hall by a member of my management in order to clinch the deal. Everything, so I was told the next day, was smooth sailing during the first two "standard" numbers, an old Italian work and a Brahms sonata. The "prospect" beamed and my manager already envisioned the buyer's signature on the dotted line, when along came item three on the programme. It was the Roussel Sonata, with its strident, leaping intervals, its stimulating, provoking, uncompromising language

E   (129)

—and the deal was off! The names of modern composers, alas, do not often figure on managerial inter-office memoranda, but Rousell's did that time—with negative comments, I am sure. And needless to say I was entreated once again to mend my already notoriously incorrigible ways of programme-making.

My Paris years mark the beginning of my friendship with Nikolas Nabokov. He would show me sketches of the ballet he was then writing for the Paris Opéra, dancing them out for me to visualize them. Some years later, in a Chicago hotel room, it was as if our Paris days had never been inter-rupted: there was no piano, and he demanded of my auditive imagination that I picture—by reading and humming with him some pages still in the blueprint stage—what his Second Symphony, later played by Mitropoulos, would finally be-come. In recent years there had been talk of a set of variations on a lovely Glinka theme he intended writing for me, for violin and piano; but, except for that typically Nabokovian *Schwär-merei* (in three languages!), things don't seem to have progressed much beyond the "find" of the Glinka melody!

Some composers show you the merest fragments, filling in the gaps with talk, gestures; others, like the Hungarian, Pál Kadosa, whom I had played in public before a note of his had been published, brought along a string ensemble to give me a preview of one of his Quartets.

Roger Sessions, Henry Cowell, Copland, Benjamin Britten, Arnold Bax, Ernst Bacon, Fred Jacobi, Roy Harris—how much stimulating shop talk I owe them! How revealing it was to hear the reticent running commentary of William Walton when we were listening to a recording of his own Symphony or his Viola Concerto . . . or to hear Vaughan Williams and Walton exchange their impressions of the Ernest Bloch Concerto after a rehearsal at Queen's Hall shortly before the recent war . . . or to sit in on a Koussevitzky rehearsal with Prokofiev or Milhaud. . . .

With all this at times embarrassing talk of what modern music owes to this or that player, one is tempted to ask: doesn't it work both ways? For what would the lives of mere interpreters be without the fertilizing influence of this vital contact with "Work in Progress"?

CHAPTER XV

BARTÓK'S meticulous timing of his compositions and Alban Berg's liberality in this matter point up the vagueness of some composers in their markings (tempo and metronomic indications, dynamics, expression marks, and so on). It has often amazed me to contrast this lack of precision and these misleading "guideposts" with the intricate and careful instructions that accompany the brain-children of other composers into the world. I have before me a manuscript of a work in two different versions: one for a wind instrument, the other for violin; the identical Scherzo movement is marked *Presto* in one, *Allegretto* in the other! Ravel in his Violin Sonata does not give metronome markings for the first and third movements, but does so in the case of the middle movement, the "Blues." One could add many more instances!*

Discrepancies are often to be found between the violin part and its duplication in the piano-and-violin score of the same work; I know of cases where "authoritative" recorded performances by the composer, under his direction, only add to one's bewilderment when one compares the printed indications with the audible realization. (It was David Popper who gave me the sound advice always to check violin part against piano or orchestral score, when in doubt.)

There are countless examples of such doubtful passages, even downright misleading indications and misprints. This

* Prokofiev, in his Sonata Op. 80 gives metronome markings for the first three movements but not for the fourth which he marks "*Allegrissimo*"; I take this *Allegrissimo* to be less a tempo indication than a signpost to its cheerful, lively spirit.

is not surprising when one finds—as I did—on comparing the texts of four or five different editions of Beethoven's violin-and-piano sonatas, and the same with Mozart's, that not even such imperishable works are free of such. Isn't it discouraging to the student of masterpieces to find in the first bar of Bach's A Minor Solo Sonata the bass note that descends from A to G changed by a French editor to G sharp? Or to find in Joachim's edition of the Beethoven Sonatas (in Sonata Op. 30, No. 1) a flagrant misprint in the fourth bar of Variation I?

In cases where the composer himself has transcribed his work into another medium, an examination of both versions is sure to yield precious clues of one sort or another to the student of these texts. To mention only a few of these transmutations into other media: Brahms's Piano Quintet in F minor was originally conceived for string quintet, then became a sonata for two pianos before reaching its definitive form; Ravel's *Tombeau de Couperin* exists in both a piano and an orchestral version, and so does his *Alborada del Gracioso*; Bach's D Minor Concerto is both a violin and a piano concerto, and in addition to these two versions its two first movements have been incorporated by Bach in the Cantata *Wir müssen durch viel Trübsal*. In Beethoven's piano transcription of his Violin Concerto he deviates from the original, fourteen bars before the end of the Rondo, by substituting for the second F a G sharp—an emendation that only my reverence for an original text of such exaltedness has kept me from adopting.

Those who believe in the infallibility of "original texts" and "Urtexts" sometimes overlook the fact that even such first editions, engraved during the lifetime of a composer, do not always represent his original intention in all details. The finale of the Brahms Violin Concerto, for instance, is marked "*Allegro giocoso, ma non troppo vivace*," but the story behind this qualifying "*ma non troppo vivace*" is that it was Joachim who added it on the proof-sheets, explaining: (to Brahms, no doubt) "*da sonst zu schwer*" (because otherwise too difficult!). Thus the tempo indication that we assume to be the composer's own turns out to be his interpreter's modification.

Discrepancies between manuscripts and "first editions" are of course very common. Bartók's MS. of the Rhapsody,

No. 1, which he composed for me (and the original of which is among my treasured possessions) contains thirty-nine more bars than the published work. And in the case of his Second Rhapsody he sent out three lithographed pages of changes that he wished to make after the first edition had already been engraved and distributed.

How understandable the confusion that might confront the player of Bartók's music, say, fifty years hence! Which is the "definitive" version: the "first edition" or the one incorporating the three loose lithographed sheets with their emendations or afterthoughts? We sometimes forget that even awe-inspiring sets of "Complete Works" may not be wholly foolproof; the score of Mozart's G Major Violin Concerto, K. 216, for instance, was engraved for the "Gesamtausgabe" of Breitkopf & Hartel over a hundred years after its composition, in 1878 to be exact.

So we take our clues wherever we find them and accept guidance along with mystification as they come our way. Charles Ives frankly says in his volume of songs: "Some of the songs in this book . . . cannot be sung." Then follow some revealing reflections of the Connecticut composer on the "rights" of a song that "happens to feel like trying to fly where humans cannot fly." A thought-provoking sentence, by the way, that leads one to muse on that abstract, unrealizable something that so often baffles one in great and eminently "practicable," playable music. . . .

Schumann's tempo marking, "as fast as possible," which he follows later by "still faster" (in the G Minor Piano Sonata), has already become a venerable chestnut in the small-talk of musicians and amateurs; but we should perhaps look on it less as a howler than as a symbol, as an expression of the creative musician's contempt for the interpreter's technical and physical limitations. Beethoven cried out: "I don't consider your lousy fiddles when the spirit comes over me!" and it is precisely to this uncompromising attitude of the trail-blazers that we owe so much in the advancement of our technical means.

I thoroughly agree with Rudolf Kolisch when he says in his essay "Tempo and Character in Beethoven's Music":

". . . if a given tempo [in Beethoven] should really prove impossible in practice, this would only indicate the inadequacy of our technique." And Schnabel, in speaking of our inclination to consider certain passages as misfits, caused by the composer's "errors in writing, incompleteness of notation, defective theoretical knowledge, physical disturbances (such as deafness), etc.," calls alterations based on such naïve judgments and assumptions unpardonable. On the other hand, one of our illustrious violinists, speaking of Prokofiev's First Violin Concerto, told me: "Yes, it is extremely interesting and I am really tempted to take it up; but, before doing so, I would feel like rewriting, rearranging the violin part." And this, as if it were the most natural thing in the world. . . .

Leopold Auer's attitude toward Tschaikovsky's Violin Concerto seems to have been somewhat similar. It is well known that though the work was dedicated to Auer it was Adolf Brodsky who first played it (in 1881). When asked about this Auer explained (in 1912, to an interviewer of the *New York Musical Courier*): "My delay in bringing the Concerto before the public was partly due to this doubt in my mind as to its intrinsic worth and partly that I found it necessary, for purely technical reasons to make some slight alterations."

The curious fact remains that while the first page of the Concerto bears the dedication "A Monsieur Leopold Auer," the cover says: "Herr Adolph Brodsky gewidmet!"

Of course there are sometimes clashes between what the creative musician demands and what the player is able (or willing) to give. During a rehearsal of one of his works, Richard Strauss petulantly insisted upon an "almost inaudible" tremolo from the violin section; the poor hard-driven players were at their wits' end. He kept calling for this, for that, for the use of less and less bow hair, for the execution of the passage at the extreme tip of the bow, and so on. At last the concertmaster could be seen whispering some instructions to the players behind him, asking them to pass these on from desk to desk; then he suggested that Strauss try again. This time the Master was entirely satisfied, telling the men that *this* was exactly the effect he had in mind. It was only years later that the concertmaster confessed to Strauss: he had instructed his fellow violinists not to play at all but, by keeping the bow on the string and looking tensely down at the right hand, to deceive the exigent taskmaster into mistaking the visual simulacrum of tremolo for the audible fact. And the Maestro with the infallible ear had promptly fallen into the trap!

There are composers who, in their minutely marked scores, guide you firmly through the realms of their fancy, with expressive, sometimes whimsically worded indications . . . they are loth to leave any margin for error. One sometimes meets with strangely evocative indications, with single words like Alban Berg's *Wienerisch* and *rustico*, or Prokofiev's *sognando* and *freddo*. How unequivocally the elusive mood of Brahms's Scherzo in the D Minor Violin Sonata is set by the marking *Un poco presto e con sentimento!*

The nearly complete disappearance from our present musical terminology of the Brahmsian *poco forte, mezza voce*, and *sotto voce*, by the way, certainly has a bearing on the trend of taste in our day and should set some of us instrumentalists to searching our musical consciences.* Although Alicia Markova's blanket indictment: "Everything to-day has to be very bright, very quick, and very loud" refers to her own field, and while it is perhaps too strong a generalization, it should give us "furiously to think." Her criticism, by the way, isn't such a far cry from Virgil Thomson's recent indictment of the "systematic employment of forced tone, of overbowing and overblowing" on the part of contemporary American orchestras.

Busoni's indication *mit absichtlichem Pathos* ("with palpably intentional pathos" perhaps comes nearest its meaning) gives the player who is to translate it into its musical equivalent a hard nut to crack; as does Debussy's when he orders the pianist, anent those three descending chords in the coda of the Violin Sonata's finale: *Cuivrez*. Some composers never seem to know exactly what they want. Indeed, Bernard Shore uses precisely this phrase in connection with Delius, going on to say: "A violinist once played a passage of his in three entirely

* The great Adagio in Beethoven's Opus 96 carried both of these indications: *Sotto voce* and *Mezza voce*.

different ways, asking the composer each time if that were what he meant. Each time came the reply—'Yes.'"

The present-day custom among some composers of dispensing with the time-honoured tradition of the Italian terminology and of using their native tongue when marking their music certainly has some amusing by-products. On one short piece that I have repeatedly played in concert, there are the following instructions to the player: "With quiet charm, demurely expressive," then "Like whistling," "With inconspicuous precision," "Archly," "Slightly detached but not staccato," and "Feathery light"—all of which doesn't seem to leave much room for any unauthorized personal meddling on the part of the executant! Yet in spite of such definiteness, one may ask whether there is any insurance for the composer against the unpredictable human equation.

The only possible "insurance" probably would be in the music of the future as Edgar Varèse visualizes it and who sees in "electronic instruments the first step toward the liberation of music." He adds: "The interpreter will disappear like the story-teller in literature after the invention of printing. . . . On these instruments, sound-producing, not reproducing instruments, the composer in collaboration with the engineer would be able to transfer his work directly. Then anyone could press a button and the music be released as conceived by the composer. Between the composer and the listener no deforming prism, but the same intimate communion as that existing through the book, between writer and reader."

But until this supposedly Golden Age dawns, the composer will be to a great extent at the mercy of the interpreter, however scrupulously he may have marked it.

Ernest Ansermet lately told me of the time he sat next to Debussy at a recital of a well-known singer Madame B. After this lady had delivered herself of a singularly "purple," overacted, suggestive interpretation of one of his "Chansons de Bilitis" Debussy turned to Ansermet in dismay and whispered *"serai-je pornographe?"*!

When one encounters nowadays indications like "freely singing," "with bite," "bouncy," and the like, one feels like offering up a vote of thanks for such concrete images. Jazz composers go one better in making their meaning clear. Don't we find terms in some jazz trumpet parts like "with bend" and "dirty"? And doesn't the jazz leader use "Sock it!" instead of our *sforzando*?

All this is especially comforting to one who has seen romantic aberrations like the personal commentary of a famous Austrian pianist, pencilled over a section of Schubert's *Wanderer* Fantasie: "*Gott tanzt mit der Natur*" (God dances with Nature). And what can one say of injunctions to the player like *Avec la fraicheur de l'herbe humide* (with the freshness of dewy grass), or *Mit tiefster Ergriffenheit* (with deepest emotion)—the latter to be found in a modern edition of one of Bach's masterpieces—? At least we are gradually leaving such gratuitous vagaries behind us, for which let us be duly thankful.

On re-reading these pages it strikes me that, strictly speaking, many of these contacts with composers were unrelated to my violinistic activities and interests. But precisely therein lies the charm of such hours, the charm that a busman's holiday seems always to have!

There was no "must" about these, no ulterior professional motive. Even when, as in the case of Ravel, the reason for our getting together was primarily a professional one (it was in New York in 1928, prior to our performance of the Violin Sonata at the "official" Ravel concert), the living memories of those hours have little to do with our actual rehearsing and playing of the Sonata.

It is probably my intense admiration for Ravel the composer that causes my subconscious to blue-pencil my memories of Ravel the pianist! As a wag put it on seeing Salzedo, master-harpist and excellent pianist to boot, officiating as page-turner to Ravel: "What a pity it isn't the other way round: Salzedo at the keyboard and Ravel turning pages!"

Ravel was somewhat nonchalant about his piano-playing; "unconcerned" might better describe his attitude. It was the confidence of the creative artist that determined his stand with respect to our task. It was as if he said: "What of it, whether we play it a little better, or in a less polished and

E* (137)

brilliant fashion? The work is set down, in its definitive form, and that is all that *really* matters."

The Sonata bears the eloquent dates "1923–27": it took the master four years to complete it.* The Duo for violin and violoncello, which Piatigorsky and I played at our "pianoless" recitals in Berlin and Frankfurt—"*ce bougre de Duo*," as Ravel called it—cost him almost eighteen months of travail.

So the rehearsal did not really absorb us inordinately—as it always does, and should, when virtuosi are bent on producing a perfect ensemble performance: we both realized the limits within which we would have to plan our performance—for better or worse—and thus I was free to indulge in one of my busman's holidays. There were intensely illuminating critical flashes in Ravel's conversation: about Liszt, the unjustly underrated composer and trail-blazer; about his (Ravel's) indebtedness to Liszt in his piano-writing; then about that Hungarian instrument the cimbalom, and the conversation naturally drifted to *Tzigane*, which Ravel had lately composed for my compatriot and former classmate Yelly d'Aranyi. I suppose my being Hungarian has something to do with it, but I have never been able to overcome the resistance I always felt and still feel toward this brilliant and (to my mind) synthetically produced pastiche of Ravel's. He must have sensed this, for I distinctly remember that his conversation swerved suddenly to Edgar Allan Poe's elaborate description of the genesis of *The Raven*. Then, if my memory doesn't fail me, taking Poe's essay as a starting point he expounded some of his pet theories of conscious cerebration, which insure the mechanical excellence of whatever a composer sets out to do, whatever idiom he chooses to write in.

My somewhat chauvinistic "hands-off" attitude when it came to Hungarian folk-lore may have nettled him, and may, too, have been the reason for the otherwise reticent master's going into such detailed theorizing. It was later that I learned how partial he was to accepting the challenge of folk-lore in his work; early in the 1900s he had entered a contest in Moscow for the harmonization of folk-songs of various

* Prokofiev's Violin Sonata in F minor Op. 80, took him eight years to complete (1938–1946).

countries. He wrote seven songs on popular themes of France, Italy, Spain, Scotland, Flanders, Russia, and the Hebrew, and won four prizes—the French, Italian, Hebrew, and Spanish.

Then we returned to the work at hand and, apropos of some fine point in the first movement of the Sonata which I commented upon admiringly, he spoke of Fauré, of the miraculous freshness that the A Major Sonata retains after more than fifty years—its première having taken place in 1878.

It is the atmosphere of that long afternoon that remains with me, *not* memories of our playing at the Gallo Theatre with a hero-worshipping audience overflowing on to the small stage. And should I want a musical accompaniment, as it were, to my recollections of that talk with Ravel, can't I invoke Koussevitzky's *Daphnis and Chloe* magic—or Lucrezia Bori's scintillating "Concepción" in *L'Heure Espagnole*—or the Capet Quartet's superb playing of the quartet one afternoon in Monte Carlo—or Horowitz's uncanny projection and analytic dissection of *Scarbo* one night at that house of the Sam Barlows perched atop the rocks of Eze on the Riviera?

When I ask myself which of the many beneficial by-products of these contacts with composers have been most helpful to me in my work, the answer that comes most readily is: learning to see things from the composer's point of view. Few familiar with our work will deny that a good deal of autosuggestion goes into our task of reproducing music. Music that we have played, and defended in words as well, with the utmost conviction, music that has filled our waking and sleeping hours (for I suppose we all memorize during our sleep to a greater or lesser degree!), may find us looking at it coldly, objectively, almost incredulously a few years later, at a different stage of our development. It is simply that the magic of autosuggestion is no longer operative at that time. If we concede—as I am inclined to do—an important role to this autosuggestive faculty in our work, what better schooling in it than commerce with new works and their composers?

Ernest Bloch told me a characteristic story that illustrates the point I am trying to make about this faculty of auto-suggestion in the performing musician. Bloch had been asked to conduct a chamber-orchestra programme at the

Library of Congress in Washington; comprising a Mozart work, a Bach Brandenburg Concerto, his own Concerto Grosso, and a *Ricercari* of Malipiero's for a small string ensemble with four violas playing *divisi*. Bloch accepted the assignment with the eagerness and enthusiasm characteristic of him; but, on studying the Malipiero work in some detail, he was so repelled by its (as he called it) abstruseness and forced ingeniousness that he felt he could not conduct it with the inner conviction and "approval" he deemed necessary if he was to "put it across." A lengthy correspondence ensued: Bloch explaining why he could not reconcile himself to presenting the work; Carl Engel (representing the sponsor of the concerts, Mrs. Coolidge) in turn explaining why it was absolutely essential that the work be performed. And at last Bloch, with a heavy heart, agreed. A period of intense study followed this initial reluctance. Bloch analysed and memorized the score, and rehearsed it with a dogged perseverance that was to offset the lack of real "flow" between the work and its interpreter—and a superb performance resulted! The Brussels Pro Arte Quartet, who were present and who knew the work from previous European performances, were amazed and told Bloch as much: "We thought we knew the score; we had played it ourselves. But you brought out new, hidden beauties." Such is the magic that this self-induced, almost hypnotic absorption on the part of an interpreter can work.

Some ten or fifteen years ago, a sort of epidemic of short suite or partita-like manuscripts was rampant among the younger composers, and many of these manuscripts reached my music rack. Busy Neoclassical toccata movements alternated with sarabande solemnity; there were cadenzas for both the violin and the piano; and it all ended, more often than not, in a "pure" transcendent apotheosis with the violin mounting higher and higher and fading away. One of the young composers, who was playing and humming his work to me (my pianist and I were reading the score over his shoulder), exclaimed ecstatically when he reached his "transcendent" hymnlike section: "*Voilà . . . le ciel s'ouvre!*" My pianist and I looked at each other, and the phrase stuck.

"The Heavens opened up" from that day on at certain points in—oh, how many!—Partitas and Sonatinas and Eclogues by different but all equally hopeful and convinced composers.

All this may sound less than respectful, but no offence is meant. I have often felt that these guiding fingers to the sometimes not so heavenly "*ciels qui s'ouvrent*" give the player an insight into many things—into the world of meaning that may lie behind mere notes, if only we penetrate the surface and develop in ourselves the faculty of *identification* with the music we are playing. An attitude without which no one should approach the "upper" regions "*qui s'ouvrent*" in the Adagios of Mozart's E flat Sonata (K. 481) or of Beethoven's Opus 96, or in the wavering *balancement* that leads into the final G major of the coda in the first movement of the Ravel Sonata.

CHAPTER XVI

MY recording experiences run like a thread through most of my four decades of professional activity, much as do the contacts with composers described in the pages just preceding. These experiences have, naturally, given rise to a number of ideas about the manifold values of the gramophone and of the very existence of recorded music itself, and it is with all these that the present chapter will deal by reprinting—in slightly modified paraphrase—two articles based on interviews of the recent past.

The first of these, "Reflections on Recording,"* published in *Listen* magazine, runs in substance as follows:

First I want to tell you about my gramophone past. My memories go back farther than I ought to care to admit! I remember the first gramophone in our village. It was a sort of market-fair attraction and reproduced only speech, no music. People stood around and gaped at it, overawed.

When I was still a boy, I met a cylinder-phonograph amateur who took records of my playing in his home. In those days this really meant engineering; he had to build the whole apparatus himself. I made records of all my repertoire—without accompaniment. Sometimes I would slip into his study and play Bach, recording myself, committing this crime of mine in secret. I learned a great deal from this.

People don't realize that I started professional recording way back in Caruso's time. A rather puerile arrangement of Sibelius's *Valse Triste* and an abridged version of the Variations from the

* Reprinted by the kind permission of the editors.

"Kreutzer" Sonata were among my most popular recordings, and —I should add—most conspicuous aberrations from good taste. Strange to say, these held the market right up to the end of World War I. Sometimes I meet old record collectors in Australia or Ceylon who have had these records since 1909. One man made me a present of one of them, which I didn't have, for my collection.

Many old records stand up very well under the test of time. There is a type of sonority that leads to "phonogenic" playing, which gets across—a kind of *plastique* in the player's articulation of a phrase or of passage work, a certain approach to one's instrument that is effective on records.

That literally *all* types of music can be successfully marketed nowadays—obscure, forgotten, experimental modern works—is (or should be) a great encouragement to all of us. This is the great achievement of our present gramophone boom and it is one that I have foreseen. I recall, in an interview printed in the *Gramophone* magazine, saying that primarily the richness and the breadth of our record repertoire depend on the record buyers. They have to extend credit and give normal support to the companies by supporting experimental ventures and not just wait for things to be released, then shrug their shoulders and fall back on some "war-horse" recorded for the umpteenth time! They have to co-operate, as subscribers to an eighteenth-century novel used to do—in advance, before publication, often before the author had finished writing it. It is this sort of co-operation that we need now in connection with gramophone recordings. People must have faith in artist or composer and allow the company to give a full picture of them.

I am very gratified by the results of my recordings of new works and new composers. I think I was the first one ever to have recorded Milhaud; in 1926 I did the *Printemps*. This became popular and started many a violinist on Milhaud. I also remember well when I first insisted on recording the Prokofiev D Major Violin Concerto. They just didn't know how to get rid of me. I told the highest official of the company: "They say it is not going to be a seller, but I *have* to do it!" He was very nice, though he had to ask, "How do you spell the composer's name?" And we did it! One just had to go through walls in those days. Fortunately, that recording has been a steady seller and has done much for the whole Prokofiev situation.*

The first record of any of Bloch's music was mine of the *Nigun*. The second was Menuhin's record of the same piece played when

* The interview here reprinted was, it must be remembered, given long before the recording of *Peter and the Wolf* and the *Lieutenant Kije* Suite, and before the re-recording of the *Classical* Symphony.

he was a little boy. Then came Sevitzky's of the Concerto Grosso. And there it stopped for years. The Violin Concerto (1939) started things moving again.

In an early issue of *Listen*, Artur Schnabel described how choked he felt in the recording studios of several years ago. To-day, conditions in the studios have improved so much that every-thing is very much alive. I often think back upon my first electric recording, when engineers allowed me to do anything I liked. Once I decided I wanted to "filter my tone" (a very foolish idea, really) and I threw a handkerchief in front of the mike. And the engineers let me do it!

We performers who have had the advantage of familiarity with the technique and material of the gramophone for many years are free of the inhibitions that bother some artists in the recording room. Recordings by people who are used to recording therefore often give you the warmth and feeling of a concert hall. Experi-enced performers don't think foremost of turning out absolutely impeccable—but cold—records, such as I call "laboratory records"; they strive after a living performance that has the impact of the moment, one that gives you almost a visual impression of the player. Some people try to produce a document. Apparently they have a legalistic obsession to get the "definitive" recording. I am always careful not to let this obsession get me. When I feel that I am losing spontaneity and am hypnotized by the fear of flaws, then I try to get around it in some way; I stop recording that section, jump to the next, and come back later to the other.

Compared with the ephemeral appearance and recognition of a big modern symphonic work in the concert hall, records provide the most durable building-up for a composer. For example, the sporadic performances of a Vaughan Williams work every two or three years are of very little help to him. In too many programmes, such works are merely tolerated, sandwiched between other more "desirable" things, and never seem to achieve what a gramophone success gives to a composer. I cannot prove this, but I have a feeling that these sporadic performances of works that are not within the reach of all simply do not get anywhere in consolidating or raising the status of a contemporary composer.

What makes the difference, I suppose, is that basic instinct in all of us, the *possessive* instinct. We may sit in a concert hall and listen to a work being played, and hardly be aware of the name of the composer, the conductor, or the player—never get the sense of the travail that went into the composing and the playing. But, as soon as we own the recording of that work, as soon as we have chosen it and bought it, this sense begins to emerge; we begin to take a proprietary pride in it. It is exactly the difference between borrowing a book from a lending library and buying it for one's own shelves. I often compare the absent-minded concert-goer to the lending-library reader, and the record-buyer to the person who browses before choosing his books, buys them, keeps them, makes friends of them—and then proselytizes for their authors!

Gramophone recordings broadcast over the air have, I think, a little of that lending-library element in them. It is true that they suggest additions to our record libraries, but there is the danger that people will remain satisfied with hearing it occasionally on the air. After all, there are millions of people who are satisfied with lending libraries.

One of the greatest problems in our present-day recording of violin music is caused by the metal E string, which has excessive vibrations. Engineers try to eliminate these by turning down the dynamics. But it is a dangerous game, when you start sacrificing the genuineness or the impact of the climax of music to pleasantness or purity of reproduction.

There is a subtle relationship between the artist and the recording room. You cannot quite put your finger on it, can hardly say that the artist "flusters" the engineer, or that the engineer "intimidates" the artist, but some such thing often occurs. An engineer who makes a sour face after a test can clip the player's wings and reduce his *élan* in the next recording. If a player who is dissatisfied with something he has done blames it on the engineer, he may influence him to do something that he would not have done by his own conviction. It is an impalpable relationship, one of the "imponderables." No—the best results are achieved when the player is courageous enough to admit errors such as faults in his playing or style, without blaming them on the engineer, and when the engineer doesn't try to intrude with his idiosyncrasies. (How can an engineer understand everything that is done in a recording room?)

It is still possible to find conductors and professional musicians who have not yet grown up to Beethoven's dynamics, who are shocked at his crescendi that end in a pianissimo, who are disturbed by the abruptness of his dynamic line, and who tone it down. This has been going on for the last century, and during the whole of that time his intentions have been misrepresented by Beethoven editors. It is really an achievement of our own age—and a great virtue of Schnabel, Capet, Toscanini, Klemperer and Furtwängler— that Beethoven's music has been re-established in its original force. Now, when you find professional musicians and artists of standing who are not yet grown up, isn't it dangerous to allow sound engineers to "edit" what we play?

Certain music produces physical discomfort in some people:

(145)

things that seem perfectly normal and are eminently satisfying to others, in percussions, tubas, and piccolos, in timbres, the position of chords, and tabu intervals. The less we meddle with each other, therefore, the better it is. The less the interpreter meddles with the composer, or the engineer with the interpreter, the greater the profit for music. The recording should be a reproduction—that is all. Too often it is merely an interpretation of an interpretation, which is not right. I have in mind the overamplification of certain recordings. You really cannot amplify, beyond a certain degree, without distorting. Most gramophones err on this side: they give too much. Therefore I always listen to my own records on cheap machines, in order to be sure that the records convey the essentials of the message even under adverse circumstances.

There is a lot to be done in the way of increasing the violin repertoire on records. Tartini's violin sonatas contain such treasures that at least half a dozen of them should be recorded. And Schubert's violin-and-piano works have not been sufficiently recorded as yet; he wrote some lovely violin sonatas. The greatest problem, however, remains the distribution of music to the people, the potential buyers.

Perhaps the answer lies in an institution that existed ahead of its time, and that doesn't exist now, when we need it most. I mean those penny-in-the-slot machines in Paris, Milan and elsewhere long before the first World War. The one in Paris was on the Boulevard des Italiens. You sat down and put earphones on. You had a catalogue, and with tokens that you bought you chose a number, turned the dial, and had it played for you. There was a large selection of records. I remember listening to Elman and Caruso and John McCormack and Emmy Destinn, just walking in for ten minutes or a half hour. I don't see why, with all the facilities and tremendous advances of our time, something similar should not be possible. There are people who hesitate at going into a gramophone shop if they are not sure they are going to buy. A solution of their problem would bring untold benefits to the artist and would enrich all of music. Juke-boxes and what they do for the ephemeral productions of Tin Pan Alley are not really analogous with the leisurely browsing I have described; for the juke-box limits the listener's choice to a handful of constantly changing hit tunes, whereas the earphone listener of my boyhood had a whole treasure store of music to choose from.

Thus, the article in *Listen*. There is one point, however, that I did not touch on in that interview and that I want to discuss here: the self-educative benefit that the recording artist can derive from listening to his own records and to the numerous test records that precede the final choice of an issued version. At the beginning of the *Listen* article I mentioned the private recordings I made in 1907 or 1908—before I started my professional gramophone career—for an old-style machine playing cylindrical records with a sapphire needle. Even then I vaguely sensed the importance it can have for a player to record himself and listen to the results with a critical ear. Needless to say, the results from such experimental recordings, on pioneer equipment, were of little value in catching fine points of playing technique. But these early efforts marked for me the start in utilizing one advantage that to-day's virtuosi have over those of the past in being able to follow their development step by step, comparing their past performances with present ones.

Often I got four or five processed test records of the same part of a concerto or sonata, and listening to the minute discrepancies in these, weighing the flaws against the passages that were more than usually satisfying to me in a certain version, deciding whether the exceptional good in some cases made up for the less-than-average quality in others, offered a schooling in critical and objective listening that only the most imaginative players of the pre-gramophone era could ever envision as an actual possibility.

I like to call snapshots and candid-camera shots "clinical pictures," and the phrase applies also to these test recordings. The habit probably stems from my Davos Sanatorium days, when my lungs and those of fellow-patients used to be X-rayed at regular intervals, and the plates studied by doctor and explained to patient. Upon these X-rays depended everything: the length of our sanatorium exile, the permission of this young woman to marry at last, after all those postponements, the resumption by that young man of his university courses, or the return of a young matron to husband and child. These unretouched X-rays, the candid-camera shots, the test records—all three seem to me clinical tests, unvarnished truth.

While some of us musicians use these "musical X-rays" in a clinical spirit, others demand of their records nothing but self-elation. There are as many attitudes toward one's own recordings as there are recording artists. Even the element of self-emulation may enter into these listening habits. I know of one fabulous virtuoso who deliberately listens to his own records, made years before, with the avowed wish to maintain his hold on those juvenile, instinctive felicities, the graces of youth, that he fears he may be losing in the process of his general development and the accrued intellectualization of his gift and powers!

Certainly the mechanical techniques that "freeze" certain performances for the artist are among the most important innovations in his schooling and evolution. The fact that such recordings, in only slightly less acoustical perfection, are available to student and teacher through home and studio recording machines is an educational factor of undeniable importance. Although I personally do not take advantage of the present-day facilities for having most of one's important public performances recorded, I agree with that conductor friend who finds such recordings of his public performances a major contribution to his own development.

If these private recordings of our own performances help us to obey the injunction "Know thyself," our commercially released records fulfil another role besides the more obvious ones: that of allowing us to get to know each other. No regular concert fan can have failed to notice the comparative rarity of the presence of our important virtuosi at their confrères' performances. Is it fear of being buttonholed at intermission time and of being forced to make pronouncements on performances just heard? Pronouncements that later on can be quoted, misquoted, distorted? Whatever the reason, the conspicuousness of their absence is undeniable. How, then, account for the fact that virtuosi on the whole are pretty well informed about each other's accomplishments, interpretations, techniques? The answer obviously is that they listen to records in the privacy of their own homes, or to broadcasts of recorded music and (in a lesser degree) to "live" broadcasts.

It is as if records fulfilled the function of those atelier visits of painters—those intimate discussions and shop-talk sessions in each other's studios which I (perhaps romantically) imagine to be an important part of a painter's life. Who knows? Perhaps the painters entertain similarly romantic notions about virtuosi's sessions!

My musings about the gramophone, prompted by a chapter in *The Magic Mountain*, by Thomas Mann, took shape in another article, this time printed in *The American Music Lover* and here reproduced (slightly modified) by the kind permission of its editor:

To find a summary of something that is still in as fluid a state of evolution as the gramophone in a work of the enduring quality of Thomas Mann's *The Magic Mountain* is an experience that stimulates me, not only as a recording artist, but as an old record collector, whose addiction dates back to the cylinder and sapphire-needle days.

Like many a hobby-horse rider, I cannot escape the feeling that an object of my enthusiasm is in some way elevated once the pen or brush or stylus of the really creative artist has tackled it. It is only then that this object of enthusiasm attains a certain "maturity."

The gramophone of 1942, though its "coming of age" dates only from electrical recordings of the mid-'twenties, is an instrument with a history of several moultings. From the quiet, groping beginnings of the 1870s, the process of capturing sound on a wax disc has developed into a major instrumentality of modern life, with a background of profound influence on the lives of men great and small. When I happened to read somewhere that Lawrence of Arabia had owned a considerable record library, it set me to wondering what role the gramophone might have played in the lives of men like Lawrence in Arabia, Grenfell in Labrador, Albert Schweitzer in Africa, and Professor Schmidt, who led a number of Soviet-sponsored Arctic expeditions. It also occurred to me that, when the history of the gramophone is written at some future date, it may well be the contact of outstanding men with the instrument, not statistical enumerations of the how many and what and where and by whom, that will ultimately tell the fuller story.

The gramophone itself will be pictured most effectively not by an exposition of the fabulous evolution and expansion of the thing, not "as rubber and science and manufacture and merchandising," as Saroyan phrases it, but by the evocative word—the image *bien trouvé* of the poet. It will be—again as Saroyan says in speaking of his records—"grace and strength and grief and joy." With the growth and attendant blasé acceptance of the gramophone, we begin to need the poet's definition of the essence of the thing—the view of naïveté and wide-eyed wonder that will lead us to its soul.

I don't know whether it is generally realized among record fans how proud a bird's-eye view of the gramophone in its heroic beginnings we possess in *The Magic Mountain*, in the chapter called "Fullness of Harmony."* Here, in this classic piece of writing, the ordinary mortal is privileged to see the magic of the instrument with a poet's (or a child's) eyes instead of merely as the casual offspring of a versatile industrialism.

Besides this brilliant insight that Mann shares with his readers, he gives, in his intensely musical description of the records, a sort of "time capsule" of the phonograph of the period around 1910. Bottles of Chablis '06, talk of the Balkan Federation being "aimed against the Austro-Hungarian monarchy," and other scattered references throughout the book delimit the time for us.

To-day one can well imagine that our costly and cumbersome records, which have not changed essentially from the days of 1910, may in perhaps a decade or so be superseded by music transferred to film and reproduced in one's own home. By that time the immense and seemingly permanent presence of the gramophone may have faded away into a mere fad for antiquaries and collectors of historical curiosa. How precious, then, to know that its spirit is perfectly preserved in some fifteen pages of *The Magic Mountain*, a work that will certainly survive a small matter like this metamorphosis of a huge industry into quite another one, survive metamorphosis and the disappearance of much bigger things too. Here is a description, from Thomas Mann's novel, of the instrument

* Thomas Mann: *The Magic Mountain*, translated from the German by H. T. Lowe-Porter, New York, Alfred A. Knopf, 1927, pp. 803-18.

which by that time will have become obsolete. The phonograph that Hans Castorp played at the Berghof was a "truncated
little coffin of violin-wood" giving off sounds

scarcely like a real orchestra playing in the room. The volume
of sound, though not to any extent distorted, had suffered a
diminution of perspective. If we may draw a simile from the
visual field, it was as though one were to look at a painting
through the wrong end of an opera-glass, seeing it remote and
diminutive, though with all its luminous precision of drawing
and colour.
. . . The vibrations, so surprisingly powerful in the near
neighbourhood of the box, soon exhausted themselves, grew
weak and eerie with distance, like all magic.

The motion of the disc was

not only circular, but also a peculiar sidling undulation, which
communicated itself to the arm that bore the needle, and gave
this too an elastic oscillation, almost like breathing, which
must have contributed greatly to the *vibrato* and *portamento* of
the stringed instruments and the voices.

This was Castorp's phonograph, a "truncated little coffin
of violin-wood" with double doors. The records that
Castorp's creator allowed him to hear in the book provide
our 1910 "time-capsule" of recorded music. One of the
recorded pieces was

an idyll, yet *raffiné*, shaped and turned with all the subtlety and
economy of the most modern art. It was . . . a symphonic
prelude, achieved with an instrumentation relatively small for
our time, yet with all the apparatus of modern technique and
shrewdly calculated to set the spirit a-dreaming.

Can it have been *L'Après-midi d'un faune?*
Hans Castorp listens to an Offenbach overture, with the
waltz, the galop, and the *cancan* described by the author in
mental images of top-hats and Parisian dancing girls, with
flashing legs, and whirling skirts. Then follows the "Largo al
Factotum" from Rossini's *Barber of Seville*, sung by a famous
Italian baritone whom—from evidence afforded by the
Victor catalogue of the time—we may presume to have been
Titta Ruffo.

Further, in quick succession, comes the kaleidoscope of what must have been considered representative records around 1910: A French horn playing variations on a folk song; a soprano warbling "with the loveliest freshness and precision" an air from *La Traviata* (I wonder whether this was Tetrazzini or Selma Kurtz); "the spirit of a . . . violinist [playing] as though behind veils a romance by Rubinstein" (which I have to confess was probably mine, this being the only recording of that saccharine piece to be found in any of the catalogues of the period); the "Barcarolle" from *Les Contes d'Hoffmann*; overtures; "single symphonic movements, played by famous orchestras" (we must remember that the first "complete" symphony recording was that of the Beethoven Fifth made by Nikisch in 1913*); an "international troupe of famous artists . . . in *arias, duos* . . ." (Caruso, Scotti, Sembrich, and Severina, perhaps). A few other numbers, which seem to point to Caruso and Anton Van Rooy, excerpts from *Carmen, Aida,* and *Faust,* and Schubert's *"Lindenbaum"* round out Mann's priceless catalogue, if one may use this word in connection with such a monumental work. But we already have a significant cross-section of the music that was available at the time for a record collector. And should we not now direct our efforts toward preserving similar cross-sections of the music recorded in the intervening decades, instead of cutting out and rendering unavailable even for connoisseurs the most valuable but little saleable documents? Only by an intensified historical consciousness on the part of recording companies, museums, and libraries can we hope that when the gramophone of the 1940s is highlighted in some literary masterpiece—say in the second half of our century—the literate record collectors will be able to use facilities like those which the historically minded film-fan now has.

The student of that day will then be able to recapture performances like those by the young Casals, Ysaÿe, Enesco, Maria Ivogün, and perhaps Godowsky (in Grieg's *Ballade* in G minor), and to clear up some debatable point in a Beethoven

---

* This performance on two 12-inch discs afforded only extracts from the four movements. The first *really* complete symphony recording was made by Albert Coates around 1920.

quartet by comparing a Flonzaley version with one by the Capet Quartet. The record fan with literary tastes will thus be able to illustrate to himself what he has gleaned from *The Magic Mountain*, for instance.

Anything that strengthens our historical consciousness with regard to what the gramophone is doing, and has already done, seems to me worth while—anything that will ultimately lead to a record library of commercially unavailable records. The inquiring music student or amateur should by no means be denied what students of painting and the plastic arts are so generously provided with, like the all-inclusive art library and reference files of the Frick Collection, America, and of several other institutions.

These musings, which I did not presume to send to Thomas Mann, nevertheless reached him. With the graciousness characteristic of the truly great he wrote me on Christmas Eve, 1943 :

December 24th, Pacific Palisades, Calif.

Professor Arlt was so kind to send me the attractive little booklet of The American Music Lover with the surprising and charming article about the phonograph in The Magic Mountain. This little meditation has given me great pleasure; it may really be that in the future the gramophone chapter in The Magic Mountain will have a certain significance from the point of view of musical technique, and, in a way, has such significance already to-day.

The development which the phonograph has undergone since the days when I wrote my chapter is indeed surprising; but ... I was perhaps happier with my black box then and the thin sounds of the records which it played than with the glorious sounds coming now from my loudspeaker.

I hope to met you personally some day and am sending you my best wishes and regards.

Very sincerely yours,
THOMAS MANN.

*

To look back upon one of one's own activities and to find that it covers not only the period described by Thomas Mann but also the groping days of the first electrical recordings of the late 'twenties and the present climactic period of immeasurably improved recording techniques—this is a lesson indeed in looking at things historically instead of being (as one is apt to be) hypnotized by the all-absorbing present and by one's infinitesimally small share in that present!

From the days of playing into the paper horn at the old His Master's Voice studios in City Road in 1908 to the present remote electrical recording when the receiving turn-table may be blocks (or even miles) away is, indeed, a vast span of activities to look back upon! But there is, remarkably enough, one constant in this looking backward on almost four decades of recording: it is Fred Gaisberg, author of *The Music Goes 'Round,* who recorded me in those City Road days, who was still on the job when in 1938 I last recorded in London, and who will—I hope!—monitor me when I go back to the Swiss Cottage Studios now that the war is over.

CHAPTER XVII

TO be a stickler for chronological exactness in a book of reminiscences strikes me as not only unnecessary but, what is worse, positively unseemly. For any attempt at chronological accuracy and completeness in the narrative is in itself so revealing of the autobiographer's exaggerated sense of his own importance that his professions to the contrary are invalidated. I may be wrong, but to give only one instance: to retell, for the *n*th time, the story of the events leading up to World War I—apropos of *one's self*—seems to me a trifle immodest, however succinctly it may be done. Whatever the gentle reader—as he used to be called—may find or miss in these pages, I do promise him immunity from this kind of chronological completeness.

It is precisely this consciousness of time in a musician that tempts him to take liberties with it, to deal with it cavalierly, capriciously, whenever he is not bound by it in his own work. On the one hand this consciousness enables him to estimate time so accurately that sometimes on a trip he will make silent bets with himself as to the exact time down to minutes, after not having looked at a watch for several hours; it also enables him to gauge practising time so closely that if he makes up his mind to stop after say 100 minutes, he generally stops on the dot. On the other hand, it constrains him to regard time entirely in terms of its inner content: of the inner content and the inherent tension of one *fermata*, of one bar, of one section of a movement, of one work—the two hours that contain all the ups and downs, the tensions, the drama of a "simple" recital . . . a content that often is out of all proportion to the actual clock time represented.

Naturally this leads to an attitude toward time that is unorthodox, to say the least, and that takes its toll when a feeling for smooth chronology is desirable. A musician acts like a man who permits himself to lose his temper with an intimate friend when he would never dream of doing so with a casual acquaintance. Time is a rather special property of the musician; he feels justified in treating it familiarly. Not quite so familiarly, though, as the Russian handyman who answered Stravinsky's telephone when I rang up the other day: "Sorry, Mr. Stravinsky out. Please, again call, he will be back an hour ago."

I have tried to apply a faculty acquired professionally to circumstances of everyday life—as, for example, to the evaluation of what a few summer months, or an ocean trip of no more than six or seven days, or perhaps a long tour of two or three years lumped together "gave" me. The faculty I mean is that of reeling off great expanses of music in the mind, silently and without the printed score, reeling off the different "*étappes*" of a composition which in the actual playing would take big hunks of time—a half-hour, three-quarters of an hour —in mere minutes. Probably the best way to describe it is to call it the opposite of the slow-motion camera technique of the movies. This reeling-off technique allows us to "see" the works in their big outlines, penetrate the inner laws of their architecture, and generally counteract some pernicious concomitants of the detail work, study, and practice so necessary for the interpreting musician.

That is why in this book I sometimes give to clusters of seven or eight years no more than two or three times that number of lines.

The four or five years that preceded World War I took me on increasingly frequent trips to the European Continent, providing contacts and musical experiences whose cumulative effect compared roughly with the university years that the average eighteen-year-old embarks upon. The radius of my travels became ever wider—my first concerts in Paris, Bordeaux, Brussels, and Bucharest supplementing the by now regular trips to Germany, Austria, and Hungary. These

REMINISCENCES AND REFLECTIONS

travels reached their widest span in the season of 1913–14, when my tour took me as far north as Helsinki and Riga, as far south as Portugal. It was during that season, too, that I played my first almost complete tour of Switzerland, which was to become my home some years later; to be the scene of my first pedagogical efforts, of my marriage, and of the birth of our daughter. When I compare the wide span of that 1913–14 tour with the lull and the restricted concertizing possibilities of the years of World War I (during which I could only tour Switzerland and Germany), and when I consider the compensatory activities which these years enabled me to go in for—reading, and the playing through of vast quantities of music not destined for "public consumption"— two words seem to bring out the difference between them: "extensive" seems to fit the 1913–14 tour; "intensive," the war years with the settling down in Geneva (in 1917) and the attendant founding of a family when still in my twenties.

I have already mentioned Mendelssohn's godson, Felix Moscheles, whose gentle and wise talk I drank in during those Sunday suppers under the portrait of Mazzini which dominated the room. It was he who explained to me the significance of the word *jingoism*, which I came upon more and more often during these years punctuated with "incidents." The caption of a caricature by Olaf Gulbransson in that very outspoken satirical weekly, the Munich *Simplicissimus* (often censored and *verboten* in those days), expressed the prevailing atmosphere very aptly. It showed a good small-town German "Michel" (or it may have been a "Michel" offspring) saying his evening prayers and kneeling beside his bed. "Lord," ran the caption, "may You grant us peace and happiness, and may our All-Highest ruler [*allerhöchster Herrscher*] *neither deliver a speech nor send a telegram* on the morrow! Amen." Didn't we have similar jitters and send out similar silent prayers before week-ends in the heyday of Hitler's power? The Saar plebiscite, the reoccupation of the Rhineland, the Sudeten, the Anschluss, the Danzig affair. . . .
Those were the days of the Zabern affair, provoked by insolent monocled Prussian officers in the peaceful Alsatian

garrison town; the days when the idea of a Channel Tunnel between England and France had one of its periodic revivals and was promptly wet-blanketed by Britons who thought that, *entente cordiale* notwithstanding, there was greater safety in some twenty-four miles of water. I listened in on some of the speeches on this subject at a City dinner at which my violin solos alternated with propagandizing exposés of this idea, possibly by the undaunted William Collard himself. One gala evening at the Moscheles studio in St. John's Wood at which I played was dedicated to the Press Association of Germany, which was just then visiting England in a body— dedicated to goodwill and understanding between the two nations. Whether this visit preceded or followed Kaiser Wilhelm's state visit to England I cannot now recall, nor can I place the much-discussed stage play, *An Englishman's Home*, in its right chronological sequence. The passionate discussions aroused by this propagandistic play (which had as its central theme the vulnerability to invasion of the "impregnable" British Isles) quickly subsided, and I had forgotten all about it until some thirty years later, until Dunkirk. . . .

Around this time a pamphlet by Tolstoy, entitled *Patriotismus und Regierung*, first printed in Germany (Tsarist Russia would not have permitted its publication), came my way through my father, whose haphazard reading—judging by this and by other examples—seems to have been guided by an admirably right instinct. Norman Angell's *The Great Illusion* (whose revised edition, years later, won him the Nobel Peace Prize) was another book that impressed me profoundly.

Not having read Tolstoy's pamphlet in all these decades, and unable to check on this and similar points, I cannot now say why this pamphlet in its green paper cover is still so real to me—almost bodily present—even though its contents are not. I suspect that what left its mark on me was the pacifistic, world-unifying *ends* and not the anarchistic *means* of Tolstoy's teachings. The fact remains that whenever—in all these intervening years—I came across the unattainable ideals of "world government, world federation, lesser federations" (as Raymond Swing enumerates them in a sad and indulgent phrase) I linked these, perhaps irrationally, with the little tract.

Looking back on the things and ideas that mattered to me all along, I now realize why the concept of the melting pot struck such a responsive chord in me when I first came to the United States in 1925; why this unifying principle which America exemplifies meant so much to me—a principle originally brought home to me by Konrad Berkovici's *Round the World in New York*, which I read on my first trip to America, and which was reaffirmed fifteen years later by *Ballad for Americans*, which John Latouche read and hummed to us at our very temporary quarters in New York during those tense, dismal days of the fall of France in May, 1940.

A virtuoso's life being what it is, he is naturally more exposed to conflicting theories than the average boy in his 'teens. For the young trouper there are few of the characteristics of the sheltered life: no conditioning through the family newspaper, and through parental airing of political opinions at mealtimes; no premature "taking of sides"; no influencing through student clans, debating societies, and the like for *him!* To me, he seems to remain on the margin of "life in earnest" for a disproportionately long time. Hence the disconcerting infantile traits that he retains long after his contemporaries in other walks of life have shed them. True, conflicting influences do sometimes help him to reach an *au dessus de la melée* attitude earlier than his contemporaries, and this feeling of being *above* partisanship does sometimes lead him to a truly supranational way of thinking. But more often than not Hugo Wolf's scathing remark in one of his letters applies to him: He who prides himself on being *above* parties is more probably *below* any one of them.

Setting out on a life of travel as early as I did when we quit Budapest for good, in the fall of 1905, it was to be expected that daily contacts, the mosaic of personal experiences, would determine my outlook on essentials. I had no thought-habits built up by continuous identification with an unchanging social, scholastic, and geographical milieu. The idiosyncrasies that colour our personality as decisively as our positive attributes—if not more so—originate mostly in early contacts and impressions, which in my case were certainly kaleidoscopic.

An everyday incident like that knock on the door of our

Berlin hotel room, early one morning in 1905 (the Prussian police on one of their routine check-ups of foreigners frequenting the less opulent hostelries), might have been the starting point for many an uncontrollable nervous reaction which I have since observed in myself, during border crossings, immigration interrogations, and the like. This knock on the door, incidentally, tallied well with stories told by a relative of ours who had returned from Berlin to Budapest; he had interesting things to say about the close check the Prussian police kept on all foreigners generally and in particular on subscribers to the social-democratic daily, *Vorwärts*.

This little incident, shocking me out of the childish sleep which goes with the age of thirteen, may have started the unconquerable distaste that all bureaucratic constraint connected with visas, labour permits, and customs formalities has aroused in me during all these decades of travelling.

Passports, which we came to take for granted after World War I, were unnecessary in the greater part of Europe during my youth, except for travel to Turkey, Russia, and Rumania, or for emigration overseas. Only in a few "police-states" like Germany, Austria-Hungary, and Tsarist Russia was there a rigid system in force, involving the announcement of one's arrival or of one's departure within twenty-four hours. These permit-questionnaires were called *Anmelde-* and *Abmeldescheine*. Furthermore this system was supplemented by such routine check-ups as the one I mentioned and, no doubt, by more surreptitious methods as well.

When we went to England in 1906, I remember being struck by the absence of check-backs of any kind. There seemed to be no need for identity cards or documents, no control worth mentioning! When my manager suggested that I facilitate the spelling and pronunciation of my name by omitting the letter "z," and when he assured us that there were no bothersome formalities involved in the process, I realized that in England a person could break with his past, could start a new life, with a new name even, if he so wished.

During my stay in England, I became very conscious of this contrast with the two police-states I had previously known; Austria-Hungary and Germany. The glimpses into police

SZIGETI AND GEORGE TEMPLETON STRONG, GENEVA, 1939

SZIGETI AT RECEPTION GIVEN FOR HIM BY VOKS, MOSCOW, 1937, SURROUNDED BY YOUNG PRI
WINNING SOVIET VIOLINISTS AND THEIR TEACHER

methods in Máramaros-Sziget, which I had gained through a police official who had married into our family, must also have been decisive in forming this distaste of mine for official officiousness so early in life; I had heard vague gossip at Uncle Bernat's table about petty police corruption and early took a violent dislike to the attributes of omnipotence which authority, personified by this minor official, by his bosses, and by the *Obergespan* of the county or province of Máramaros, represented to me.

I knew too well, even then, how the rubber stamp or signature that spelled freedom to trade or to settle somewhere depended upon the goodwill of petty officials bound together by an intricate system of corruption; a goodwill that the ignorant Ruthenian peasants or Jews who had migrated into Máramaros from Rumania or Austrian Galicia had to buy, more often than not at a price which, on their level of subsistence, was exorbitant.

It may be irrational to put down that episode of the early morning police check-up in Berlin as partly responsible for my distaste for anything even remotely linked to bureaucracy and constraint—as irrational as it is, conversely, to try to account for some of the pleasurable reactions awakened in me by sights and actions tending to dissolve the suspiciousness and hostility that a national or racial or linguistic group displayed to members of another group. For certainly my feeling of contentment at seeing and reading a trilingual poster of the Châtelet Theatre (in French, English and German) on a *colonne d'affiches* on the Paris boulevards some time in 1908 or 1909 was also irrational. There was no more reason for my being inordinately pleased over this than there was for my dislike of questionnaires, permits and visas. It was simply that the former symbolized welcome, and the latter restraint, restriction and limitation.

I seem to have been inclined, from those early days, to associate confining and regimenting factors with German territory; circumstances somehow led me to this association of ideas. The mental discomfort I felt in the lovely and so characteristically Lorraine town of Metz, when I played there under a German municipal *Musikdirektor* around 1910, was indefinable but persistent. The German garrison just did not seem to belong; the typical red brick of the post office or railroad station or high school—in the so-called "Wilhelm II" style—was a jarring note in the town, as were the stance of the monocled officers and the attitude of their wives. Although the music we played bridged the gulf between Lorrainers and Prussians—as good music will always and everywhere—the set-up of the concert association did not seem to stem from the soil of the place, but gave one the uneasy feeling of being grafted on; one had the vague and suspicious thought that music was being used for purposes of "peaceful penetration."

As chance (the young player's principal tutor) willed it, I got to know at about this time Rudolf Rotheit, a music-loving Berlin journalist who filled a distinguished post on the *Vossische Zeitung*. He happened to cover the events that led to the forcing upon the mountain people of Albania the rule of the German Prince von Wied. Rotheit accompanied the German expedition which culminated in the setting up of this incongruous ruler, and on his return gave me some picturesque descriptions of these seemingly *opéra comique* events. However, as Pierre van Paassen points out, they were far removed from the realm of *opéra comique;* they were, rather, one of the preparatory moves prescribed by the pan-German Geopolitical Institute to pave the way for world conquest. (These long-range plans had been evolving since 1897 though, as van Paassen comments sadly, they were discovered by the world only in 1939.)

Rotheit also gave me his book entitled *Aus Albaniens Werdetagen*, describing his experiences. Thus, through the hazard of a young fiddler's career, I, who in the normal course of events would hardly have been aware even of the existence of Albania, became an interested listener and reader about events that formed an instructive chapter of Pan-German and later Nazi techniques. No wonder that when I played in Metz or in Prague such distrustful and suspicious interpretations of everyday things should have flashed through my mind!

Travelling and concertizing often pointed out to me conflicts similar to those I sensed in Metz. In Prague—when it was part of the Austro-Hungarian Empire—the Czech violinmaker Lantner explained apologetically to my father why he could not hear me on the following day at the symphony concert of the Deutsches Landestheater, much as he desired it: no self-respecting Czech would set foot in the German opera house! Of course, this worked the other way round, too: no "true" German would attend the Czech theatre.

Such tensions among the different racial elements of a given territory were brought home to me in particularly graphic fashion during my three visits to Riga. The first of these occurred in 1913, when Riga was a part of Tsarist Russia but at the same time a stronghold of that typically Germanic and Hanseatic culture of the Baltic provinces. During the second, in 1927, the national consciousness of the newly founded Latvian Republic had probably reached its zenith. And the third was in 1937, when the incorporation of Latvia into the Soviet Union loomed large on the political horizon.

How instructive to compare the three different interpretations given to me by three different sets of friends! In 1913 my host was the poet and critic Hans Schmidt, friend of Joachim and of Brahms; it was he whose poem Brahms used for setting as the *Sapphische Ode*, a page treasured by all interpreters and lovers of the Lied. In his conversation, and in the countless anecdotes he told, Schmidt naturally stressed the Germanic cultural elements of Riga, a tendency that my own reading of the staid *Rigasche Rundschau* still further confirmed. It was in this same *Rigasche Rundschau* that Hans Schmidt wrote that he found "something Apollonian" in my playing and in my attitude toward music.

The age-old division into two opposing camps: the "Apollonian" and the "Dionysian" conception in art! Stravinsky, in his Harvard lectures in 1940 ranged himself on the Apollo side and explained: "the Dionysian elements which set the imagination of the artist in motion . . . must be properly subjugated before they intoxicate us, and must finally be made to submit to the law: Apollo demands it."

But to return to my three visits to Riga in the 'twenties: a friend, Lina Grosvald, descended from old Latvian patrician stock, whose father and brother represented the newly founded republic at Paris and Stockholm respectively, just as naturally interpreted everything from the Latvian national angle. And in 1937 some Soviet-inclined friends in Riga did their best to make me realize what they termed the folly and futility of the brief experiment of Latvia's secession from the immense Russian commonwealth.

The news-stands with their Latvian, Russian, German, Yiddish, and (I believe also) Polish papers, as well as the second-hand bookshops with their multilingual wares, further emphasized this continual tension and flux of which my profession happened to give me three distinct *aperçus* on these three occasions.

Travelling inevitably enmeshed me in the red tape that snares the touring virtuoso when he tries to get his person, his violin, his honest earnings, *and* his accompanist across frontiers—especially if the last be, as mine was for several years, travelling on a "Nansen" passport issued to so-called stateless persons.

The customs officer in Saigon, French Indo-China, who would not let me "import" my Guarnerius had a particularly objectionable way of exercising his function. Single-handed he managed to conjure up around him the atmosphere of a penal colony. It was the day of the concert too! Every minute counted. I had lurid visions of my Guarnerius being impounded and tossed into a store-room cluttered with the fantastic accumulation of oriental contraband. It took the president of the Concert Association, who happened to be the "sugar king" of Indo-China, to prevail upon the chief of the customs bureau to overrule the minor official and rescue me.

When we settled in Paris in 1925, I had just as much trouble explaining my status at the Ministry of Labour as I had had explaining my violin to the man in Saigon. I could not make it clear to a certain estimable functionary that I was neither a *rentier* (a person living on unearned income) nor an *employé* (a salaried worker); nor could I—from his point of view—be an employer. He recognized no other categories and insisted I must be one of the first two. If I lived in Paris on my earnings in other countries, he did not see why I should be allowed to appear professionally here as well. It was a case of either one thing or the other, and the twain could not, in his opinion, meet. I tried to show him how illogical and unworkable this interdiction was.

"But, Monsieur," I said, "when I play here in Paris, perhaps once or twice a year, say at the Concerts Colonne, it is more in the nature of a gesture to my French colleagues than for pecuniary compensation, which comes to a negligible fragment of my yearly income, not worth mentioning."

I presumed that this rigid pigeon-holing had some connection with the intricate income tax laws of the country. If I remember rightly, the income tax of a foreigner living on his income (unearned in France) was computed by taking some percentage of seven times the amount of the rent he paid. To avoid a confusion of categories they were adamant about making sure that the *rentier* earned nothing in the country.

At this stage of our altercation I seemed to be classed as a *rentier*, but mention of the Concerts Colonne had pricked his Parisian ears and catapulted me into his one remaining group. "If you play at the Concerts Colonne, Monsieur, you are an *employé*, and you must get your employer to make an application here."

After all this we were back where we started. Even the Légion d'Honneur ribbon I wore (usually handy in these cases) was of no help. A good deal of expostulation back and forth wore us both out needlessly until some higher-up (I don't remember what his title was) came and untied the bureaucratic knot, and I was rescued once more.

If ever I needed proof that bureaucracy forms a truly supranational freemasonry, with the same quirks, the same incalculable workings of the mind, and the same lack of logic, I found it in Boston, where the Saigon customs incident repeated itself with uncanny similarity of detail.

I had entered and left the United States many times with my two Guarneri and they had never been suspect as "import" or "export." Only a week before, I had left Boston for engagements in Nova Scotia without any difficulty about this; but on my re-entry that morning I ran into a snag. I was anxious to make a railway connection to upstate New York for my concert that night, and I could not afford to miss the morning train. To my consternation I heard this spiritual brother of customs officers the world over pronounce the shattering verdict.

"You must put up a bond for your violins," he said. I don't remember the exact amount, but it had to be in cash. This was about seven-thirty in the morning, and my train was leaving before I could get my cheque okayed or wire to my New York bank or concert manager for cash. I was taken from department to department and ended up in a warehouse with countless rugs, carpets, and pieces of old furniture. Here the final decision, which none of the other departments would take upon themselves, was put up to the official in charge of the warehouse.

Bureaucratic logic had it that, as my two Guarneri were over two hundred years old, they came under the office listing of antique furniture. The expert in charge had—fortunately for me—a sense of humour. He admitted his incompetence in appraising "merchandise" of this kind and after a phone call or two released me.

On the other hand, a contrasting experience during World War I, which ever since has somehow represented for me the essence of an understandingly liberal interpretation of the dead letter of the law, was the cutting of red tape by a high British government official, Chancellor of the Exchequer, in charge of duties similar to those of the American Custodian of Alien Property during World War II. I was technically an enemy alien living in a sanatorium in Switzerland, and I conceived the wild idea of writing to the office of the Chancellor in London that I was undergoing a cure in Davos, had been rejected by the Austro-Hungarian military draft board, and was in need of the royalties accruing from the sales of my gramophone records (His Master's Voice) in the British Empire. I asked if, under the circumstances, he would consider releasing these half-yearly sums to me. There was very little conviction behind this letter of mine; it was simply one of several half-hearted efforts to alleviate the stringent financial situation created for me by the war. Imagine my surprise and elation when an answer came from the Treasury in that Old World calligraphy of high British offices of thirty years ago, asking me to execute some simple document. I think my doctor's certificate, or the recruiting bureau's, sufficed; and soon afterward I, an "enemy alien," began receiving these more than welcome royalty cheques for the duration of the war. Incidentally, in those days, a certain type of correspondence requiring the personal touch of the Chief himself would usually be written by clerks in their typically unindividual handwriting and then submitted to the Chief for signature; typewriters seemed to be considered inappropriate in a certain stratum of officialdom.

To mention another instance of the cutting of red tape —not of minor importance like the preceding one, which merely involved royalty cheques, but of major importance, involving fundamentals. I remember this particular *deus ex machina* with genuine gratitude. While I was teaching at the Geneva Conservatory in 1919, my fiancée and I decided to get married and applied to the Austro-Hungarian Consul General, Baron de Montlong, for the necessary papers. During the Russian Revolution the Russian girl who became my wife had been left stranded in Geneva at the finishing school for *jeunes filles* that she had entered with her sister in 1914. They had no news from their parents in Russia, were unable to get into contact with them at all; so we agreed to go ahead without parental consent—simply on the not very authoritative green-light signal of Madame Dourouze, the headmistress, and of my fiancée's elder sister. Wanda was to be "given away" by those who had little sanction to give.

Once our minds were made up, there remained still the legal formality of posting banns, which were unobtainable during the revolution-troubled months. This is where the Consul-General's paternal generosity and understanding came in. By insisting on the rigid application of the law, he could have retarded and (who knows?) perhaps annihilated our plan; for how often the simple postponement of an action means its deferred but eventual cancellation! Especially one like ours, which had little to do with weighty reflection or common sense or any of the "wise" measures two young persons in love find boringly irrelevant.

Baron de Montlong smiled at us. "How can I give you the marriage dispensation?" he asked. Then turning to me: "For all I know, you may be a bigamist!"

Smiling back, I felt a bit of a fool, trying to get both a clear conscience and a plea for quick action into my wordless answer.

"We shall see," continued the Baron, and calling in his legal adviser he said to him: "Herr Doctor, these are the facts of the case." He enumerated them. "Let us not, if we can avoid it, fall victim to the dead letter of the law. I don't want to postpone the happiness of these two youngsters if we can help it. All laws have been twisted and tortured out of all semblance of law, what with war and revolutions. For once let's twist and turn one for a good cause, yes?"

The Herr Doctor nodded and promised to find the necessary loop-hole. Soon afterward we were eating our wedding breakfast in a most incongruously operetta-like setting—the dining-room of the young bride's boarding-school, among her giggling schoolmates. Nothing could have been less romantic. Instead of the scent of orange blossoms, I inhaled the severely hygienic smell of the varnished pitch-pine of austere boarding-school refectory furniture. Instead of chiffon, lace and satin I was surrounded by forbidding starched, prim school uniforms. The wedding breakfast was equally heavy going: orangeade for champagne, cold ham for *mousse de pâté de foie gras*. It was nothing if not dietetically correct.

I moved from my small bachelor apartment into roomier benedict quarters where my meagre furniture looked somewhat forlorn. This furniture had barely sufficed for my small bachelor apartment—which was, by the way, of a kind that had distressed many a well-meaning friend at the time I settled in Geneva. These good people naturally expected their "artist friend" to occupy some handsome old house on one of the tortuous little streets surrounding the Cathédrale de St. Pierre; it was toward this neighbourhood that artist, littérateurs, and bachelors of both sexes with Bohemian penchants gravitated, and it was a shock to my banker friends with wish-fulfillment dreams of a Bohemian life that I firmly declared I preferred sunshine and plumbing to the Poe-esque atmosphere of *la vieille ville* and settled in a modern, sunny little apartment in what was considered the "wrong" neighbourhood, peopled by petty bourgeois, artisans, mechanics, and the like.

My nonconformist attitude dictated the choice of my first family apartment, too. It was in a healthful, tree-studded section in Champel, with a fine view of the two Salèves. Villas, girls' schools, and sanatoria dotted the vicinity—as little satisfying to my atmosphere-craving banker friends as the former shopkeeper-artisan neighbourhood had been. (Near by was the Hotel Beau Séjour, in which the mentally sick Guy de Maupassant had ended his life.)

The way my bride bridged her schoolgirl and her married life was refreshingly idyllic. The installation of *my* things in our new flat took only a couple of hours; hers took considerably less. As all her belongings could be crammed into the one old-fashioned trunk with which she had set out from her father's estate in Russia five years before, and as our apartment was barely five minutes' walk from the school, her moving was effected by the old school gardener and his wheelbarrow.

This idyllic informality was characteristic of these war- and revolution-tinged years in our staid but cosmopolitan little world of Geneva. What could have been more unconventional, for instance, than Isadora Duncan's connection with this finishing school, which was called "Pension des Hirondelles"? Isadora did not hesitate—when departing for a tour of America in 1915 or 1916—to leave some twenty of her child troupers of different nationalities (but all bearing the adopted name of Duncan) in this school, paying for them for a few months, then—when the money ran out—forgetting all about it. She simply dumped them, so to say, into the lap of the directrice and among this flock of Hirondelles, without giving much thought to how the directrice would cope with the problem. The 'teen-aged pensionnaires—my future wife and sister-in-law among them—exercised their maternal instinct on these children with their page-boy haircuts and their tunics of exquisite texture (though too often they lacked the essentials of sturdy wearing apparel, such as stout shoes!), and also assisted the teaching staff in giving the little troupe a semblance of an education. Eventually, when the situation became insoluble, the various consulates took charge, and most of the younger children were repatriated to their respective countries, the older ones ŏrganizing themselves into a dance troupe and giving performances to eke out an existence of sorts.

CHAPTER XVIII

———— ✺ ————

I T is primarily the sudden changes of environment that can
make the seemingly sterile years of the young player, with
no schooling to speak of, so fruitful. Let me give a typical
example. I set out from a small Hungarian village (the poor
man's summer resort) to play at the Fiesta de San Fermin at
Sarasate's birthplace, Pamplona in Spain; from there to the
Bavarian Highlands, ending up with a couple of engagements
at the Pier Pavilion, in Douglas on the Isle of Man. What a
multitude of contrasting impressions crammed into a bare few
weeks: the Hungarian village, glittering Catholic Spain, the
Wagnerian romanticism of the Bavarian Highlands, and the
gay, teeming crowds from Liverpool and Manchester and from
Arnold Bennett's "Five Towns" on the beach and pier of an
English holiday spot. . . . Surely, here in this unplanned trip
was more stimulation than in many a normal student's summer
holiday, however "educationally" planned!

Pamplona's famous son, Sarasate, who had died some time
before, used to play, year after year, without fee, at the
concerts that were part of the renowned Fiesta de San Fermin,
dedicated to the patron saint of Navarre. It was an offering,
something wholly apart from his glamorous world career, to
the patriotic and religious significance of the Fiesta.

For me, then barely twenty years old, without even a
smattering of French or Spanish, this trip and this assignment
(several violin concerti which I had to prepare at very short
notice, for the contract came through almost at the last
moment) turned out to be quite an adventure. The bull-fight

—with famed Chiquito as the "star"—I will pass over. I was totally unprepared for such a spectacle; these were pre-Ernest Hemingway and pre-Henri de Montherlant days! A glass of green chartreuse, gulped down at the buffet after I had, somewhat ignominiously, quit the box, helped overcome the nausea that threatened me. But the picturesqueness and the novelty of everything else! The folk music; with fifes and drums; the frenzied dancing in the Plaza del Castillo around the bandstand all lit up by coloured bulbs; the crowd sipping iced drinks in front of the Plaza cafés while watching the dancing; the glimpses into Sarasate's career, of a brilliance unequalled in the second half of the nineteenth century, vouchsafed to me by his friend and biographer, a career made a palpable reality by visits to the Sarasate Museum where everything relevant and otherwise—his violins, orchestral scores and parts, even his collection of shirt studs and walking sticks, down to his calling cards (nothing but the magic name "Sarasate" on those bits of pasteboard*)—was proudly preserved; the novelty of the food; the fruity red *vin ordinaire* placed in front of one in huge carafes without being ordered; the complications I encountered in everything and anything, from taking of a bath at the public baths to the mailing of a registered letter—all this fascinated me. Incidentally, it was the deferential courtesy of the bathing master, when he learned that it was the "soloiste de la Fiesta" whose bath he was preparing, that first made me realize the importance of an assignment which I—with the unawareness of my twenty years—was taking as merely a matter of course!

To be able to send my father several of the French hundred-franc notes that I earned made one of those moments in a boy's

---

* I am unashamed to admit that such relics start me on many a train of thought. So, for instance, when I was lately shown a likewise beautifully engraved calling card with the name "Ludwig van Beethoven" on it. This appurtenance of a more *mondaine* life than we associate with Beethoven made me ponder: Hasn't the romanticizing nineteenth-century biographical style made him out somewhat more *farouche*, more nonconformist with the social amenities, than he really was? What seemed to me an indispensable adjunct of Sarasate's glittering *mondanité* was rather surprising in connection with the Beethoven of the innumerable anecdotes that show him so rebellious and disdainful of worldly conventions.

life which seem to mature him and to create a sort of demarcation line in the transition from boyhood to young manhood.

These registered letters containing money had to be sewn
with criss-cross stitches right *through* the sealede nvelope,
letter, and banknotes, and the tape ends sealed with wax for
good measure, to prevent their being tampered with in transit.
It wasn't so very many years since that the Spanish postman
expected a tip for every delivery, and anybody at all familiar
with the custom knew that to disregard this tradition would
mean the non-receipt of all mail addressed to the nonconformist! The resignation with which the Spanish people
accepted such petty corruption astounded me when I heard
of it. It was interesting to contrast such a custom with the
admirable discipline of the honour system in England. I
thought of the unwritten code which allows the passenger in
England to have his baggage labelled (though without getting
a receipt), and put in the guard's van free of charge; it is then
dumped on the platform at his destination, where everyone
picks out his own, with never a traveller violating the code. It
is this same code, I suppose, that allows a couple of million
pounds sterling in coin or gold bars to move through the
streets of London in an open cart without police protection, as
Simeon Strunsky points out, contrasting this with the armoured
cars that carry out similar operations in New York City—in
broad daylight.

From Spain to Upper Bavaria, to the well-ordered, stiffly
bourgeois routine of a family hotel where I was awaited by
Swiss friends whose daughter was to get some lessons from me.
Visits to the weirdly romantic castles of mad King Ludwig of
Bavaria (Richard Wagner's fanatical patron); Ludwig's
swan-obsession expressed in the ever-recurring swan motifs
of the castle's decorative scheme—I remember especially
Schloss Neuschwanstein; the legends about him, which were
still alive then and were told in hushed voices around one. . . .

Who knows but that the impressions that I gathered then
helped me to realize better and much sooner than I would
have otherwise the morbid romanticism, the monomaniac
traits in Ludendorff's mysticism and in Hitler's obsessions?

The trip to Douglas, Isle of Man, soon afterwards brought

me a very different experience; a general strike, while I was on that leisure island situated between England and Ireland. To reassure the inhabitants of the island and the thousands of holiday-makers from near-by Liverpool and Manchester that they wouldn't starve even if the strike continued, a Dreadnought was dispatched and was anchored in sight of Douglas; notwithstanding the anti-jingoism and anti-Kiplingism of my venerable friend Felix Moscheles, it was a comforting sight! And when, soon afterwards, the strike having been called off, I joined the other holiday-makers in a rowboat trip to the Dreadnought, almos tspilling into the sea while transferring to the rope ladder, about the first thing I saw on deck was—an upright piano. Prominently displayed on this was a cardboard sign painted by one of the sailors and reading PLEASE GIVE US A TUNE! Soon the warship resounded with music-hall songs, clog-dance tunes, and ballads, contributed by eager if not very skilful hands. Boatloads full of merrymakers kept plying back and forth, sight-seeing parties guided by officers or sailors were made up; incidentally one of the gun turrets was made to turn around at my special request—and a grand time was had by all.

It made me understand a famous old *Punch* drawing often quoted in those days; it showed a Cockney in costermonger outfit, all bebuttoned, with his "lidy," approaching the sentinel standing guard at the gangplank of a British warship in port. Upon the sentry's asking the Cockney on what ground he seeks admittance, comes a self-assured: "Tell the Admiral *one of the shareholders* wants to look hover 'is bloomin' tub."

I suppose it was the wide diversity of daily experiences like these that pedagogues of another day had in mind when they counselled parents to send their sons abroad, around the world, whenever possible; I presume this is what was really meant by the linking of the concept of the *Wanderjahre* with that of the *Lehrjahre* which we come across in German literature. As for myself, it was practically the only education that ever came my way, and if it left me with some rather shocking gaps in my equipment, the fault lies in me and not in any set of conditions.

It often amazed me how the hazards of a profession like mine, of my travels and contacts, combined—or one might say, *conspired*—to drive lessons home to me. How often did one hazard seem to continue what the other had started; how well everything seemed to dovetail: information, reading, personal contacts, the encountering of just those out-of-the-way types that were still missing in my collection. I say "collection" advisedly, because there seemed to me to be a parallel between this gallery of types one keeps adding to and the old-time waxworks à la Madame Tussaud. Isn't the forming of a collection of this kind the first and indispensable step on the road to anything even vaguely resembling *Menschenkenntnis?* It is primarily to make clear to myself these processes, hazards, whatever you would call them, that I dig out some of these trivia.

Newspapers, with their danger of forming habits and thought-patterns (according to how one uses them), could, I think, come in for some consideration at this point. As Lincoln Steffens said: "Nobody can read a newspaper every day and not be influenced by it; we read our paper in our quiet, relaxed moments, when we might be thinking, and thus unwittingly let the editors form our minds."

Can there be a better guard against this danger than a virtuoso's wandering life? Imagine him on a trip from Manchester or Liverpool, say, to Warsaw—quite a routine trip in those far-off years of peace. I see him buying papers, glancing through and discarding them as his train takes him across the different frontiers. How things loom big or pale, according to where you read them! What symbolic significance the charwomen at the various borders seemed to have as they swept up the accumulated litter and all the crumpled dailies in my compartment! There were those bought at my departure, the substantial, dignified *Manchester Guardian* and the *Liverpool Daily Post*; the so much "louder" London afternoon papers, picked up en route a few hours later; then the Paris papers, and *L'Indépendance Belge*, and the *Nieuwe Rotterdamsche Courant*, and the *Kölnische Zeitung*, like so many gusts of wind blowing at me from different points simultaneously! Thus, gradually, I confirmed to myself my arrival on the other side of the Channel; now at various stops news-stands beckoned with the *Berliner Tageblatt, Frankfurter Zeitung*, and so on until I reached my destination. There I was, enclosed in the neutrality and impersonality of one and the same compartment—the enamel sign attached outside reading: "Flushing-Warsaw" or maybe: "Calais-Warsaw" —but exposed, through these papers, to the stresses and preoccupations of all these regions the train was passing through or just skirting, stresses cancelling each other in quick succession. And, once at one's destination, how completely absorbed one became in the immediate task, how all-important just *this* city, *this* public, *this* country seemed. . . .

Then, on the way back or farther on, the same process in reverse, perhaps with some variants dictated by mood or curiosity or sudden homesickness for country, city, or public perhaps farthest from one: a London *Sunday Times* or a Vienna *Neue Freie Presse*, probably four or five days old, picked up at the lobby news-stand at Warsaw's Hotel de l'Europe. How quickly the virtuoso's necessary and exaggerated all-absorption in the present is, as if by magic, suddenly set right, a proper perspective re-established!

Obviously the foregoing does not apply to the United States. Here we may go on a transcontinental trip of three thousand miles, and the papers snow into our observation or club car in upstate New York, in Ohio, in Kansas, then in New Mexico, and as we go over the Sierra Nevadas—and everywhere papers with the same news-service releases, the same syndicated columns, the same national advertising, and one of two political outlooks. . . .

I feel like adding a footnote to this rambling comment on newspapers, about the *other* reading done on such trips: books and magazines. There must have been some method in the seeming disorder of reading most of the time in a language *other* than the one spoken in the country I happened to be touring and playing in. I know it wasn't done deliberately, but I found myself reading Hungarian in England, French in Soviet Russia, English in Germany, and the

German-language Soviet literary monthly while touring, say, in Italy. There must have been some method in all this....

As newspapers on such a trip cancel each other, so do many things in a virtuoso's life. Our travelling mode of living contradicts or attenuates influences so constantly that we are protected from the danger of becoming inordinately used to any one thing, of getting into a rut of any kind; protected from prematurely arriving at conclusions, convictions, at ingrained habits of thought—in a word, at *des opinions toute faites*.

Lincoln Steffens in his *Autobiography* suggests that "convictions are identical with hardened arteries." Come to think of it, doesn't all "arriving," all "achieving," seem premature and regrettable when we compare it with the joys inherent in the fluid, nascent state of almost anything that is still in progress, whether it is success, friendship, or accomplishments?

CHAPTER XIX

————— ·{◊}· —————

THE many forms of hospitality enjoyed, and sometimes stoically borne, in different countries could probably help me to map out a substantial slice of my travels, if I were a little more methodical and could choose just the right examples from the many and give just the right amount of space and spice to each.

"Being entertained" has I don't know how many connotations for the travelling virtuoso. In some it is pleasurable; in others it is barely distinguishable from a chore. In my case it covers a wide range, from that Biblically frugal evening meal served in enamelled tin cups and plates at a long communal table in the agricultural colony of En'charod in Palestine, to the cup of tea, "petit fours," and hothouse muscatel grapes that Queen Elizabeth of Belgium offered me at the Palace the first time I played for her. Or it may mean a sumptuous *déjeuner*, typically "Bordelaise," like the one I shared at Monsieur Delor's, President of the Société Philharmonique of Bordeaux (I have since seen his name on the label of many a grateful and comforting *fine bouteille*)—a meal, by the way, that marked my initiation into the ritual of wine-tasting with its obbligato of connoisseur-talk and respectful silences, each in its rightful place: the one after, the other *during*, the act of what the French call "*déguster*."

Again, it may refer to a feast, modest yet generous—and lasting into the small hours of the night—in some overcrowded Moscow "Kwartier" of a university professor or of a musician, with, say, Paul Lamm the musicologist, and the composer-pianist Samuel Feinberg; threshing out some fine æsthetic dialectic point across the table with Artur Schnabel, whose tour happened to coincide with one of mine. Or it may be Tairov, founder of the Moscow Kamerny Theatre, with Erwin Piscator. It was in the pre-skyscraper, pre-"Moscow Subway" days of 1925 or 1926. In those days there were what seemed to me an unimaginable number of name cards pinned to the doors of the subdivided apartments, each card representing a family unit; after each name was a number indicating how many rings would bring to the door the member of the family you were calling on. The overcrowding of Moscow, the housing shortage of those days, not to speak of the lack of servants, the resulting complications in the simplest of daily routines (these bell-ringing mathematics are but *one* example), stagger the imagination of anyone used to our ways of living. Each apartment with its several family units represented a bewildering diversity of human case-histories—each one a "Grand Hotel" in miniature.

There were beds everywhere, covered with old-fashioned white crochet bedspreads. Yet somehow, then and there, the ideas of "bed" and "feasting" did not seem to clash; one was conscious only of the long table, heavy laden, with all kinds of zakouskis, salade-Olivier, smoked sikh-fish, caviare, vodka, sweet Crimean wines, and, of course, the ubiquitous samovar.

I remember also ceremonious *rijstafel* meals in Batavia with perhaps a dozen or more native servants passing the score of auxiliary dishes and condiments that make up this meal, passing them with that unfailing, innate sense of decorum and charm of the Javanese. Then, there comes to my mind that luncheon at the Sassoons' Park Lane house, when Lady Asquith, next to whom I was sitting, gave for my benefit a brilliant improvisation of the Wildean paradox that "Life imitates Art far more than Art imitates Life," and that "a great artist invents a type, and life tries to copy it, to reproduce it in popular form like an enterprising publisher!" It was apropos of the portrait Sargent had painted of her—one that was not a good likeness, so Lady Asquith told me, but which prompted the young girl she was at the time to "live up to" it, grow up to it. . . .

Few things seem to reveal such essential differences, even when outward forms resemble each other, as this business of being entertained. Could, for example, the contrast be greater than between the "Alt-Wien" Sunday suppers of the patrician family in Pötzleinsdorf, where places were set for three, four, or more friends who might drop in unannounced, and hospitality as it was understood and practised in Geneva? Staid, solemn, estimable Genevese gentlemen who spoke to me on this subject said they would no more think of dropping in at mealtime, even on their own brother than—I forget the horrific comparison!

Still, I had to admit that *their* hospitality had its points too, its somewhat frozen formality and its elegant frugality notwithstanding. This tolerant and understanding attitude toward differences of approach is essential to the touring virtuoso; how otherwise could he "take it" when a well-meaning president of a women's college considers it a perfect ending to a perfect day for all concerned to have the luckless artist of the evening stand in the receiving line with him and his lady, while a hundred or more students line up in an endless procession of twos, are presented to him, mutter something about the thrilling "program," and have their hands shaken by the virtuoso—if, indeed, his hand muscles are still capable of this performance? Or when a Ladies' Something-or-other Club in a far-flung part of the British Empire considers it an ideal way of entertaining its musician guest of honour to give a formal tea with offerings by the young musical hopefuls of the town, and to summon the guest to pronounce critically, encouragingly, constructively, and inspiringly on what he is about to hear?

These were trying moments, to be sure, and they had to be coped with as they came along. But, on the whole, I have been spared any of the really painful and embarrassing misadventures that sometimes jinx formal gatherings. That of Frau Professor Einstein at one of the New York banquets tendered to her illustrious husband seems to me to top them all. The preliminaries of the banquet were interminable; and even when at last everybody was seated, still the presumably principal business of banqueting—eating—did not get under way. The hungry but near-sighted lady started nibbling at what seemed to her a terrible-tasting salad. To her neighbour she said: "I'm afraid you won't find this salad very good," only to hear the disconcerting reply: "That's not a salad; you are eating an orchid!"

Occasionally, as in a pleasant little town in Wisconsin, a hastily improvised gathering turns out to be the perfect "after concert" party. A dozen or so congenial people with the indispensable sprinkling of gramophone-record fans among them—the collectors, who are almost invariably the best informed, musically, in these smaller communities. Sausage, cheese, and beer are by no means a negligible part of the proceedings. There is lots of good, animated talk, and one leaves refreshed and relaxed, and—I am willing to wager—not only with a pretty accurate estimate of the musical climate of the little town, but with the knowledge of how one's own offerings have fitted in with what has been going on there musically in the past.

There were parties that somehow epitomized for me a whole phase of a city's life. A dinner in Vienna, which I shall presently describe, did just this for me. And now, after two decades, it still typifies those nightmarish days of inflation with their attendant fantastic aberrations. I had already seen more than my share of what there was to see, had heard about the hungry crowds that broke the plate-glass windows of the elegant hotels on the Ring, giving vent to their impotent anger at seeing the lounging, tea-drinking, cocktail-sipping, unchanged and unchangeable tourists who seemed oblivious to the misery that surrounded them. I had been told by salespeople about the systematic plunder that went on. A sales girl at the music store gave me a specific instance of this. She described how a foreigner, probably quite illiterate musically, walked in, pointed to the shelf packed with pocket scores, and demanded to know "how much?" And when, naturally, she asked which of the scores he wanted, he replied with a sweeping gesture: "The whole shelfful!"

Those were the days when Dutch, Swiss, American, English, or Scandinavian currency was designated *Edelvaluta* ("noble" currency) in the countries where inflation had wrought such havoc. They were the days of grotesquely inflated buying power for the possessors of these *Edelvaluta*, and conversely, of tragic devaluation for those compelled to sell. One could hardly escape a sense of guilt over being there at all. Even to stay in one of those impoverished countries gave one the feeling of adding (if only in an infinitesimally small degree) to the misery and the moral disintegration all around, by exchanging *Edelvaluta*, by "competing" with the natives who couldn't "compete," who sold their valuables for ridiculous prices, and who starved.

To take a party of Viennese friends after one of my concerts to a restaurant that was now beyond their means, to encourage them to "indulge" to their hearts' content, to be able to do all this with the quarter or fifth part of a modest Swiss hundred-franc note, was an experience that struck me as being in a sense humiliating—humiliating because of the tragic line of demarcation between buyer and seller. You bought, let us say, a treasured autograph, letter, or page of music manuscript of Johann Strauss from a Viennese patrician family; for the seller, this transaction was not a sale, but a barter—barter for milk and bread or the resoling of his shoes.

But to return to that dinner party just mentioned. It was given by a friend of ours, a pretty young widow who hailed from one of the "privileged" monetary regions: that of the Swedish kroner, the pound sterling, Dutch florin, or American dollar, never mind which. She had rented an apartment furnished in fastidious taste by some aristocrats who had left everything: ancestral portraits, silver, and knick-knacks to serve as a décor for the pretty representative of the new, moneyed élite whose turn had now come.

She did things handsomely, one must admit that; there were none of those clashes of taste one fears in such cases. She looked the part, spoke her three languages with the best of them, had a more than adequate knowledge of music; this last being almost indispensable in a capital where the opera was, in a sense, the centre of attraction of society—or, let us say, of that specifically Viennese cultural *mondanité*—but where, in addition (as Křenek points out) "the affairs of the

opera house used to be the permanent topics of popular discussions in street-cars and grocery stores." But the men we
saw around her when my wife and I, a little late, entered the
already well-peopled drawing-room! Who *are* they, we
wondered? Sharply cut, characteristic faces: determined, the
traces of stormy living in every one of them, a nonchalance in
their attitudes that irresistibly recalled the seedy elegance of
Monte Carlo croupiers and the poor, down-at-heel confirmed
gamblers there who follow a system. Not a single woman
among the guests—only men, men in well-cut but too-tight
dinner jackets, rakish clothes and accessories that showed up
their lined, disenchanted faces all the more. High-sounding
titles, names so century-laden that they might have been
invented by a playwright. There were casual references (they
seemed to me *too* casual!) to foreign diplomatic posts one or
two of them had held, to naval units one of them had commanded in World War I, and so on. The eldest of the guests,
an Altgraf (whatever the distinction between Count and
Altgraf may signify!) to whom the younger men seemed to
look up, spoke of some commemorative mass at St. Stephen's
Cathedral which Court etiquette required him to attend on
some date hallowed by Hapsburg tradition.

All this seemingly ostentatious talk filled us, for no valid
or logical reason, with an indefinable malaise, made us anxious
for our naïve, still girlish-looking friend. We exchanged
glances, my wife and I; our suspiciousness must have been
evident to this worldly-wise (and "wise") team—for they
looked just that: a team working on some prearranged scheme.
Was it a gambling outfit, we asked ourselves? Were they
out to palm off on our innocent friend some huge, rambling
estate at a preposterous price? Or were they merely currency
traffickers? Or were they biding their time until one of their
crew should land the heiress in a marriage that would benefit
all of them? This last seemed to us the most likely. We left
very early, left our friend to her "fate"—as we thought—but
determined to have a heart-to-heart talk with her the next day.
As we walked out of the apartment house, relieved, what did
we see but a policeman standing on guard before the building!
In our wrought-up, nervous state, we half expected him to

accost us and ask for identification papers or information about the apartment and the company we had just left; however, nothing of the sort happened.

Next day, during our heart-to-heart talk, the laugh was on us. Our naïve friend—evidently more inured than we were to the shabby elegance and the somewhat (shall we say?) *relaxed* moral code of the Austro-Hungarian ruling classes— was amazed and amused at our panicky state. She explained that they were all bona fide aristocrats; impecunious, to be sure; out for a wealthy marriage, perhaps yes, she admitted with a charming pout; but nothing seriously wrong with them as far as she had been able to find out. As for the policeman, he was assigned as a special mark of distinction to the old Altgraf, as a sort of guard of honour whenever he went out in those troubled times.

To admit to such a grotesquely false evaluation of a given milieu is hard on one's self-esteem, and we often laughed over this mild attack of persecution-mania to which we had succumbed. But strangely enough, although the facts were against us, we still cling stubbornly to that unmotivated, instinctive judgment in the face of all evidence to the contrary! Just as one may cling to dreams in broad daylight, imagining them more valid and significant than reality itself.

Post-concert entertaining of the player is often considered an integral part of the musical event, at least in the estimation of the party-giver and of some of his guests; fortunately it is only in rare and extreme cases that such a party assumes proportions and a subjective importance that completely overshadow the *raison d'être* of the party itself. Overshadow it, I may add, only in the opinion of the party-giver and a certain number of his particularly thirsty guests. To paraphrase the classic riddle that asks whether the chicken or the egg came first, it is difficult to determine in these cases whether the party is an appendix to the concert or vice versa.

If I follow these jottings on hospitality with some on applause, it is because I feel, rightly or wrongly, that the two have a common denominator. It all depends on the point of view, but I know how much it means to me personally (and

to many other performers that I have discussed this with)
when I am made to feel not only the guest of the concert set-up
but its host as well. When this happens it is an added bounty.
The cheque seems written with a sympathetic hand, so to speak.
Moreover this gracious gesture has a salutary effect. Naturally, like every good host, the performer feels bound by the
most elementary laws of hospitality to study the reactions of his
guests and make them feel happy as far as it is in his power to
do so.

Applause is one of those concomitants of public music-
making which virtuosi, and especially their entourage, often
tend to consider in a somewhat distorted way as an end rather
than as a by-product. (Although, I admit, a pleasant and
heart-warming one!) To paraphrase the former Soviet
dictum about religion, one could say that applause is the opiate
of these people. How much thought—that could be applied
to more worthy ends!—is expended on foolproof, "sure-fire"
programme sequences, and how much that is outdated and
reactionary in our repertoire and in our programme-patterns
is due to the obsessive preoccupation with this business of
provoking applause! It doesn't seem to help much that time
and again these foolproof programme blueprints are disproved
by the public itself, which, as an entity, is so much more often
instinctively "right" than are its component parts. But the
Prelude to *Die Meistersinger* still continues to be placed at the
end of a symphony programme, and some venerable chestnut
at the end of a piano or violin recital, even though every so
often a number in the middle of the programme unexpectedly
steals the show. The inertia of habit still wins out and we are
reluctant to admit our miscalculations.

Applause, then, was another of those things which, like
hospitality, I soon learned to consider from several angles and
to take as it came along in all its varieties.

I got to know the purists who would like to dispense with
it altogether whenever possible, seeking as they do that
sanctified atmosphere which alone reconciles them to having
to listen to music in the promiscuous company of the uniniti-
ated. (Didn't B. H. Haggin recently describe the atmosphere
of some of our subscription concerts in New York City as

"heavy and noisy with the ostentatiousness" of its audiences?)

At the opposite pole was applause as the naïve trouper looks at it. For him it is one of the few measurable things in his modest endeavours on the concert stage, and as such he watches and evaluates it jealously. It is one of the few means of advancement that he has.

I remember John McCormack telling us, one night on tour, a story about one of these, a Lancashire tenor. This typically provincial ballad singer was having the time of his life one evening at a small concert somewhere in the sticks, giving encore upon encore. The audience clamoured for more and more. He listened to the applause with the happily fatuous and appraising smile of his kind before "obliging them with his next rendition." Then, suddenly, pointing to his some-what fatigued dress-shirt with a knowing wink, he blurted out to the members of the concert party standing around him back-stage: "See? This is me loocky shirt. Worn it t'night for the *ninth* time, and, by golly, triple encores every time!"

As for myself I have had my share of more than fifty-seven varieties of this seemingly all-important commodity—applause. In some Latin countries, at the wrong places, at some brilliant passage occurring in the middle of a movement, just before a *tutti*—all this condoned by the clapping enthusiasts' entourage. I can testify from personal experience that in former days, before "music appreciation" reared its unlovely head and made purists and pedants out of too many music-lovers, the end of the 32nd-note variation in Beethoven's "Kreutzer" Sonata was invariably the signal for an outburst of applause. I heard this happen at Sarasate's, Ysaÿe's, and Kubelik's performances of the "Kreutzer."

In some musically overbred set-ups, on the other hand, in places where they pride themselves on waiting lists and where season tickets are inherited and season-ticket holders constitute a kind of aristocracy, I have "heard" silence at the close of a joyous clarion ending to an allegro first movement of a Mozart concerto—a frozen void after an allegro that is as divinely *allègre* as only Mozart could make it.

At one playing of a Mozart concerto, Richard Strauss

conducting, the Master and I exchanged happy glances at the conclusion of the serenely joyous first movement. Naturally we expected a similarly happy reaction from our audience and when we met with polite and stony silence instead, Strauss turned to me and muttered, in his thick Bavarian dialect: "The so-and-so newspaper scribblers and commentators! This is their work—making people skeered to clap when I know they feel like doing it."

I confess to being especially interested in one phase of applause: not in its volume or length but in its reflex-like quality. The number of seconds that elapse between the last chord or flourish of a piece and the applause-reaction is a fairly accurate gauge of the nervous sensitivity of the audience, of the rapt tension the player has succeeded in generating in his hearers, and also an indication of the collective responsiveness of a crowd. It is a case of innate musical sense versus assembly-line conditioning by music-appreciation courses and other so-called educational means.

During World War II in America when I almost invariably started by playing *The Star-Spangled Banner*, I had an interesting point of comparison between the temperamentally different types of audiences by judging the number of seconds it took my audience to recognize the melody consciously and to transmute recognition into action—that is, to rise from their seats. I found this more revealing in the smaller communities, not too familiar with recital routine, than in the larger, where this clinical test (somewhat along the lines of the laughs tabulated in dead earnest by the motion-picture industry) did not apply. I found that the alertness an audience showed by its reflex-like reaction at this prelude to the concert was in exact ratio to the quality its audible appreciation would have throughout the evening.

When I auditioned for Angelo Neumann, one of the great impresarios of all time, then director of the Prague German Opera (which, largely through his prestige, became a "breeding place" for outstanding conductors such as Mahler, Muck, Leo Blech, Schalk, Zemlinsky, Klemperer, and Bodanzky), he told us a story "on" Richard Wagner and applause. My audition for the great impresario, whose days were numbered, took place at a sanatorium near Dresden. He was in a wheelchair that in my mind turned into a throne every time his wife and daughter entered the room and humbly kissed his hands. But he was friendly in a somewhat gruff manner and used the familiar "thou" indiscriminately, even to me, meeting him for the first time. After he had me (proud youngster that I felt) sign the contract, he brought to my attention a new word for my professional vocabulary: option. He explained it carefully and then began to reminisce.

Shortly after the first Bayreuth festival, he took a Wagnerian touring company on the road into Italy to do the entire *Ring*. He was the first impresario to do so and it called for temerity and courage. The melody-loving Italians invariably encored the Rhinemaidens' Song, and Neumann—overawed disciple of Wagner that he was—shuddered at the "sacrilege." Hans Richter, who conducted the troupe, if I remember rightly, snorted. "Sacrilege? Just you wait and see the old man's eyes light up when I tell him! Sacrilege indeed!"

Verdi, according to Franz Werfel's novel about him, went so far as to say that in some music applause is so much a part of the context that it should be written into the score. I don't know what the source is—whether it is based on an authentic anecdote, a passage from a Verdi letter or diary, or on the poet's divining instinct—but I subscribe to it.

CHAPTER XX

———— ··⟨⟨✽⟩⟩·· ————

IT may have seemed to some that I spoke with undue emphasis of that scourge of the years that followed World War I: inflation. But the vividness of my memories is probably intensified by the fact that history seems, unfortunately, to be repeating itself. For haven't we, within the past two or three years, heard similarly macabre stories? In Belgium a second-hand bicycle is sold for the equivalent of $800,000 worth of "old style" francs, and $40,000 worth of these francs buys four dollars' worth of the new currency. In Budapest—so we read in a *New York Times* article in 1945—"a hundred-pengö note, once the equivalent of twenty dollars, is worth less than a match," so that "a young American officer lit his cigarette with a hundred-pengö note." And in Greece the English sovereign was lately reported to have bought thirty billions of drachmas! My apparent insistence on that earlier period of inflation is therefore understandable, personally involved as I was in many of its phases and forced as I was to shape my life during those years according to these mad financial phenomena.

Let me explain how "Inflation I" (so I am tempted to label it as a parallel to the phrase "World War I") influenced my personal fortunes. The post-war years found me in Geneva where I had been appointed in 1917 to head the violin master classes, and where my pianistic colleague on the faculty was José Iturbi. These years also coincided with my founding a family, and thus for the first time in my life I was forced to take a realistic view of material things—all the more so as I found myself saddled with a not inconsiderable debt to a Swiss bank when my father passed away. During the war years he had pursued the chimera of financially assuring my future (as the good man termed it) by steadily buying Austro-Hungarian war bonds at a tempo that increased at the same rate as the krone crumbled in relation to the Swiss franc. As he bought short at this Swiss bank, the situation that faced a young couple when these bonds had ceased to be valid collateral can be easily imagined.

We would not consider the too easy expedient of repudiating a debt incurred in good faith by a "provident" parent, so we started paying it off—laboriously, in small instalments, like the woman in Maupassant's story of "The Necklace." But there was a difference: all the while we were repaying the bank, we knew that we would be getting worthless paper in return, once we had finished paying off the debt.

All this meant pursuing my career thenceforward on three distinct, superimposed levels simultaneously. The teaching position in the Conservatory was the material foundation on which I could base the economy of our little household and also the resumption of my European career, so abruptly cut short by the War. This was the first level.

My concertizing activities in Switzerland, with its disproportionately numerous music-loving, music-consuming small towns, could be called the second level. These concerts, mostly self-managed and sometimes mounting up to the astounding number of thirty-five to forty-five a season, squeezed into Switzerland's mere fifteen-thousand-odd square miles, meant security, plus the opportunities of the concert platform—so important to the playing trim of a young virtuoso, especially after the lean concert years of 1914–18.

They also produced the money to finance the resumption of my concertizing across the borders, away from the safe haven that was Switzerland. This was the third level.

These latter trips—and it is here that I return to the point I am trying to make; i.e., of the effect inflation had on my personal fortunes—simply did not count from a material point of view.

The seemingly substantial fees that even well-known and "desirable" soloists were paid in inflated marks, in Austrian or Hungarian or Czechoslovak kronen, in zlotys, lei, Finn marks, and so on were barely sufficient to cover the costly, often zigzagging trips, hotel charges, and other overhead expenses.

But how infinitely precious these first international trips were to me after the long years of enforced repression of my wanderlust into the small area of Switzerland! How I rejoiced at every new or renewed contact with still another capital: Warsaw, Vienna, Bucharest, Rome, Belgrade! What did it matter if I returned home to Geneva and to my pedagogically not very rewarding duties, flushed with the excitement of these new experiences, but with little else to show in the way of material results? When, for instance, I came back clutching a bottle of eau-de-Cologne Russe and a "lamé" blouse for my bride: the final yield of those two resplendent concerts in the Filharmonja in Warsaw! What did such meagre material results matter when a trip, like this one to Warsaw and to other Polish cities still bearing visible scars of the very recent German occupation, gave me the lift of playing to some of the most responsive and sympathetic audiences in Europe?

Besides, this one had brought me closer into touch with Karol Szymanowski and also marked the renewal of my friendship with the Busoni disciple, Josef Turczynski (teacher of young Witold Malcusinsky. I had not seen Turczynski since those memorable Busoni concerts and rehearsals in 1913 or 1914, mentioned in a preceding chapter. It was at that gay after-concert gathering at his house that I had my first glimpse of a manuscript violin concerto by a young Russian composer, one Sergei Prokofiev, a work that even then at a casual reading fascinated me by its mixture of fairy-tale naïveté and daring savagery in lay-out and texture. This was in the very early 'twenties, remember!

Thus "lucrative" tours up and down Denmark's Jutland coast, through Spain, through Holland, would alternate with trips that were undertaken literally "for art's sake" and nothing else; for the sake of a performance under Furtwängler or Ferdinand Loewe or Hermann Scherchen, or for the sake of playing Brahms chamber music with Elly Ney and others at the Munich Brahms Festival, or for an Ernest Bloch première with Carl Friedberg at that Salzburg Festival which marked the inception of the International Society for Contemporary Music. These were heady pleasures indeed, and probably I could not have indulged in them had not these staid and substantial, if somewhat unexciting, concerts in small, prosperous Swiss or Danish or Dutch towns paid for them. If I am to pursue that figure of speech about the "three superimposed levels," I would say that these heady pleasures belonged to the third and highest level.

But I always tried to remember that it was these somewhat unexciting concerts in Switzerland, Denmark and Holland that enabled me to stage come-backs in London, Paris and Brussels (in the last-named city at the invitation of Eugène Ysaÿe), partly in self-financed recitals, partly, as in Paris, at those Sunday Symphony *matinées*, with their chronically shaky financial set-up, at the Châtelet or the Opéra Comique, at the old Trocadéro or at the venerable Société des Concerts du Conservatoire, playing at these of course without a fee worthy of the name!

For these co-operative concerts were considered a labour of love even by the members of the orchestra, who were satisfied with the pitifully inadequate share that came to them after the season's final count was made. How then *could* a soloist, invited by the executive committee whose every member was a fellow musician, stoop to the discussion of mere money matters!

These fellow musicians, too, not unlike me, earned their bread and rent and clothing *elsewhere*, in less congenial ways: by rounds of lessons, by playing in cafés and cinemas, so that they might be able to indulge in this more glamorous and satisfying music-making of the *grands concerts dominicaux*. . . .

During those years a "double life" like mine was probably the only solution of the problem, to anyone who wanted to avoid the financial sponsorship of some munificent friend of the arts.

It was certainly strenuous this way, but, I think, more satisfying in the long run than other more expeditious methods of relaunching one's career would have been. Sometimes this

THE MUSIC ROOM AT WIMBORNE HOUSE
From a painting by Sir John Lavery
(In the foreground in white, Alice, Marchioness of Wimborne)

CONCERT HANDBILL ANNOUNCING THE PERFORMANCE, JANUARY 9, 1939, OF BARTÓK'S *RHAPS*
(LATER CALLED *CONTRASTS*) BY SZIGETI AND BENNY GOODMAN

living almost simultaneously according to two different standards made one's head whirl, as at the time when I interrupted a group of concerts in Germany to fill an engagement or two in Holland; I had received ridiculous quantities of inflated marks at these concerts and had of course rid myself of them as best I could as I went along, buying music, books, presents, and so on. The fees in hundreds of thousands and later in millions of paper marks that we virtuosi received in those days were based upon our pre-1914 fees, which in Germany had seldom reached a four-figure sum in the "gold mark" days. But not having had time to exchange—or, better!—spend this last batch of banknotes of fantastic denominations which, as I knew from previous experience, had about as much substantiality as snowflakes gathered in a warm hand, I resigned myself to bringing them back with me four or five days later when I was to play in Frankfurt-am-Main. On returning to Germany I took a rickety horse-drawn cab from the French-occupied zone to non-occupied Frankfurt, a drive of some few miles, and my wad of banknotes "earned" less than a week ago barely sufficed for the cab fare, for porter's tips, for the morning paper, and for my breakfast of ersatz coffee.

Living in wholesome, sheltered Switzerland during those troubled years and returning there after these trips to the ravaged parts of Europe was a continuous series of object lessons and of contrasts that often made me wonder. To arrive at the scrubbed and varnished, clean-smelling frontier railway station of Basel, from Poland or Rumania, for example, and to be firmly, though courteously, invited to undergo an inspection by the Swiss sanitary authorities—this gave me quite a shock and made me realize the extent of disease-breeding filth, poverty, and degradation that huge territories of Europe were still fighting, ineffectually, after so many years. It was only lately that I came across some terrifying data from these years: about conditions which the insouciance of youth made me entirely ignore at the time, about—for instance—the typhus epidemic which raged practically unabated from 1917 to 1921; one writer estimates that there were ten million persons infected, and three to six million deaths.

This, then, was the explanation of the orders of the Swiss frontier medical officer to examine closely every Eastern European and Balkan passenger's overcoat and coat collar, even going to the length of examining every seam, in search of typhoid-carrying lice. The doctor, who happened to be a concert-goer and had often heard me, was apologetic while going through the motions of this check-up and gave me some of the reasons for this regulation. (I seem to have heard of cases where passengers of those days had to strip for a thoroughgoing check-up.)

Or could contrast be greater than getting home to Geneva from the Berlin of the Kapp-Putsch nightmare in the early spring of 1920? This is one date I remember accurately without having to look it up, and for a very good reason. My wife, expecting our baby, was in Geneva, alone, with no relatives around her except an unmarried sister; and here was I, stranded in Berlin for I don't know how many interminable days. Dr. Wolfgang Kapp, worthy predecessor of the Nazis, had struck in lightning fashion, and the morning after my arrival I found myself in a city paralysed by a general strike that extended even to the chambermaids of the Fürstenhof where I was staying. From its windows I watched the barbed-wire enclosed Anhalter station for signs and portents. I dutifully made my daily, and constantly less and less hopeful, inquiries as to the resumption of railroad traffic, and tried, unsuccessfully, to draw the bayoneted, sheepishly uncomprehending guard at the station into a semblance of conversation; then, frustrated, I returned to my room for a little practice, for reading, or for one of my frequent, tasty, though less than dietetically correct meals. Let me explain: My sole nourishment consisted of pre-Putsch pumpernickel (the bakeries were of course not baking any bread), a jar of Strasbourg *pâté de foie gras*, and a bottle of old Tokay which I got from the Weinhaus Huth near by; it was one of Busoni's former favourite haunts. But the impossibility of communicating by phone or wire with my wife—whose condition I pictured with the somewhat lurid pessimism usual with young prospective fathers—was certainly a greater torment to me than all the other discomforts put together.

Carl Friedberg, the partner of my scheduled sonata recital,

was naturally unable to travel to Berlin from Cologne where he was then living, but I went through with my project nevertheless, improvising the programme with the pianist Frau Kwast-Hodapp, then greatly admired in Central Europe. As all means of intra-city communication were suspended—whether buses, trams, or taxis—and as electricity was not functioning either, we played our Beethoven, Brahms, and Schubert to a bare few dozen of the faithful from a candle-lit platform that was, I must admit, most *stimmungsvoll* and congenial to the chamber music we were playing.

The train that, after interminable days of suspense, eventually took me to Munich and from there to the Bavarian-Swiss border was entirely blacked out, as there was still some sporadic shooting at moving trains from among the ranks of the most resolute of the railroad strikers; the diehards among them did not countenance the gradual easing up of the general strike.

This reactionary Putsch, which aimed at the restoration of the monarchy, seemed to me at the time to have in it more comic, or at least tragi-comic, elements than was good for a thoroughgoing, full-fledged Putsch that wanted itself respected, and no mistake! It was engineered by three Putschists: Dr. Kapp, General von Luttwitz, and Major Pabst, who headed a mere handful—8,000 soldiers, to be exact—on that 13th of March, 1920. But in the light of what has happened since, I have somewhat revised my too juvenile impressions of those days. I know now how the stirring manifesto by Reichspräsident Ebert, and his great prestige with the workers, which resulted in this wholehearted and spontaneous general strike, had saved the day, at least for the time being.

I have since had the experience in Havana of hearing some bombs go off in the middle of the Andante cantabile of Mozart's D Major Concerto, and—later in the evening while walking along the grass-bordered promenade—of being brushed (along with other promenaders) into the side streets by the unperturbed and—for such exigencies as these—well-conditioned police of this beautiful and perhaps too eventful capital. But the Kapp-Putsch still remains Number One among my few revolution- or war-tinged souvenirs!

CHAPTER XXI

WHILE it probably *is* true that my teaching activities in Geneva could be called unrewarding because of the mediocre level of the pupil-material, there were some compensations, as there always are in work done with zest and regardless of results. Some of my pupils were older than myself, belonging to that archtype of the roving "eternal student," always in quest of a "new method" which will at long last lead to the goal. Most of them were semi-amateurs, relatively well-to-do young people from Yugoslavia, Turkey, Syria, England, Finland and Palestine; some, in less easy circumstances, went in for courses at the Polytechnic University in addition to their musical studies, like the young Pole who, while he was studying with me, became an expert chemical engineer specializing in wool dyes, having worked his way through the two educational institutions by playing on late afternoons and evenings in tea-room or café orchestras.

Another pupil, an Anglo-Saxon, later hit upon the idea of becoming an expert flyer and of complementing his by no means negligible violinistic accomplishments with the prestige and publicity value of piloting his own plane on what the letterheads called the "First Aerial Concert Tours of the Flying Violinist So-and-so."

Two of my better pupils ended up by marrying and becoming trusted members of Ansermet's Symphony Orchestra in Geneva, playing at different desks of course! I saw them there as recently as the fall of 1939 when I played the première of Ernest Bloch's Violin Concerto in the composer's home town.

So my teaching years were not quite without consequences of one sort or another! Which reminds me of the resigned and philosophical smile with which Busoni summed up the results of his years of directing the famous Liceo Musicale of Bologna. "You ask me what I achieved during my directorate? Musically, very little. Yet there *is* one achievement I can be proud of: I succeeded in having plumbing installed in the lavatories!"

Entrance examinations were lax, to say the least, and so we were often left stranded, Iturbi and I, with some pretty hopeless pedagogical cases on our hands. When we got together for some sonata-playing—Iturbi always amazed me by his sight-reading prowess!—we used to compare notes, and we came to the melancholy conclusion that the general level of pupil-potential could not have risen appreciably since Liszt's days at our institution. Liszt, who took refuge in Geneva with the Comtesse d'Agoult in 1835, had taught at our Conservatoire for some time, and it was inevitable that we were shown the sort of class-book in which our illustrious predecessor had recorded his observations on his pupils; this showing of the Liszt relic was a ritual of quite a little solemnity, as one can well imagine. Some of these notes, destined to guide the Director in awarding the credits at the end of the school-term, were rather revealing as to the kind of pupil even a Liszt had to contend with at our school. Here are a few samples:

"Ida Milliguet. Genevese artist, flabby and mediocre. Good enough appearance at the piano.

"Marie Demellayer. Vicious method (if it *can* be called a method), great zeal, mediocre temperament, grimaces and contortions. Glory to God in the highest and peace to men of good will.

"Jenny Gambini. Beaux yeux." That was all. . . .

Some of my pupils would have rated less complimentary remarks, like that young man from the Balkans with the completely bald pate and reckless lady-killer manner, or that woefully plain young girl from the Near East with whose afflictions (chief among them rebellious and hardy tufts of hair on chin and upper lip, and—I suppose one would say—sideburns!) I duly commiserated, but who nevertheless subjected my eyes to not a little anguish during lessons.

It was this incurably persevering (and hopeless) pedagogical case that caused me one day during a private lesson to make an exclamation that my wife happened to overhear and which she was fond of telling of me. "Mademoiselle," my wife heard me splutter and stutter, after a particularly excruciating agglomeration of sounds brought forth by her peculiar, stiff, rapier-like bowing, "Mademoiselle! . . . *Vous jouez comme* . . . you're playing like a . . . like . . ." (my wife held her breath, fearing the worst) ". . . like a naval officer!"

What must have gone on in my mind during the outraged moments that preceded this outburst, what made me sublimate the insulting comparisons which were bubbling up to my lips into "naval officer," must remain one of those minor mysteries of the subconscious that no amount of psychological insight will ever fathom.

Still, as I said before, there were compensations in those years of teaching. To prepare an ensemble performance of one of Corelli's or Geminiani's Concerti Grossi, to coach the quartet classes, to use as teaching material many a work that was outside routine virtuoso repertoire—all this made me conscious of gaps in my equipment which, I tried to console myself, were all but inevitable in the usual virtuoso career.

Sometimes in classes there were performances by pupils which, though far from being virtuoso achievements, moved me by their deep awareness of the musical and expressive content of the composition. Even now, after all these years, I can recall moments like that heavy-set Bernese girl's playing of the slow movement of a Bach concerto; it had an inwardness, a touch of that something which is so rarely projected from the concert stage—something of what looks out at us from one of the kneeling "donor's portraits" on the side panels of a Van Eyck or a Van der Goes triptych; or, to find a comparison nearer our times, out of the eyes of some Modigliani child-model. Years later I saw her, even heavier than she used to be, married, maternal, her violinistic ambitions relegated to the distant past. But nothing can alter what to me still seems a fact: that she had been visited by moments of grace in those student years.

To witness such moments is rarer than one would think, even in a lifetime of concert-going, and to recognize them while they are happening is one of the things I have learned from those contacts with amateurs. (*Dilettanti* really seems an apter word, because it is nearer to its root, *dilettare*: "to take delight in.") I sometimes contrast *their* "raptness" with some of the scintillating, impeccable performances that recall Virgil Thomson's devastating indictment of "the machine finish that is dead and horrid" in so much of our concert-hall music-making.

The lung specialist in Davos under whose care I was during the early war years was one of those amateurs who could show us professionals something when it came to real devotion to music, a certain intransigeance in evaluating performances, and above all an enthusiastic curiosity about any good work off the beaten path. When I became, so to say, attached to his household—repaying his medical services and hospitality by playing duets with him evenings and trying to improve his playing technique—he rode his hobby-horse more royally than ever: he signed up with a music-circulating library in Zürich which allowed us the run of its violin literature, and we could ask this library for anything and everything every fortnight; this, by the way, helped *me* to fill many lacunæ in my musical background. When my doctor-musician auscultated my lungs periodically he used to be amused at the way my musical ear co-operated with him: when he tapped my collarbone to check on the difference of sound over right and left lungs, I listened in on the tapping and gave him my findings, which he often smilingly acknowledged to be right.

The doctor was not the only musical amateur who helped fill blanks for me. It is almost embarrassing to have to admit that I owe my first revelation of the Mozart sonatas to a Hungarian baron of exquisite musical taste who reminded me in many respects of Proust's Baron Charlus.

Speaking of violin literature, I was amazed, when I visited Professor Einstein in Princeton and went through the stacks of music on his shelves and piano, at the catholicity and unerring good taste of this "amateur." The Professor pointed out with a smile that his Bechstein grand was one of the two presented to distinguished Germans as a gift of honour: the other recipient being—incongruously enough—Hindenburg.

After I sent the Professor my edition of Tartini's Concerto to add to the stacks, he wrote:

July 1, 1943.

"My hearty thanks for sending me the concerto which you played so incomparably. I hope it will give me fresh courage to manhandle my fiddle with my old fingers: the fiddle, incidentally, doesn't deserve anything much better!"

I cannot be positive, but I seem to remember Ansermet's telling me that it was Diaghilev who introduced Pergolesi's music to Stravinsky. Thus we owe to the initiative of a musical amateur that jewel-like score of Stravinsky's that is a quintessential transmutation of Pergolesi: the *Pulcinella* Suite, composed in 1924.

To live in a place as Stravinsky-conscious as Ansermet's orchestral headquarters were bound to be, had its very real advantages. The fact that I had become aware of this far-reaching influence as early as 1911, when Stravinsky's *Fire Bird* burst upon the unsuspecting and unprepared listener that I was then (this was at one of its first performances at Covent Garden), naturally made me all the more receptive to this *ambiance*. Characteristic of this Stravinsky consciousness around Geneva, where he was living at the time, was the gesture of our Conservatoire president, Jean Bartholoni, toward him. The composer was at that time in rather straitened circumstances, and more to alleviate these than for any other reason Bartholoni bought from him the original manuscript score of *The Fire Bird* at a figure which took care of Stravinsky's pecuniary worries for a long time to come.

Incidentally, it was these pecuniary worries and the propitiousness of little Switzerland for barnstorming (I have already referred to the disproportionately high number of concerts one could give in that small territory) that were to a great extent responsible for the composition of *L'Histoire du Soldat*. As the composer puts it in his autobiography: "I was now also in a position of the utmost pecuniary difficulty. . . . It was imperative to find some way of ensuring a tolerable existence for my family. . . . I got hold of the idea of creating a sort of little travelling theatre, easy to transport from place to place and to show in even small localities."

Ansermet at the time elaborated substantially upon the ideas that (so he said) were at the back of Stravinsky's conception; there was (always according to Ansermet) an element of protest against the artificiality of our contemporary music set-up in this venture, a return to the earthy, functional quality music had in former times when it was more an integral part of everyday life than in ours, particularly in the early part of our century. I distinctly remember Ansermet's enthusiasm over Stravinsky's and Ramuz's idea of a sort of tent show that would play continuously (as cinemas do) with people dropping in for a half-hour or so, for an admission price of a few coins, the way one used to drop in at puppet-shows, open-air "Guignol" shows, Chinese theatres, fairs, and the like. As I see it now, all this may have been a gesture of protest against the orchestral mammothism of Mahler and Richard Strauss; for these ideas of Stravinsky's seem to have been in the air at that time—or, conversely, it may have been Stravinsky who gave them a definite impetus. Anyway, the period following the first World War saw a crop of new works for chamber orchestra and still smaller instrumental combinations, and saw also the emergence of the concept of *Gebrauchsmusik*, particularly in Germany among composers of Hindemith's circle.

These romantic, barnstorming plans of Stravinsky's were never realized because (as he told me lately in reminiscing about Geneva days) the epidemic of Spanish influenza laid low all of his collaborators, including himself and his (and my) impresario, Adolph Henn.

The Stravinsky-Ansermet ideas about the wholesomeness of old-time, modest barnstorming were a determining factor in my own pattern of concertizing in those Geneva years.

The modesty of the apparatus that sufficed for such tours is probably the reason that it took me so long to get used to the high-pressure promotion that has since then become unavoidable. A few postcards to the various towns to engage the local concert hall, or sometimes church; an advertisement or two in the local papers; a few posters which the same printing shop turned out for the whole tour—these, combined with the two- or three-hour distances between the different concert towns (Berne, Biel, Olten, Aarau, Winterthur, and so on), gave to such a tour an almost idyllic simplicity. I can't help feeling that these years, with their sturdy, unartificial tone, had a lasting and important effect upon me. After such little tours I would come back to my Conservatoire classes, to shop talks with Ansermet after rehearsals and concerts, the whole constituting a well-balanced musical diet.

The Mussorgsky and Debussy enthusiasm that radiated from Debussy's friend Robert Godet, who was often with us, also formed an important ingredient of this musical diet; it meant a healthy counterbalancing of the very Central European, not to say Germanic, slant of my musical orientation up to then. Godet, a man of amazingly wide culture, often liked to heckle me, to draw me out, as he did after a performance of the Brahms Concerto in which I must have seemed to him to be particularly wrapped up. At a gathering after the concert he asked me, with inimitable mock-seriousness and a malicious glint in his eye: "Do tell me, what *exactly* is it that you see in this work?"—a question well calculated to cause the Brahms player of barely an hour ago to sputter and make several false starts before gathering his wits. Such bouts, however, prepared one in a quite subtle way for the time when musicians (and not the least among them!) would begin to question more and more the sacrosanctity that, gathering around the very name of Brahms, came to obscure the real and magnificent musical values we owe him. Who hasn't come across the objectionable type of music-lover who mouths that name in a peculiar way, while the smirk that accompanies his "Ah . . . Bwahams!!" implies proprietary rights in the great man.

Godet's attitude toward Brahms came vividly to my mind

in 1947 when the British Broadcasting Corporation sponsored a series of six concerts to commemorate the hundred and fiftieth anniversary of Schubert's birth and the fiftieth of Brahms's death. (A series in which William Primrose, Pierre Fournier and myself had the privilege of collaborating with Artur Schnabel.)

Reviewing this series Eric Blom had this to say: ". . . perhaps this was Brahms's last chance to stand on a level with Schubert; I predict that in another fifty years he will be ranked with Mendelssohn as one of the immediately secondary masters, still in good company, for Schumann and Weber, not to mention several non-Germans, will be there too."

Godet, consummate German scholar though he was, spread around him in a hundred different ways a very healthy, critical scepticism toward many aspects of German culture. That this extended to Richard Wagner goes without saying, especially during those years when it was quite in order for Darius Milhaud to review a Wagner programme at one of the Paris Symphony matinées in three words: "À bas Wagner!"—plus the critic's signature.

Shortly after I came to Geneva in 1917 I heard Godet tell the following story with infinite relish. The Munich publisher, Bruckmann, had commissioned Godet around 1911 or 1912 to translate *The Foundations of the Nineteenth Century* by Houston Stewart Chamberlain, the renegade English writer— a work that became one of the ideological bases of Nazism and of the so-called "race theory." In the early years of World War I, in 1914 or 1915, Godet must have been—I suppose— again approached by Bruckmann, this time to write something in line with the Chamberlain ideology or perhaps to lecture on this subject. (Godet's prestige and his brilliant scholarship, as well as his work as translator and commentator of Chamberlain, of course made him an eminently desirable recruit to the vast propaganda machine of the Pan-Germanists.) But this time Godet refused. His eyes flashed whenever he told and retold the story of *how* he answered the publisher's query as to the fee he would expect to get for this assignment. It was short and to the point: "The thirty silver pieces of Judas!"

I think this is an appropriate place for Nicolas Slonimsky's succinct characterization of Houston Stewart Chamberlain, in *Music Since* 1900, under the date of January 9th, 1927:

> Houston Stewart Chamberlain, English Wagnerite naturalized in Germany (and married to Cosima Wagner's daughter), who expanded into a full-fledged doctrine Wagner's philosophical views on the superiority of the German race and the inferiority of the Hebrews, dies in his spiritual birthplace, Bayreuth, at seventy-one, only six years and three weeks before the advent of the millennium he awaited in Germany.

Not long before Chamberlain's death Adolf Hitler made a humble pilgrimage to the author to whom Rosenberg, Strasser, and he himself "owed" so much.

To come back to Godet's musical beliefs, I think he was the prime mover behind that series of *Pelléas et Mélisande* performances in Geneva with Rose Féart (who had studied the role of Mélisande with Debussy) in the title role. I suppose that Godet's presence and proselytizing among us must also have been responsible for that first performance of Debussy's Violin Sonata, a few weeks after Debussy's death in 1918, in the strangely moving atmosphere of a little parish assembly hall in the shadow of Geneva's cathedral.

Frequent trips to Paris, which was to become our home in 1925, sometimes for concerts, at others to sit on the jury at the Conservatoire examinations or to judge the contests for the Prix Edouard Nadaud (a contest comparable in importance to the American Memorial Award), gave me a gradually clearer insight into the musical ideals and practices of this great centre. My sitting on the jury at these examinations and contests afforded me particularly rich opportunities to observe stylistic and technical trends. To compare notes with fellow jurors of the stature of a Lucien Capet, the great Beethoven-quartet player, of a Thibaud or an Enesco, was always a stimulating experience that sent me back to Geneva refreshed and eager for activity.

Among the diverse stimuli of these Geneva years—Ansermet, Godet, Jaques-Dalcroze, and others—I count as one of the most germinal my friendship with the painter Maximilian Mopp (which was the name he contrived from his real name,

Max Oppenheimer). He it was who not only gave me some insight into the technical inner workings of the painter's craft, but who—lover of beautifully fashioned antiques, porcelains, bindings—served in a certain measure as æsthetic mentor at this comparatively late stage in my development. A fanatical devotee of the violin, both as an amateur fiddler and as a connoisseur of the *luthier's* art, he was, I think, one of the first to realize the dramatic pictorial potentialities of portraits of string quartets, in which the protagonists are not only the four tense playing figures, but also the four instruments with their varied masses and rhythmical tensions. His portraits of the Rosé, the Klingler, and the Willy Hess quartets and others are widely known, as is his monumental portrait of an orchestra, "Symphony," exhibited at the Golden Gate Exposition at San Francisco and in most American and European museums. It was in 1917, when he painted my first portrait, which in format and conception is somewhat a companion piece to his Busoni portrait, that a friendship began which has spanned three decades.

Mopp, who now lives in New York, recently completed my second portrait for which he urged me to sit, coaxing me and reasoning with me thus: "You must really find time for a few sittings, Joska! I must paint you *now*! It is only after a man is past fifty that he *begins* to have a face. . . ."

CHAPTER XXII

USUALLY it is the browsing reader who does the skipping, but I find that I myself have indulged in this amiable weakness by skipping decades at a time! This may be pardonable in the customer (who I have been told is always right), but it is reprehensible in the person who caters for him. However, in telling of that Sunday afternoon in Felix Moscheles's studio in 1907 at which Maxim Gorky gave me his signature, I couldn't resist giving some anticipatory glimpses of the tours of Soviet Russia that I undertook quite regularly, twice a year, in the early fall and spring of the second half of the 1920s. Now let me tell about these a little more fully.

The first invitation to visit the Soviet Union reached me in 1924 while I was rehearsing with Maestro Fernández Arbós at the Teatro Real in Madrid for the somewhat belated Madrid première of the Brahms Concerto, incredible though the word "première" may seem to us in such a connection. Its first performance in England had taken place on March 6, 1879 with Joachim as soloist. It was conducted by W. G. Cusins. Dramatic contrasts are linked in my mind with this invitation to Soviet Russia; contrasts give certain dates their contour and significance—I almost said their symbolic significance. I received the wholly unexpected and thrilling invitation to visit the new world which Russia was building out of ruins in—paradoxically—one of the foyers of the anachronistically regal, red-plush-and-gilt, crystal-chandeliered Madrid Opera. Incidentally, the next day I was presented to members of the royal family, with the petrifying ceremoniousness usual at the Spanish court, and doubly painful to the flushed and wilting-collared player of the Brahms Concerto.

It wasn't so many months afterward that I played at another opera house, an opera house also with gilt and red plush and crystal chandeliers. The setting was the same, but what a dramatic difference! It was at the concluding session of the *Sjezd Sovjetov*—the plenary meeting of all the Soviets—at the Bolshoi Theatre in Moscow. For this occasion I exhumed from the limbo of my forgotten repertoire Wieniawski's *Souvenir de Moscou*, playing it with the Opera Orchestra under Golovanov. The "Honoured Artist of the Republic" Nishdanova sang. Then there was an interminable pause for deliberations and speeches before the concluding musical programme could begin. I wanted to go back to my hotel and wait there in comfort, but this was impossible; the bayonet-bearing guard at the stage door who had checked me in by comparing my pass-card with the admittance list nailed on the door would not have let me in a second time.

The brilliantly lighted Opera—row upon row of boxes packed with the chosen representatives of the many Soviet republics; Kirghiz, Tatar, Bashkir, Turkmen, and many another exotic physiognomy or headgear gleaming out of the loges; the uniforms; the colourful national costumes; the simple red head kerchiefs of some of the women delegates; the Mongol beards and the drooping moustaches and the young clean-shaven Red Army men—the picture of this swarming crowd, swaying, moving, talking, applauding between numbers, remains unforgettable to me.

When I recently read of Serge Koussevitzky's suggestion that the peace deliberations which are to follow World War II should be interspersed with the eternal values of our symphonic music, played by the great orchestras of the world, this plenary session came back to my mind with particular vividness. Such a suggestion seems to me so characteristically Russian and such an apt extension of this other politicomusical manifestation! It is heartening to note that the San Francisco Conference was opened by a symphony concert with Yehudi Menuhin as soloist.

Between 1924 and 1929 I made eleven tours of Soviet Russia, an average of two a year. With the tightening of foreign-currency export regulations, however (my fees had previously been paid in American dollars), these tours became more and more impracticable, and in the following decade I played there only in 1931, on my way to the Far East, and again in 1937.

One of the reasons I, am doing less than justice to these trips, which left on me an indelible impression of positive achievement on the part of the Russian people, is the discouragement I feel on reading the wholly misleading descriptions by some of my fellow artists of their tours there. How, for example, can I hope to correct and counteract misstatements like those in a book published in America as late as 1942, referring to conditions in Russia in 1928—conditions with which I think I may consider myself fairly well acquainted!

As I read amazing statements like: "I was hungry all the time I was in Russia"; So-and-so "had his shoes snatched out of his hands while he sat bent over in his compartment ready to put them on"; or ". . . as much of the city as had not been possessed by the deluge was *overrun by convivial commissars*" (my italics), all desire to rectify them leaves me, and I say to myself, "What's the use?" with an almost Russian shrug of resignation. So I shall limit myself to affirming that I personally did not suffer any pangs of hunger on these eleven successive tours, which lasted usually from three to four weeks each, and took me as far as Baku and Tiflis. Nor, for that matter, were things snatched out of my hands in railway coaches or elsewhere.

My statement about not having gone hungry should, however, be modified to this extent: I did almost starve (not quite, but almost) on the May Day that invariably seemed to find me in Moscow, my spring schedules being more or less the same each year. On these May Days restaurants, groceries, and pastry shops were closed, and even the simplified rolls-and-coffee-breakfast service at the Hotel Savoy was virtually suspended. However, the joy of the crowds, the carnival-like spirit, were such that I can't imagine that even the most callous tourist could have had it in him to expect "business as usual" on such a day of popular rejoicing. To the newcomer to the Soviet scene that I was, these May Day celebrations were a liberal education in themselves.

The endless processions, with their floats, with their huge caricatures (the texts of which I had translated to me), gave a rough-and-ready popular interpretation of current events of the year and of recent history seen from the Soviet vantage point, which was invaluable to me, especially when comparing trends and leitmotifs from May Day to May Day. (I assisted at five from 1924 to 1928.) The blown-up caricatures carried by the marchers gave one a kind of overall Soviet comment on world affairs, a somewhat crude and crushing simplification, true, but one well calculated to drive the message home to both the indigenous peasant and worker and the sophisticated foreign tourist whose political education and maturity were, more often than not, rather skimpy.

As to those "convivial commissars" mentioned in the book that started me on this train of reminiscences, I can only oblige with the description of the modest dwelling of the one I got to know: Lunacharsky, the intensely-cultured, polyglot, widely-read Commissar of Education. It was a home containing the same comfortable, well-worn, and by no means ostentatious furnishings one would find in the parlour of (say) a professor in some small mid-western college, with the difference that Lunacharsky's Gramophone, instead of being the latest model, was of the 1912 vintage! The table was laid with only as much "opulence" as one might expect in practically any cultured wage-earner's, musician's, or writer's home.

Altogether, conditions were not very different from those I found at the house of Nadine Auer, Leopold Auer's daughter, who had invited me to hear a young, up-and-coming violinist. I heard a fabulously gifted young man, who seemed diffident about his impending first trip across the borders to Berlin. Reassuring him enthusiastically, I told him that "Evropa" (as the Russians call all countries beyond their frontier to the west) was waiting for artists of his stamp. It turned out that America was, too! The young man was Nathan Milstein, and he was accompanied on the piano by Vladimir Horowitz's sister.

If I feel rather strongly about statements like those mentioned above about foreign artists going hungry in Soviet Russia, and other equally thoughtless bits of reporting, it must not be taken to mean that my own early trips could have been called de luxe! When in 1924 I made my first one, the organized "Intourist" tours were still a long way off—those tours taken by so many Americans and other foreigners in the late 'twenties and 'thirties, which gave birth to such endless books and travelogues, informative, misleading, all kinds.

When I arrived, the Hotel Savoy was barely in shape to receive foreign travellers, and rebuilding and redecorating were still going on with a vengeance. I used to be awakened regularly early every morning by the hammering that accompanied the business of relaying the torn-up parquet floor in the corridors and in adjoining rooms.

The housing shortage in those days was such that I was first scheduled to camp out in one of the offices of the Bolshoi Theatre Administration, in a room they intended to rig up for me into tolerably comfortable living quarters. However, at the last moment arrangements were made with the Savoy and I was deprived of the novel and exhilarating experience of having my bedroom in the administrative offices of the former Imperial Moscow Opera!

It was this spirit of improvisation, of making the best of any situation, that gave such zest to whatever was undertaken. Almost everything was a "first"; everything started from scratch. To be in on these comparative beginnings was bracing and tingling like the cold, snowy Easter weather I found there.

Mention of Easter and of snow brings back vivid memories of the crowds attending church services on Easter evening, of the overflow that could not find room inside spilling way out in front of the church, whose portals remained open, the worshippers bareheaded in the sparsely falling snow. We must remember that this was contemporaneous with the inscription—since vanished—that proclaimed in giant letters on one of the walls overlooking Red Square: "Religion is the opiate of the People."

The Russian people still had to make the best of what

they had. Sometimes I would be accompanied on an upright piano with many of its keys missing, but my pianist played on undaunted. I used to marvel at the way violinists like Milstein and Naum Blinder (now of San Francisco) managed to play beautifully in tune on strings that—one would have thought—precluded any such possibility.

Shaving soap and safety-razor blades were considered munificent gifts in those days. The peddlers who stood at the kerb near Kitayski Gorod displaying their pathetically modest wares were like portents of better days to come, even though all they had to offer were narrow leather belts, baskets, so-called "strawberry" soap that smelled to high heaven, primitive pieces of luggage made of wood, canvas, and about five per cent leather, shoelaces and pathetically rudimentary brassières of coarse white linen devoid of the remotest semblance of frills or frivolity. The incongruous assortment of these wares showed better than any commentary could how these people were rediscovering what we take for granted—rediscovering or discovering, as the case might be. Take pencils for instance. Under the new social order so many millions of Soviet citizens—not only children, but grown-ups who had remained illiterate under the Tsars—were learning to write, and the demand for pencils was so enormous that in 1925 an American was given a Soviet concession to set up a pencil factory. Soon the Hammer factory was turning out over half a million pencils a day!

The tendency to self-sufficiency and the Russian people's pride in every step achieved toward that end was understandable in a vast country as surrounded by non-co-operation and hostility as Soviet Russia was. But it is significant that, in spite of this trend, the government did not consider the country "self-sufficient" enough in virtuosi or conductors. It made very real sacrifices in that scarce commodity, American dollars, in order to give the young generation in the Conservatories—to whom the pre-war heroes of the concert stage: Nikisch, Busoni, Josef Hofmann, Ysaÿe, Kreisler, Casals, Mengelberg, were no more than names—the stimulation that foreign artists invariably bring after a long period of isolation.

How near their Civil War days were to them was brought home to me in particularly dramatic fashion in Odessa. Seeing from afar an unwonted commotion and crowds milling about on the imposing, bastion-like promenade overlooking the harbour, I went nearer and was still more puzzled when I saw young boys in anachronistic cadet-school uniforms of the Tsarist régime perched high on the lamp-posts that line the promenade. They were waving their caps and frantically throwing bouquets of flowers. The explanation came when I was close enough to see the movie-camera crew and the director in riding breeches, megaphone at his lips. They were shooting a scene showing the "triumphant" entrance into Odessa of an anti-revolutionary Anglo-French-Italian interventionist column. In this sequence, generals with their portly wives decked in elaborate flowered hats were seen riding in open landaus and receiving the tribute of the "liberated" crowds and of the Tsarist cadets who had climbed up the lamp-posts.

To witness a scene from such recent history, re-enacted at the identical place—and not so many years after the actual happening either!—struck me with an impact that no amount of documentary evidence can produce.

Such flashbacks to the recent past only reinforced the impression of the many efforts I saw around me, all co-ordinated to the building of their world of to-morrow. I was to have played for the thousands of workers and engineers of the Dnieprostroy power works, but my prearranged and closely knit schedule made this impossible. However, fragments of the saga of this stupendous technical achievement were brought to me by spokesmen who came to Rostov-on-the-Don to negotiate this appearance with the official of the State Concert Bureau who always accompanied me on these tours. It is curious how the physical proximity of such projects made them loom large in my consciousness, even though they were no more visible or, for that matter, understandable to me twenty miles from the spot than, say, at a distance of five hundred. I observed this time and again. (For instance, some ten years later, during the period of sanctions that were meted out to Fascist Italy after her aggression against Abyssinia, I played at the Engineers' and Officials' Clubhouse in Ismailia, heart and brain of the Suez Canal. At that time the legend of this gigantic creation, and its political importance, became much more of a reality to me, during talks with the music-loving engineers and officials—mostly Parisian—than it had been during the physical passage of the Canal by boat some years before.)

A technical achievement more in my line, though just as difficult for me to follow as the vast conception of the Dnieprostroy construction had been, was Leon Theremin's ether-wave instrument, which I got to know in Moscow in the spring of 1928.

I stumbled upon Theremin on the stage of the Moscow Conservatory Hall one afternoon when I went there to rehearse. The shy young scientist was busy assembling his incredibly intricate instrument with its countless wire connections (or whatever one calls them). We were introduced to each other and I listened (somewhat incredulously, I admit) to my pianist's claims of what Professor Theremin's magical-looking contraption could do. It was said to produce—or, rather, to capture out of the ether, by "controlled static"— musical sounds of an almost unlimited scale and of an infinite variety of timbres, linked together with a legato beyond the scope of the human singing apparatus and, still more, beyond the capacity of bowed instruments. Also, it was endowed with a vibrato like a string instrument or human song—and all this without strings, without finger-board, without sounding-board, simply by moving one's hands in front of the two metal bars projecting from the instrument, one of which controlled pitch and the other volume.

The claims sounded fantastic to me to a degree difficult to realize now, after an interval of some eighteen years, when one takes the theremin as a matter of course, along with thereminists like Lucie Bigelow Rosen, Clara Rockmore, and others, and theremin concerti with orchestral accompaniment and the like. I of course would not rest until I got Theremin to play me a few snatches of melody and, immediately, I tried my hand, or rather my hands, at it myself, with somewhat dire acoustic results. Soon afterward Theremin took his wonder instrument to Berlin. Paris and London followed, then came the trip to the United States, preceded by cabled dispatches—some a column long—that apparently whipped up an excitement of which we had palpable proof on the ocean trip my wife and I happened to share with Theremin and his secretary-collaborator.

Our loungings in the winter garden of the ship, during which the Soviet inventor indulged in the romantic pastime of composing little Russian poems in the form of anagrams, were every so often interrupted by wireless messages bearing some of the biggest industrial and commercial names in America, offering Theremin Caruso-like fees (I distinctly remember one offer of $5000) for the privilege of a "preview" of the invention during a soirée in their homes or, in the case of a cable signed by the owner of a great department store, in the auditorium of that store.

As Theremin and his secretary spoke no English, my wife and I had to convey to him the meaning of all this competition between Chicago's Mr. S., Detroit's Mr. F., and Philadelphia's Mr. W. But all we succeeded in conveying to him was names and figures, which did not seem to interest the young Soviet scientist; we could not get across any of the excitement that *we* felt—vicariously!—at these cabled offers, which to us seemed pretty fantastic. (My own fees had not then gone beyond the modest three-figure stage.)

However, Theremin, imbued with the socialist ideology, was calmly emphatic in his refusal to consider any of these offers and stuck to the original plan of giving the first demonstration free of charge in the presence of the Press, of noted musicians, scientists, radio engineers, and the like. We saw a good deal of each other after this initial excitement had subsided. Later we followed the ups and downs of the experiment with friendly interest, as well as the attempts at commercial marketing of the instruments, Theremin's resistance, and his scruples—for he always remained the researcher who tried to perfect his invention before thinking in terms of marketing. It was all very instructive to me and taught me something about the natural history of "sensations" and of their aftermaths, often so anticlimactic.

How little Theremin was interested in marketing problems and in capitalizing on his inventions is shown by his whole-hearted and disinterested collaboration with Henry Cowell on a completely uncommercial project. This collaboration resulted in an instrument which would do for rhythmic combinations what the keyboard had in the past done for the development of harmony. Cowell's aim was to devise a keyboard for the control of rhythm so that various rhythmic combinations, such as three against four, four against five, etc., would not offer technical difficulties but might be employed and enjoyed in cases where they enhance the musical and expressive values. Cowell had already made a crude instrument in which wheels turned, and percussive sounds in various rhythms were produced and continued as long as a key was held down; but Theremin, with his usual genius, was fired with the idea and suggested that he would like to develop it much further in the working out, so that one might have combinations of rhythm up to seventeen simultaneous rhythms (this was the final result in the instrument) and in which each rhythm might be attached to a particular pitch. In the final instrument, there were seventeen keys—the first key playing whole notes as long as it was held down, the second half-notes, the third three notes to a measure, etc. A lever controlled the tempo, which could be made fast or slow. A rhythmic figure, such as a half and two quarters, could be made by playing the half-note key for half a measure, and the quarter-note key for the remainder of the measure. So the music for it does not consist of notes all of the same value in the same part! The pitch is arranged so that the normal pitches are in overtone relationship—that is, a rhythm of two is an octave higher than a rhythm of one, a rhythm of three is a fifth higher than that of two, etc., just as is the case in overtones. Besides, the pitches can be also raised or lowered by a special lever.

Two such instruments were built. One belongs to Cowell, but is lent by him to the psychology department at Stanford University; the other was built for Nicolas Slonimsky, was sold by him to Joseph Schillinger, and is owned now by Schillinger's widow Frances Schillinger. Cowell found the instrument stimulating musically as well as unique, and wrote for it a concerto with orchestra accompaniment, which to date has never been played. He also wrote several solos, which he played in demonstrations through the country. Schillinger and Professor Farnsworth at Stanford University have used it more for scientific experiments and psychological research. Theremin claimed that it was the first instrument ever to employ the principle of the "electric eye." When one presses a key, a light is lit, which shines through two whirling wheels. An electric eye is at the other side of the wheels, which revolve so that one wheel produces the rhythmic pattern, and the other produces the pitch, when the flashes of light through holes in them irritate the electric eye.

Though other scientists—perhaps before Theremin—had worked on the principle of disturbing a magnetic field by the introduction of a human or animal body, to my knowledge he was the first to apply it to a musical instrument. All through World War II, I kept wondering whether it was not precisely this principle which provided the basis for the death-bringing device used by our enemies in such shocking fashion: I mean the hidden mines that were set off whenever the unsuspecting victim approached the minetrap. As we know, these were used extensively in places where the mines could not be set off by any of the usual automatic means.

However, the possibility that some of the detecting apparatus too that saved so many lives on our side, can in some way be traced to Theremin's and his fellow scientists' experiments and achievements is a compensating, consoling thought. . . .

CHAPTER XXIII

EVERY time I returned from Soviet Russia I was amazed
and amused by the questions put to me about the externals
of concert-giving there. My questioners were surprised
to hear that these outward conditions were similar to ours:
with ticket-selling, bill-posting, newspaper advertising, and
all the trimmings. But then, in those days, many supposedly
well-informed people still clung to the idea that life in the
Soviets was the life of robots who earned ration cards instead
of money, whose leisure was regimented, who went to
theatres or concerts herded in groups. They had evidently
never heard of the N.E.P.—in Russian, *Novaya Economicheskaya
Politika*, the "New Economic Policy" with which my eleven
tours coincided. Though the externals of these concerts,
then, were identical with those that prevailed almost everywhere, within this framework I found audiences of a sensitivity
and a quickness of nervous reaction I have never encountered
anywhere else.

I was told by those who remembered audience reaction in
Tsarist Russia, like Josef Hofmann, Chaliapin, Koussevitzky,
and Prokofiev, that this special quality, which I somehow
ascribed to the Soviet pattern, was not something specifically
linked to the present Soviet temper, but a timeless attribute
of Russian audiences as such, irrespective of political creed.
Where else would one see crowds like those waiting—
sometimes in the rain—in the courtyard of the Moscow
Conservatory or in front of the Borse (Stock Exchange) Hall
in Odessa, half or three-quarters of an hour by the clock,

waiting just to have that last glimpse of their artist and to send up that final shout as he gets into the droshky waiting for him at the stage door?

Or where else would the departure of a member of the audience before the end of a theatrical performance, something quite usual in our part of the world, be pilloried so indignantly as it is in Soviet Russia? A prominent American playwright who recently (in 1945) committed this *faux pas* in a Moscow theatre found out to her dismay that taking French leave in the middle of a performance does not go unpunished in Russia. As she reached the exit she was besieged by a score of irate ushers who indignantly demanded to know where she got her nerve, how dare she leave before the final curtain? They made it plain to her that such behaviour was—to put it mildly—inexcusably "uncultured" and that no one in the history of that theatre had ever before acted so boorishly.

If such behaviour is considered inexcusable in Russia, while looked upon indulgently elsewhere, there is *one* kind of group reaction in a theatre or concert hall that I have never heard of except in Soviet Russia. This is the antithesis of the gradual emptying of a hall during a less than satisfying performance: the gradual *filling up* of a hall during a surprise revelation of an unheralded artist. This is precisely what happened to a young Italian pianist while making his Moscow début some years ago. His first numbers were played to almost empty benches, though applauded with enthusiasm mingled with amazement. After his first numbers many of those present slipped out to the telephone booths to tell fellow music-lovers of the unexpected revelation they were missing, urging them to hurry and come. And, at intermission time, more and more telephoning. The young pianist ended his concert, so inauspiciously begun, before an almost crowded, wildly cheering Conservatory Hall.

The devotion and patient insistence of these Soviet crowds does not exclude discipline and an innate sense of the fitness of things. A story told me by Mary Pickford in 1945 well illustrates this. We were reminiscing about our visits to Soviet Russia (hers took place in 1926), comparing notes about this essentially Russian quality that sets the adulation of these crowds entirely apart from similar mass demonstrations elsewhere.

From her innumerable Soviet memories of that epic trip she singled out this one as showing how tact, which we usually associate with the individual, can manifest itself even in a crowd. She had been driven ragged, she told me, by an unending schedule of teas, appearances, etc., and neither she nor Douglas Fairbanks could find it in their hearts to disappoint the child-like expectation of each succeeding group by a refusal. How was one to discriminate? It was either all or nothing. One afternoon, during one of these receptions, her strength gave out and she collapsed; the doctor who was summoned was adamant in ordering the immediate cessation of her activities.

The crowds waiting for her in the streets in a compact mass were notified from the balcony that she would not re-emerge from the building as her afternoon schedule had to be curtailed. Still they waited, incredulous, and suspecting some ruse to evade them. The mounted police edged their horses into the crowd in a vain attempt to disperse it, but the solid mass of humanity re-formed after every such attempt. Eventually Douglas Fairbanks came out on a balcony and explained the situation through an interpreter. The crowd listened with hushed respect, barely dared to applaud for fear of disturbing their beloved patient, and quietly melted away. It was *this* reaction of the crowd that left Mary Pickford with an indelible memory—not the hysterical adulation, which was no different in its essence from that which went out to "America's Sweetheart" everywhere and anywhere.

For my own part I was touched when at a Leningrad rehearsal the violin section of the orchestra gave up its smoking recess in order to stay grouped around me and, with naïve insistence and typically Slavic urgency, called out to me collectively and individually to play for them the Paganini 24th Caprice during the rest period.

If such manifestations were typically Russian rather than Soviet, one set of musical experiences during my tours *was* indigenous to the new social order which the Revolution had created: the conductorless orchestra called Persymphans.* Some of the most unorthodox musical challenges of these trips to Soviet Russia I experienced in regular appearances with this unique body of musicians. After decades of concerto-playing with conductors who co-ordinate a soloist's performance with that of the orchestra, who synthesize the whole and mediate between the two when there are discrepancies in conception, I found the contrast of these entirely new working conditions stimulating.

Sometimes, in the nineteen-twenties, after an appearance in Berlin or at the Leipzig Gewandhaus, and still under the spell of the music-obsessed, frenzied Furtwängler, or of the infinite song that flows from Bruno Walter's baton, I would stand only four or five days later on the platform of the Moscow Conservatory Hall rehearsing with this conductorless orchestra. Playing the same works that Furtwängler had directed for me so recently—with that suggestive power of his that swept away every obstacle, even long-standing convictions of seasoned orchestra-players and soloists in matters of tempo and interpretation, when those convictions were contrary to his own—I stood there in front of musicians without any spokesman, any intermediary, any canalizer of the forces at work that the concerto conductor is. There was no one to shape things in his own image, Furtwängler-like.

At the Persymphans rehearsal, on the contrary, there was a workshop atmosphere generated by proud artisans bound together in the common task of making good music. Each man had the right to have his little say on occasion. Mutual respect, in the knowledge that careful sifting of the highest available talent had brought them together, rather than pull or favouritism or regard for past achievement (the achievements of orchestra players of high repute are often, alas, *long* past), gave them a serenity unwonted in other orchestras. Bickerings, backbitings, sycophancy had no place in their set-up.

I rehearsed and played with my back turned to the orchestra, of course, the strings grouped in a semicircle around me,

* The name Persymphans was made up thus: from *pjerva* (first), *symphonichny* (symphonic), and *ans* (from ensemble).

the half-dozen or so immediately to my right and left having their backs turned to the audience, and the woodwinds and brass behind me, vertically across the inner part of the semi-circle.

These performances were to one's overall musicianship as the tempering process is to a steel blade. Anyone will understand who has ever attended a rehearsal *with* a conductor, or who has listened to an orchestra performance with even a little imagination as to the spadework which goes into it.

We even gave a world première: that of Casella's concerto, dedicated to me; the composer, conscious of the unusualness of this première, had all the data pertaining to it engraved on the fly-leaf of the score.

The rise in Soviet living standards from year to year became a reality to me, returning as I did every six or seven months. I shared the joy of my friends the Romanovs (he was a well-known author of short stories, many of them translated into German, French and English) when they moved into their new co-operative apartment, built to the specifications of the art workers—writers, actors, dancers—who inhabited this housing unit. The peddlers who in 1924 had offered for sale their pathetically primitive wares were no longer the principal purveyors of manufactured goods. State department stores had sprung up. The state cosmetic industry made quite a showing in its display windows, and the "strawberry" soap that had offended my nostrils in 1924 had evolved into a fragrant product. Russian reprints of foreign music had begun to appear, though it was necessary to write out by hand all the orchestral parts of a Hindemith composition from a pocket score that had somehow found its way into the country; I saw this being done by the orchestra librarian in Moscow—at the time it was the only way to make that performance possible.

The awareness of the young generation of what was being composed across the borders was quite remarkable. It was during my second or third visit that Lev Knipper—best known in America as the composer of *Meadowland*, popularized by films, radio, and Cossack choirs—came to me on behalf of the newly founded Soviet section of the International Society for Contemporary Music and asked me to play Ernest Bloch's Sonata for them. My first performances of Prokofiev's Concerto in D created a great stir and evoked an almost physically palpable response which I have never encountered elsewhere when I have played this work; the Scherzo, as if by a prearranged signal, invariably had to be encored. That the venerable Glazunov ostentatiously walked out of the hall during my Leningrad performance of this concerto did not detract in any way from the popular and critical acclaim. Nor could Glazunov's walking-out be interpreted as an unfriendly gesture toward me, for soon afterward I received the following official letter signed by the venerable composer, in his capacity as Director of the Leningrad Conservatory, countersigned by the assistant Director, Professor Ossovsky, and the Secretary, A. Alexandrov, who later achieved wide fame as creator and leader of the Red Army Choir.

Very dear Maestro, 26 January 1928

The board of the National Academy of Music of Leningrad has the honour to send you the following proposal:

The Academy, since the World War, has been deprived of one of its best teachers and pedagogues in the person of its violin teacher Monsieur Leopold Auer, who has gone abroad.

His influence during the long years of his professorship in Russia has been of the greatest, not only at the Academy, but also in the Russian world of music. As pedagogue, he created an independent and original school of the violin, known now in the entire world, of which the most brilliant exponents gather laurels among the nations of the globe. As violin virtuoso, Monsieur Auer, through his concerts given in Leningrad and in all Russia, has greatly contributed to enhance the artistic musical level of the country and to popularize the art of the violin. Also, as a great artist, through his personality, he had a favourable influence on the musicians who, with his help, aimed toward perfection.

The National Academy of Leningrad is extremely anxious to include among its pedagogues a maestro of the same value, or even of superior value, a pedagogue and a player at the same time, who can assist in the great problem of deepening musical culture in the country renewed by the revolution.

Therefore, in this difficult situation, the Academy, appreciating highly your authority as an artist universally known, appeals to you, dear Maestro, and asks you to do it the honour of becoming teacher of the master class.

In case this offer is agreeable to you in principle, the Academy begs you to let it know what practical material and academic conditions you would consider satisfactory, in the event of your coming to live in Leningrad.

To make your stay, from a material point of view, as acceptable as possible, the Academy would undertake to facilitate the organization of your annual concerts in Leningrad, Moscow, and in the other towns of the Union, and, in consequence, will await the expression of your wishes.

In the hope of a prompt reply, we beg you to accept, Sir and dear Maestro, the expression of our highest consideration.

The Rector of the Leningrad Academy
Professor A. Glazunov
The Vice-Rector, Inspector of Classes
Professor A. Ossovsky
The Secretary of the Administration
A. Alexandrov

Though I interpreted this offer as a great honour, I felt it to be somewhat premature and inacceptable to the young virtuoso that I was then, who had just embarked upon his annual American tours.

When I played the Prokofiev Concerto in Kharkov the principal daily assigned two critics to cover the première, one belonging to the conservative camp, the other to the progressive young school; and they gave their conflicting opinions, for what they were worth, side by side on the same page!

Such was the youthful earnestness with which "firsts" of any kind were treated in those heroic days.

Once I programmed the Second Roussel Sonata, which I have already mentioned. I was somewhat dubious about doing this, Roussel's name and standing being unknown to my audience, but the response was so immediate and so warm that I had to repeat the rhythmically intricate Finale. Cases like these convinced me that the notion of *succès d'estime,* so prevalent in musical sets where only lip-service is paid to contemporary music, was non-existent among these musically perceptive people, who accepted or rejected entirely according to the dictates of their innate musical instincts.

Now, in our better informed days—1945—it is difficult to imagine or to believe the kind of talk my first trip to Soviet Russia elicited from even normally well-informed people. They entreated me to take numerous precautions against all kinds of disasters likely to befall me on this "hazardous" trip. Their recommendations ran along these lines: "Be inoculated against infectious diseases," "Make your will before leaving safe Switzerland," "Use only a cheap grade of envelope when writing to your wife so that she can detect any 'steaming open' procedure on the part of the censoring secret police," "Don't talk to anyone on the train on the way from Berlin to Moscow," "Look out for hidden microphones in hotel rooms," and so on.

Even later, when I had already made several safe trips, devoid of any E. Phillips Oppenheim complications of international intrigue, these well-meaning die-hards remained sceptical. They would not believe how little the average Soviet citizen or the musical organizations with which I had dealings indulged in proselytizing. These European friends kept harping on the old tune that foreigners of distinction are shown only "what the authorities want them to see," and repeated similar clichés.

The fact is that I was not "shown" anything (my projected visit to the Kremlin never came off), nor were any explaining, interpreting apologists assigned to me. I was considered a "specialist"—that was all; as long as such a specialist, whether

GETI, LILY PONS, AND EUGENE ORMANDY REHEARSING ARIA FROM MOZART'S *IL RÈ PASTORE*
FOR THE ANN ARBOR FESTIVAL OF 1940

SZIGETI WITH HIS WIFE, WANDA, IN THEIR GARDEN AT PALOS VERDES, CALIFORNIA

an oil-well engineer, an electronics researcher, or a violin virtuoso, did his work to the best of his ability, the authorities were not much interested in his private opinions. A Hungarian engineer whom I met in Baku, whose very stance, Austro-Hungarian "officer chic," patent-leather shoes—everything, in fact—was "out of tune" with his environment, confirmed this to me in so many words.

My visits to museums and theatres were entirely unguided, and were decided upon whenever I was in the mood; I was rewarded with some of the most lasting impressions of my many years of museum and theatre experience. The Shtchugin Gallery of Modern Art; the Leningrad Eremitage, which I had first visited in December 1913; Nemirovitch-Dantchenko's *Carmencita* with Bizet's music, remarkably conducted by Vladimir Bakaleinikov; Alice Koonen's superb performances at her husband's Theatre Tairov (where I first saw Eugene O'Neill's *Desire Under the Elms*); the Meyerhold staging of Ilya Ehrenburg's *D. E.* (Destruction of Europe); the nerve-shattering expressionism of the Habima Players' *Dybbuk;* a *Hamlet* with Gordon Craig's scenery . . . these are but a few of my outstanding memories.

I have no notes from these earlier trips, but when we came to America after the outbreak of World War II I did happen to bring with me my 1937 diary. Here are some short entries taken from it:

Kiev—September 27, 1937. Bouquets of flowers presented to us [my wife and me] on our arrival at the Kiev railway station.

September 28. Two rehearsals. Afternoon *izvoshtik* drive around town. Sophia Cathedral empty, in process of restoration. Stylistically an imposing job, this restoration. Countless gay, somewhat ragged young people, two tiny girls singing at the top of their voices. . . . At streetcar stop, well-disciplined queue. Sat in on rehearsal of Ukrainian national dancers, who are working in smaller room, adjoining the "Hall of Pioneers" where I shall be playing to-morrow.

Moscow—October 2. The five prize-winners of the Brussels Ysaÿe contests welcome me. [How characteristic of their sense of "community" that they, whom I saw at the Brussels contest *together*, should greet me here *in corpore*.] Professor Schmidt, hero of the Arctic, and Prokofiev at concert. Pushkin centennial exposition. See crowd of 1500 in front of Lenin's mausoleum. Looked for John Reed memorial tablet on Red Square wall, where it was in the 'twenties, but it is no longer there.

October 5. At reception given for me at VOX [Society for Cultural Relations] Jacob Flieher and Zak, prize-winning pianists, play with incredible suggestive force and brilliance. Young fiddlers Kogan, Josip Meister (12 years old), Latinsky (15 years old); Kalinovsky plays Chausson *Poème*, young Boussia Goldstein plays Tartini, Poldini, Dvořák enchantingly.

October 6. Two concerts to-day; matinee recital at 1 p.m. *and* orchestral concert (Beethoven and Brahms concerti and Corelli's *La Folia*) in the evening.

Leningrad—October 7. Concert ends after midnight.

October 8. The trumpet player of the Philharmonic is pointed out to me: a redeemed *bizbrizornyi* [one of the waifs and strays who roamed the country in packs like wild dogs after the civil war]. To think that he *may* have been that sub-human-looking ragamuffin I saw ten years ago in Kiev! I was walking in the Park with my pianist Strasfogel when I saw the lid of a green refuse box, about the size of a bridge table, begin to bob up and down. A pair of wild, furtive eyes looked to see whether the coast was clear, and up popped one of these *bizbrizornyi*, smiling, refreshed after his obviously long and happy sleep, and relieved to see us instead of the cops he had feared. . . . Visit in radiant sun to Peter and Paul bastion prison; cells where Gorky, Kropotkin, and Vera Figner languished; and the cell where in 1897, in order to escape third-degree questioning, the girl student Wistrova poured lamp oil all over herself to burn to death. On the banks of the river under the walls of the prison a young student, his torso uncovered, sun-bathing and reading aloud, memorizing some algebra. (I glanced into his book.) . . . Asked to write two dozen lines for *Izvestia* on this visit in German or French. [This little article appeared in *Izvestia* of October 17, 1937.]

CHAPTER XXIV

—————·{❖}·—————

DURING the years of the early twenties, while I was rebuilding my European concert career the hard way, there were already intimations of coming events: repeated nibbles from America. Though even as far back as 1911 or 1912 I had had an offer to tour America with Marcella Sembrich, it was Martin Hanson, Busoni's American manager, who was the first to approach me after World War I. Another offer came from the concert set-up sponsored by the Brunswick Record Company, the organization that was responsible for the return visit, around 1923 or so, of Richard Strauss and of other European big-name attractions. Bill Murray, the genial artists' representative of the Baldwin Piano Company, former critic of the *Brooklyn Eagle* and a discriminating music connoisseur, also sought me out after one of my London recitals and made arrangements with me on behalf of his company long before any managerial contract with America had been drawn up. (At about the same time he "discovered" Gieseking for his firm, and it was he who, at the beginning of Gieseking's American career and of my own, sponsored a sonata recital by the two of us in the old Æolian Hall. He was also responsible for a broadcast of the Debussy Sonata and, I believe, of a Mozart sonata by Gieseking and myself—a rather courageous gesture for those early days of radio broadcasting.)

For a good many years there must have been a trickle of news in American papers about my doings in Europe, but this was long before the much better organized period of the 'thirties, when musical observers like Herbert Peyser were fulfilling a useful and necessary mission, travelling through Europe, covering and reporting all important musical events for their American papers, and acting as weather vanes—or perhaps seismographs if you like—for the purveyors of music in the United States.

It was only lately that Howard Taubman of the *New York Times* who interviewed me for a national magazine told me that Fritz Kreisler, with characteristic generosity, had brought tidings of me to the American journalists who met him at the dock. This was shortly after he had heard me in the Berlin Philharmonie Saal under Fritz Reiner in 1922 or 1923. The same music critic, incidentally, said that the first reference to me in the morgue of his paper dated from around 1910 when I had played for Queen Elizabeth of Belgium. Such things, however, were quite unknown to me and were therefore unexploited by my entourage, who naturally could have speeded up my coming to America by these and other publicity breaks! But, whether consciously or not, I bided my time and was not over-impatient to hasten the date of my American début. I do not claim to have been an exception among young European virtuosi, all of whom consider this début a most desirable and glamorous goal, but still I waited for signs and portents and did not interpret as definite offers the managerial nibbles of Hanson and others.

As in so many things, I must have been influenced by Busoni in this wait-and-see attitude of mine, whether I knew it or not. Intimations of many clashes between the uncompromising nonconformist Busoni personality and the American concert set-up of those early days—the first fifteen years of our century—came my way in talks with the master and his associates.

There was the "incident" of the "Emperor" Concerto, for instance. During the Mahler tenure at the New York Philharmonic in the first decade of this century, Busoni and Mahler, intransigent purists if there ever were any, decided to cleanse the masterpiece of all the interpretative accretions of past decades and give a model performance based entirely on the score and not on "tradition." ("*Tradition ist*

Schlamperei!"—Tradition is slovenliness !—had been the battle-cry of Hans von Bülow in rehearsals.) They wanted the work to emerge in its original freshness and purity and started at the rehearsal to "undo" the harm that had been done, by removing those interpretative accretions (pencil markings in score and parts and so on) that dim the lustre of a musical work just as surely as successive carelessly applied coats of varnish dim the glow of a masterpiece of painting. After the lengthy and somewhat stormy session over the first movement, a prominent woman member of the Music Committee ostentatiously got up and left the rehearsal room, saying indignantly in a loud voice: "No, this will never do!" The rest of the incident—Mahler's and Busoni's reaction or quick repartee—was left to the imagination of the disciples gathered around the Master when he told of this and similar experiences. Some of these young people naturally drew rather hasty and lurid conclusions from this case, which—I now see—must have been a more or less isolated one, even for those days.

There were less painful incidents, too, told and retold at the Busoni table or in the Busoni library, like the anecdote about the gentleman who heard Busoni in a Liszt concerto when the pianist was already advanced in years, his hair streaked with grey. In those days Busoni's long Prince Albert coat gave him a very Lisztian appearance.

"That was very good," the man was overheard to remark to his wife. "Now I should like to see him as Mozart in a Mozart concerto with a wig on."

Stories like the one I heard about Franz von Vecsey, in the early 'twenties at the height of his popularity and drawing power in Europe and South America, may also have influenced me by corroborating the ones about the Busoni conflicts. It appears that Vecsey was so incensed at the presumption of a big American gramophone company which dared to suggest that he, Vecsey, the adulated virtuoso, should make *test records* before being signed up, that he preferred to let the important (and even to him desirable) contract go by the board rather than submit. To understand his reaction one must remember that his drawing power in Berlin, for instance, was so great that the largest available concert hall, the Philharmonie, no

longer sufficed and he had to give his recitals at the Scala Music
Hall, which was to the Philharmonie what the old New York
Hippodrome was to Carnegie Hall.

The event that brought things to a head and provided me
with those "unmistakable signs and portents" for which I
had been waiting during all the protracted and inconclusive
negotiations with Martin Hanson, the Brunswick Company,
and others, was my meeting with Stokowski a year or so
earlier. This meeting I owe to the good offices of César
Saerchinger, who, before his present political and historical
broadcasting activities, had been devoting most of his time
to musical journalism and editing. I had played the Bach
Chaconne for Stokowski (it was at the Hotel Baur au Lac in
Zurich, shortly before he was to embark for the States), and
all he said was: "I am sailing next Wednesday, I'll be seeing
my manager about you approximately a week later and you
will have a cable from him about ten or twelve days from
to-day."

I had had too many sobering experiences with conductors
who made unfulfilled and in some cases unfulfillable promises
to young players and composers to be unduly excited over
the possibilities inherent in this simple statement. When
the cable from Stokowski's manager *did* arrive—and within
the specified twelve days, too!—it is easy to imagine my
delighted surprise and my gratitude for such exemplary
regard for his own given word. Those other conductors—
alas, all too numerous—who promise the ever-hopeful composer or soloist to "bear him in mind" for another season, and
who more often than not fail to do so, made me appreciate
Stokowski's scrupulous timing all the more. The German
equivalent to this ever-postponed "bearing in mind" had
become quite a joke among us young musicians. The Herr
Generalmusikdirektor would benevolently assure us: "*Ich
werde Sie im Auge behalten*," and we wondered sometimes:
"Good Heavens, how *can* the exalted conductorial 'eye' hold
(*behalten*) all this load?"

By a neat coincidence—a coincidence such as a novelist
might fabricate—it was not at this audition in the Zurich

hotel that I saw for the first time the man who was to give me the "break" of an American début with the Philadelphia Orchestra. As it happened, I had been present at that memorable Stokowski début in London one spring afternoon in 1908, when the organist from St. Bartholomew's, New York, electrified a Queen's Hall audience. I still remember the already then typically Stokowskian sound of the London Orchestra in the concluding number—Tchaikovsky's *Marche Slave*—and the feline suppleness of the orchestral support that the young conductor gave to Zimbalist's playing of Glazunov's Concerto, then still a comparative novelty. I believe it was only after this concert that Stokowski was "graduated" to his first major symphonic assignment—the Cincinnati Orchestra, which he took over in 1909—to be followed in 1912 by his creative activity at the helm of the Philadelphia Orchestra. So I had in a way been "in" on his conductorial beginnings some fifteen years before he was to usher in *my* American début with the impressive playing of the orchestral statement of those ineffable themes that precede the entry of the solo violin in Beethoven's Concerto.

When I call the playing of this orchestral exposition of Beethoven's themes "impressive," I should add "intimidatingly impressive." For that was precisely its effect on me as I stood there at the Philadelphia rehearsal—it was in December, 1925—my fingers cold, awaiting the redoubtable entry of the solo violin. I was getting weaker and weaker at the knees as the silken sheen of that orchestral introduction enveloped me—me, who had never before heard an American orchestra. After all, a violinist playing with an orchestra in a new world submits to a kind of ordeal by fire in front of some half-hundred string-players. Most of these have started their playing careers with the same high hopes, often with the same natural equipment; and not a few among them believe—rightly or wrongly—that at some period of their development they reached approximately the same level as the soloist now standing before them. Thus, unlike a pianist or a singer, the violinist has to pass muster before a critical fraternity of his *own* kind, however great his fame. At least one-third of the orchestra, the fellow-violinists, come to such a rehearsal with a decided "show me" attitude. That much is certain.

Naturally, I don't claim for these very personal reactions anything like general validity. All I want to convey is that to me, subjectively, such first rehearsal contacts with an orchestra and particularly with its body of fellow string-players had more importance than the débuts themselves, although objectively I fully realized that the latter were more important.

I may, however, be unduly stressing the negative, the cramping, aspects of the situation and failing to make clear some of its joys. To stand in front of dozens of one's fellow craftsmen, all initiates to whom the hows and whys of the soloist's doings are an open book, to earn their acquiescence, their approval, their admiration, as the work progresses—this can bring incomparable moments of elation to the soloist. Naturally, it depends to a great extent on his own attitude, on his musical *Weltanschauung*. Some play *in front* of an orchestra, not only in a literal but also, alas, in a figurative sense; whereas others play *with* the orchestra, rejoicing in that mutual interpenetration which alone constitutes real concerto-playing. The elation has some physical, sensuous components, also, like everything into which enters the element of unanimity, of impulse and initiative passed to and fro.

You ask how this acquiescence, admiration, and all the other infinitely nuanced reactions are conveyed to the soloist? Exactly in the same way in which the judgments—whether of censure or of admiration—are passed by the orchestra players to their conductor, whose severest critics they are, as is well known. There are a thousand subtle avenues of communication from orchestra player to soloist: nudging the player at the same desk, taking over in the soloist's identical manner some melodic fragment he has just played—these are but a few of the signs the violinist has that his message has reached his most understanding and most exacting audience.

To return to my American début, I don't remember how this particular rehearsal in Philadelphia went off, beyond the fact that between the rehearsal that had ended around noon and the concert scheduled for three o'clock I found myself back in my room at the Bellevue-Stratford, fiddling away at some passages which presumably had not satisfied me. While I was engaged in this wholly irrational activity (if indeed it was not downright harmful—I should have been relaxing and fortifying myself with a leisurely light meal before the crucial début), in walked Carl Flesch, his jovial, quizzical eyes flashing at me from behind eyeglasses.

"Well, of *all* things . . . to be practising at this hour! And after all the fine things I heard about your rehearsal this morning, too! Yes, the grapevine *has* reached me already; some of my Curtis Institute pupils were at the rehearsal."

And he went on scolding me for being so unnecessarily tense and apprehensive before this début, playfully muttering imprecations and "Donnerwetters" on those managers, confrères, and the like who magnify the importance of such events out of all proportion and thus lead to puerile behaviour like mine.

"Why," he went on, "you should look on it as just another concert. Have confidence in your American audiences. Assume that merit will be recognized even if minor accidents do happen. Consider my own case: I played this same Beethoven Concerto with this same Stokowski in this same Academy of Music two years ago. Incredibly enough, my memory failed me—for the first time in *you* know how many decades of a concert career—at this place—" and he hummed it while I stared at him wide-eyed. "I had to stop," he continued; "I had to go over to the conductor's stand. We resumed then—and, you see, Szigeti, that it didn't harm my standing in the least, did it? Here I am, head of the violin department of the Curtis Institute, playing more concert dates than I intended taking, and everything shipshape—in spite of that painful happening!"

Little did kindly Carl Flesch know that by his well-meant reassurances he had only succeeded in adding one more obsession to my numerous others: the obsession that *my* memory might fail me, too, at precisely the same place he had pointed out.

CHAPTER XXV

WE hear a lot of talk nowadays about "planned economy," "planned publicity campaigns," planned this and that. When I look back on my first American season, its salient and (I will confess) to my mind most sympathetic feature is that it was so utterly unplanned! I can describe it best by the things that *weren't* there and that *didn't* happen. I wasn't interviewed, or photographed. There were no receptions. I had almost no contacts with New York society. My adult recording career had not yet begun. That there were in those days—1925—no national news magazines, no broadcast interviews, no broadcast performances to speak of—all this simplified matters still further. The absence of these short cuts to fame, as well as (I may add) the absence of the now ubiquitous press agent, made an appreciable difference in impact and in quick returns, by contrast with what obtains at the present time.

I went to America without my wife and without an accompanist, and thus was generally less surrounded, advised, and monitored than is commonly the case. Even a solo recital, that most planned of all planned things ephemeral, was given only as an afterthought, as it were. No date for it had been set before my Stokowski début and I began thinking about it only after Carl Friedberg called me up the next day to ask *when* I intended following up the Stokowski concert with a solo recital. It was only then that I really knew I had every reason to be grateful for the way things had gone off; generally such knowledge comes to the virtuoso through his overeager circle, or let us call it bodyguard. Little by little, however, the début began to produce results.

Mr. Bagby, whose Morning Musicales at the old Waldorf had for some half a century been a sort of barometer of metropolitan (or rather "mondaine") acceptance of new-comers to the New York operatic or concert stage, engaged me very soon after my solo recital. When the meticulous little gentleman, with his twirled, waxed moustaches, came to discuss the programme, the interview turned out to be quite an eye-opener for me. Not only had I to confess that I was not prepared to play most of the "salon" pieces he suggested —Poldini's *Dancing Doll*, the "Meditation" from *Thais*, Chopin nocturnes, Spanish Dances by Sarasate—but I was somewhat crestfallen when he asked me to be sure to wind up my group with Hubay's *Zephyr*. I had played this as one of my last encores at my recital, after a substantial list of Bach, Corelli, Mozart, and so on, and now I heard from the music arbiter's lips: "It's *Zephyr* with which you got *me,* and it's *Zephyr* with which you'll get my audience, too."

And the old gentleman *did* know his audience; one must hand that to him. This of course was not surprising, con-sidering that while "his" artist was performing he sometimes used to sit on the stage, almost hidden behind decorative screens and palms, scanning with opera glasses the faces of his audience, most of whom had been known to him for years, and evaluating the artist not only by the applause, but by the glances and nods, the ecstatic expressions or their reverse, which the playing elicited.

Early experiences like these fortified me for certain sub-sequent clashes and conflicts roused by my programme policies, though in justice to all concerned I must admit that these were not frequent. True, there was the well-meaning executive of one of the biggest concert circuits in the country whose supreme "trump" during a somewhat heated argument was: "Well, let me tell you, Mr. Dzigedy—and *I* know what I'm talking about—your Krewtser Sonata bores the pants off my audiences!"

This classic description of the effect Beethoven's "Kreutzer" had on the essential apparel of some hearers quite naturally leads me to a digression involving some of my ideas on building programmes. Perhaps a good way of approaching the question is to look around in other fields where the juxta-position and the sequence of the material presented are important. In drawing up a programme, I feel that the player should at the same time be something like an editor: must assemble works that he believes in, and that, with all their diversity, still express something fundamental in the editor himself—with the not inconsiderable difference that, in the case of the recitalist, the "editor" not only makes but also defends his choice in the reproduction of these works.

The "hanging" of an art-gallery wall is an operation that can make or mar a painter's showing. It calls for deciding how to let one work—or sometimes one splash of colour—dominate the wall, radiating outward and enhancing the lesser works around it, or to let the others explain and lead toward the dominating work. In musical programmes, this policy is preferable to following and perpetuating concert formulæ that may have been successful in their day and for a particular exponent of that time but which will probably spell disaster for the imitator, who more often than not imitates at the wrong moment.

I may recall here the advice given me when I first came to the United States in 1925, by a manager who—as he thought —had his "finger on the public pulse" and who was somewhat dismayed by the programmes I presented. "Start a pro-gramme," he once told me, "with the Vitali *Chaconne* and follow it with something like the Wieniawski D Minor Concerto." The suggestion was well meant, but somehow I had never thought of playing just those two works at any of my concerts in America. Presently the explanation of his advice dawned on me: these were precisely the two works that Heifetz had played at that legendary début of his in 1917. . . .

When I compare programmes—particularly violinists' programmes—of the past few seasons with those of my first years in America, I am struck by their variety, enterprise, and awareness of contemporary production. Chronological se-quence seems less important now than it used to be. The criterion in placing works on our programmes is rather their density, weight, mood as they follow each other. Did we not recently see a programme where the pianist placed Debussy's six Ètudes early on the list, to end up with the Bach-Busoni *Chaconne*?

In my series of three matinées, called "A Survey of Three Centuries of Violin Music," at the Town Hall in New York in 1937, I did not go to such lengths as this, but I did contrast styles and forms rather more freely than I had in my Berlin series in 1928. At that time my three programmes consisted in the main of a different Tartini sonata each time, one Bach solo sonata (with a fugue in each instance), one French sonata (those by Debussy and Ravel, and Roussel's, No. 2), and shorter pieces in a somewhat more formalized scheme which I have since more or less discarded.

Since these series of programmes, I have tried to diversify my programmes still further by calling upon composers to collaborate with me in their works (Bartók in New York, Milhaud in Paris, Pál Kadosa in Vienna, and so on), thus creating a little "oasis" in a recital programme where the composer and not the reproducing artist is the centre of interest. I have also enlisted the help of fellow artists like Fritz Stiedry's or Max Goberman's string orchestras for the performance of works like the Mozart Divertimento, No. 17, and Bach and Tartini concerti, a horn-player for Brahms's Horn Trio, and Benny Goodman for the performance of Bartók's *Contrasts* for clarinet, violin and piano; and I have invariably found that, after these excursions into different media of sound, my audience seemed to listen to the rest of the programme with an added zest.

It would perhaps be worth while to investigate such leavenings of the traditional programme with works that call for the collaboration of a guest artist. I do not see why a violin recital should not include the Trio by Ravel, for example, or Mozart's Trio in E major, or one or two Bach arias from the Cantatas with violin obbligato; why a viola-player should not take pride in presenting Debussy's Sonata for Flute, Viola and Harp; and why a pianist should not essay what Artur Schnabel and Alfred Cortot have done so memorably—

collaborate in one of the imperishable song cycles with a partner of his choice. This, however, for just one section of the programme—for that "oasis," as I think of it, for the "let-up" that is needed perhaps oftener than we egocentric performers are willing to admit!

Moreover, even without resorting to these interludes on the regular recital programme, which may entail expenditures in rehearsal time and money beyond the concert-giver's means, there are still many untapped sources of the solo literatures to draw upon.

How many performances of Ernest Bloch's violin-piano sonata, or of one of Biber's violin sonatas, or of Chabrier's Suite for Piano called *Scènes pittoresques*, or of the 'cello version of Bartók's Violin Rhapsody, No. 1, have been listed in the avalanche of New York's recital programmes these last three or four years? Has Tansman's Suite of Four Pieces (violin and piano), or Joseph Achron's *Stempenyu* Suite (recently played by Heifetz), or Theodore Szanto's piano transcriptions of excerpts from Stravinsky's *Rossignol* and *Petruchka*, or Prokofiev's set of *Songs Without Words* for violin and piano— has any of these had its quota of performances by the young performers? How is it that Benjamin Britten's early Suite, Op. 6, published in 1936, had to wait for its first New York performance until 1949, when I presented it in Carnegie Hall? And what about that lovely Duo in A major by Schubert so superbly recorded by Kreisler and Rachmaninoff?

The list is inexhaustible; all that the increasingly improving standard of our recital programmes needs is still more confidence in the constantly expanding audience and in its taste.

An article on programme building by Alexander Fried (apropos of one of my programmes in San Francisco) catalogues his desiderata for a good programme as balancing "the heavy and the light, the smooth and the harsh, the long and the short, the cool and the ardent." He says that a programme listing "old music promises comfort. By offering new music, it arouses curiosity, suspense. . . . And suspense is as valuable in a concert as it is in a story or play."

I have found that the best ideas for my next programme in

a particular city come to me immediately after—I almost said during—the concert I am playing there. It is then that it is easy to imagine how some other work of one's repertory would have shaped up in the present context, instead of the one actually played. It is then also that it is easy to plan a programme that will have exactly the right points of similarity and contrast with the one just played, or with the ones recently presented in that city. This makes for the larger continuity and variety which I think should govern the player in the ensemble of his programmes in cities where he appears annually, just as it should govern the building of each of these programme-units.

This probably is the reason why recitals like the series already mentioned by Josef Hofmann in St. Petersburg in the first decade of this century, or Busoni's Berlin series, or Ignaz Friedman's Copenhagen series during World War I, have yielded such memorable material and remain so vivid to all who attended them. The same observation applies to those cities where my contemporaries and I were able to present five, six, nine, ten different programmes within the space of a few weeks, as in Sydney, Melbourne, Tokyo. It is only in such cases that we approach the enviable status of a painter who in one retrospective show is able to assemble and juxtapose under one roof the fruits of several years or even decades of work. What does the average concert-goer know of our *Gesammterscheinung*—our development on the basis of performances scattered over many years, sometimes with gaps of whole years between? Performances that by their very nature are almost impossible to weigh against each other? (Although some omniscient critics do attempt this seemingly impossible thing, with results that are there for all of us to read and ponder.) Of course, the gramophone and the radio have to a certain extent remedied this situation and made the comparative evaluation of our performances somewhat more feasible.

This comparison of performances (whether of those by the same player spread over a given length of time, or of performances of the same works by about equally qualified players, massed within a short period) should be one of the self-imposed tasks of all conscientious critics. I don't quite know how they could manage it; perhaps by attending contests, examinations, and the like, taking a kind of post-graduate course in performance-criticism. As far as my own experience goes, my duties as member of the jury at the Paris Conservatoire contests and at the Brussels Concours International Eugène Ysaye provided me with invaluable object lessons in the field of critical listening.

It is almost a commonplace to remark on the howlers and "juridical errors" committed by oracular critics of all times and climes and with respect to all sorts of masterpieces. A framed sheet listing the edifying critical judgments passed on Beethoven (by Spohr), on Weber, and on other masters, which I lately saw on the walls of Stravinsky's study (some of which he comments upon in his Harvard lectures entitled *Poétique musicale*), reminded me of certain judgments of this nature that came my way at various times in my own career—and still continue to come. I often consider having some of the particularly choice ones framed and hung on the wall of *my* study!

The headline characterizing Prokofiev's First Violin Concerto as "Farmyard Noises at Queen's Hall" when I first played it at the Royal Philharmonic Society in London in 1924 or 1925 is one of these. And a worthy pendant is the following attempt at critical humour, by a reviewer in one of the largest American cities, after a recent performance of the same work: "It was a musical equivalent of sawing wood that might have contributed substantially to the war effort if the wood had been real, for then there'd have been something to show for it." The opinion of the New York critic of the 'twenties whom the sound patterns of Roussel's Second Sonata reminded of a carpet being beaten also belongs here; I forget his exact words, but I know that at the time they vastly diverted Roussel when I relayed this piece of descriptive criticism to him. That such critical howlers are not confined to our own time is well exemplified in Hanslick's now famous dictum regarding the Tchaikovsky Violin Concerto: "The violin is no longer played, it is yanked about, it is torn asunder, it is beaten black and blue." And later: "Tchaikovsky's

Violin Concerto brings us for the first time to the horrid idea that there may be music that stinks in the ear."

I wonder how a recent so-called witticism I read in an important daily after the broadcast of Stravinsky's Second Symphony, will stand up before the eyes of posterity—or even the generation that follows us: "I was kept in my chair Sunday beyond the end of the [Stravinsky] programme. The back porch water heater had come on. I took it to be another Stravinsky selection and listened for ten minutes before I discovered the difference."

. But perhaps one should be grateful for these would-be obstacles in the path of every good work: they serve to point up the irresistible momentum of these works, as is so unmistakably shown by the present popularity of this same derided Prokofiev Concerto, and of how many other similar works! If regard for the critics' reactions is able to curb the adventurousness of the player in planning his programmes, then the adventurous streak in him must be only skin-deep!

This adventurous spirit must remain steadfast not only in the face of the bogey of reactionary concert reviewers, but also in one's dealings with the powers-that-be who operate before one's recording sessions come to pass. What influence sales statistics have on the suggestions, decisions, and vetoes of the director of repertory, how much of his directing is in turn "directed" from higher up, how his personal artistic credo affects the shaping of the catalogue—all this is still, after many years of recording, a mystery to me. Happy examples are Goddard Lieberson of Columbia, who is a composer in his own right and was a contributor to advanced musical monthlies long before he became director of the Columbia Masterworks Division in America, and Walter Legge, to whose catholic taste, musical sensitivity and amazingly keen ear the English H.M.V. and Columbia catalogues owe so much.

On the whole, my long recording career—dealt with in an earlier chapter—has been singularly free from vetoes and interdictions on the part of these "powers," or repertory-round-table conferences, or whatever one may call them. The story of how I succeeded in getting my way in the case of the Prokofiev Concerto proves that the rule has its exceptions.

CHAPTER XXVI

TO come back to my first seasons in America—after these digressions on programme-building—things soon began to happen, things that had significance for me and that seemed to presage a long and lasting connection with America. Contrasting significantly with Mr. Bagby's somewhat depressing insistence on *Zephyr*, for instance, was a request from Artur Bodanzky and Mrs. Harriet Lanier that I should play Busoni's Concerto during the following season of their admirably planned Friends of Music Series.

This second season and the following ones brought me many other musical satisfactions, like the joint concert with Alfred Cortot at the Library of Congress on Mrs. Elizabeth Sprague Coolidge's birthday, the already-mentioned sonata programme with Gieseking, a similar one with Gabrilowitsch, orchestral appearances under Furtwängler, Fritz Reiner, the Ysaÿe pupil Henry Verbrugghen, Mengelberg, and others. I had already played with Koussevitzky and the late Frederick Stock during my first season. As luck would have it, an attack of the flu forced me to play my Boston Symphony appearance without a rehearsal, my physician having authorized the trip only at the last possible moment and on condition that I skipped the rehearsal scheduled for the day preceding the concert.

A rehearsal-less Beethoven performance was clearly something of a rarity and could have been attempted only with a supreme body of players like the Boston Symphony and a masterly leader like Koussevitzky—though, whatever the outcome of such an emergency performance, the soloist feels cheated of the thrills of a rehearsal such as I described in connection with my Philadelphia Orchestra début.

A rather unusual appearance topped the end of this first season: a repeat performance of the Beethoven Concerto under Stokowski in Philadelphia—a re-engagement during the same season, which naturally meant a great deal to me. Incidentally, my first appearance with the New York Philharmonic during my second season (1926–27) resulted in another such reappearance during that same season; I played under Furtwängler at one of the spring concerts.

This same "unplanned" season brought me another thrilling experience, one that could come about nowhere but in America: the two concerts sponsored by Rodman Wanamaker in the Auditorium of Wanamaker's Department Store in New York. They were given to introduce the priceless Rodman Wanamaker Collection of Stradivari, Guarneri, Amati, and Guadagnini instruments which Thaddeus Rich (then Stokowski's concertmaster) had assembled for him. I played on the "last" Strad, the one called "The Swan," and it was the first time the voice of this incomparable instrument had been heard in that hemisphere. The members of the Philharmonic Orchestra, who accompanied me under the baton of Alfredo Casella, also played instruments of the Wanamaker collection; altogether a galaxy of masterpieces brought to life in one body of sound that remains, I think, unique.

Naturally I was not allowed to take the "Swan" Strad to my hotel room on account of insurance-policy restrictions. It was up in the dust-laden rooms storing Mr. Wanamaker's private collections that I had to practise. They were full of mementos, relics, curiosa; on the walls were photographs of the Pope and of General Pershing, and framed autographs of Napoleon, Edison, and other notables. I seem to recall some Madame Tussaud-like features, too: wax figures of Napoleonic soldiers in authentic uniforms; historic swords and saddles; death-masks without end. And I, walking about these rooms, which were peopled only by memorabilia, conjuring up a ghost-like past, practising fragments of the Bach *Chaconne* on what was also a relic, but a relic that sang out, a living thing amid the dust-covered museum pieces.

As I have indulged in so little fiddle-lore in these pages, an enumeration of the instruments used on these two occasions should follow here, I think, for the record. It is the unexpected find of the programme of the March 30th, 1926, concert in one of my scores that enables me to do this. The players who accompanied me were: First violins: Scipione Guidi, concertmaster, playing a Montagnana, 1747; Hans Lange, playing the "Joachim" Stradivarius, 1723; Arthur Lichstein, playing the "La Chesnaie" Stradivarius, 1687; and Edward Tak, playing the "Dancla" Stradivarius, 1710; Second violins: F. Kuskin, playing a Tecchler, 1722, and Nicolai Berezowsky, playing a Guadagnini; Violas: J. J. Kovarik, principal, playing a Guadagnini, 1780; Leon Barzin, playing a Goffriller, 1727; and M. Cores, playing a Guadagnini; 'Cellos: O. Mazzucchi, assistant solo 'cello, playing a Ruger, 1675, and H. Van Praag, playing a Tecchler, 1730; and Basses: U. Buldrini, principal, playing a Gagliano, and A. Fortier, principal, playing a Testore. The bows used were by Tourte, Voirin, Vuilleaume, Lamy, and Peccate.

The programme also gives the following data on the four Stradivari used on this historic occasion:

1. The "Comte de La Chesnaie" (1687), from the master's early period, when he was still somewhat under the influence of his great teacher Amati, but had already begun his career as an independent *luthier*. Formerly the property of the noted French violinist, Léon Reynier, who sold it in 1869 to his pupil and friend, M. le Comte de La Chesnaie.

2. The "Dancla" (1710), from the "Golden Period," which reached its climax in 1715. Formerly owned by M. Florent, a renowned violinist under the Second Empire, and later the property of Jean Baptiste Charles Dancla, who for fifty years was professor of violin at the Paris Conservatoire.

3. The "Joachim" (1723), from the "Golden Period." For many years the property of Joseph Joachim, who played it in concert all over Europe. It was sold by Joachim to one of his prominent pupils, Enrique Fernández Arbós.

4. The "Chant du Cygne," or "Swan" (1737), from the

final period. Famous as the last violin made by Stradivarius —in the year of his death, when ninety-three years old. So proud was the master of his workmanship during the last years of his life that he formed the habit of writing his age beneath his name on the labels inside the violins of that period.

In his famous book on Stradivarius (1909 edition), Hill refers to this violin in these words: "Several other instruments have been seen by us on the labels of which Stradivari recorded his age. These are : first, a violin dated 1732, "d'anni 89"; second, a violin dated 1735, "d'anni 91"; third, a violoncello dated 1736, "d'anni 92"; fourth, a violin dated 1737, "d'anni 93." This last is probably the instrument mentioned by Count Cozio as belonging in 1822 to Professor Bertuzzi, of Milan. Later the property of M. de St. Senoch, of Paris, it is now owned by a distinguished Brazilian violinist, M. White." Joseph White, who was private violinist to the Emperor Dom Pedro of Brazil, parted with this violin in 1913. Until recently it was held in the private collection of a wealthy European collector. This is perhaps the opportune moment to mention in passing the instrument I am at present using (since 1937). It is the Petrus Guarnerius of Mantua (dated 1701) called the "Count Baldeschi" after its original owner. The definitive work on the Guarneri Family by Hill lists it among the outstanding examples of the master and it has the unusual feature of carrying beside the Guarneri label a hand-written one by the proud original owner stating "Proprieta del Conte Baldeschi."

My former instrument, the one I made many of my recordings with, between 1926 and 1937 was a Petrus Guarnerius of Venice, formerly in the possession of Henri Petri, father of the distinguished pianist and Busoni disciple Egon Petri. It was first used by Henri Petri and later by his son Egon who at that time was still undecided which career to follow, that of a pianist or that of a violinist, being equally proficient on either instrument.

When Egon Petri and I recorded the Brahms D Minor Sonata in the middle 1930's at the Swiss Cottage Studios there was an almost sentimental *rencontre* between Egon Petri and his former beloved Guarnerius !

Those first seasons seem to me in retrospect almost idyllic; so unexacting, thanks to the absence of overorganization, overpromotion, overeagerness of any kind; unstrenuous and comparatively leisurely.

I was a frequent visitor at the Metropolitan Museum of Art, often having my lunch there in the cafeteria among art students, teachers, and museum officials. There must have been something of "make believe" in this predilection of mine, game elements quite unbecoming to my age, I admit, something akin to the sport of children's dressing-up. I was on my first American concert tour, in New York—yes, but was this a reason for denying myself pleasures somewhat outside the pale of West Fifty-seventh Street? I enjoyed being among these vigorous, white-overalled youngsters marked with paint or plaster spots. But perhaps it was simply that I liked playing hooky from the haunts, occupations, and preoccupations associated with a first tour!

Whatever the reason for such escapades, my first two or three seasons brought me enriching experiences that complemented those gathered in many years of museum-going in Europe. There were visits to Miss Helen Frick's gallery, Mrs. Havemeyer's collection, Mr. Widener's home in Philadelphia, Mr. Henry Goldman's roomfuls of masterpieces. Mr. Goldman's eyesight at that time was almost completely gone, and the way in which he nevertheless pointed out to me beauties and felicities of composition or colour or plastic masses visible only to his mind's eye made a poignant impression on me. Mrs. Havemeyer's reminiscences of Mary Cassatt, of this or that Impressionist, of how she had happened on some of the pictures on the overcrowded walls—such were among the valuable by-products of my gallery excursions. At that time, these treasures were not accessible to the general public, and such visits therefore necessitated quite a few preliminary efforts on the part of anyone who, like myself, was not yet well versed in American ways—which, human nature being what it is, only enhanced my receptiveness and awareness.

Although already a much-travelled virtuoso who had toured all European countries, I still seemed to have retained provincialisms and leisurely habits little in keeping with my new environment. I used the telephone as little as I possibly could—a habit traceable to my not having had one installed in my Geneva apartment during my first five or six years there; telegraphed still less; wrote everything in longhand (I still don't use a typewriter); thought even a part-time secretary a luxury to which only politicians, bankers, and industrialists are entitled; and (besides all these impedimenta) I clung to that disconcerting European custom of dropping in on people unannounced.

Once, having a date with Bob Simon to meet him in the lobby of Carnegie Hall—I believe it was to hear Gershwin play his Concerto in F with Walter Damrosch—I decided to advance the time of our meeting by half an hour or so and went up to his apartment, unannounced, just as in those days one would have dropped in on a writer or painter or critic on Montparnasse or in Munich or in the studios of our *vieille ville* section in Geneva. The immediate consequence was some little embarrassment on the part of all concerned, but it quickly wore off and—thanks to this intrusion—I had my first glimpse of the inner workings (kitchenette, fruit juicer, and all) of the ménage of a young, newly-married couple of the literary and musical set in New York. By the way, it was on this occasion that I first came across Mencken's *The American Language*, and I remember well that my amazement—no doubt due to the years I had spent in England, where I had never heard of such a thing as an autochthonous American language—in turn astonished and amused my young host.

I committed another and similar *faux pas* in my early New York days. Having, on the night of my Carnegie Hall début under Stokowski met a young book publisher and his wife who had asked me to look them up, I decided one fine afternoon that I would like to drop in at their office, browse in their library, and have a little chat. I vaguely imagined that a New York publisher's quarters could not be greatly dissimilar to those rather romantic dens and cubicles of some European music publishers I had penetrated before World War I. There was Bartók's publisher, Rozsnyai, in Budapest, whose little office at the back of his modest music shop I remembered; and Hamelle, César Franck's publisher, to whose combined store

and publishing set-up on the Boulevard Malesherbes in Paris
Hubay had introduced me, and whose well-worn black alpaca
jacket and antiquated business methods seemed so well to go
together.   Adding to these memories some less precise ones of
small book-publishing houses in London that I had seen from
the outside only, such as those of Martin Secker, John Lane, and
others, I went expectantly on my way.   Amid the clatter of
typewriters, adding machines, and buzzing telephones and the
constant coming and going among the various offices of this
to my mind *un*bookish atmosphere, I presented my card to a
forbiddingly efficient receptionist, to be told—after a few
minutes' wait—that Mr. and Mrs. X regret, but they are in
conference, and will I come to dinner one night next week? . . .
And I was the poorer by one more shattered, all-too-juvenile
illusion.

I went in, too, for certain other similarly irrational and
wasteful pursuits.   In order to deliver in person a letter of
introduction from a Geneva banker friend to a Wall Street
magnate, I went from West 71st Street all the way to Wall
Street in a taxi—of all things, instead of going by subway
express and avoiding all those innumerable, enervating traffic-
light stops.   The addressee of the letter of introduction—in spite
of my having chosen the (to him) probably least convenient
time, the noon stock-trading hour—received me courteously
but somewhat blankly.   Not belonging to the concert-going
set, he had apparently never so much as heard my name,
and must have taken me for either a potential investor or a
job-seeker.   He asked me what he could do for me.   I was
at a loss to reply, except that I would like to have him attend
my recital.   The banker—who had no interest whatsoever in
music—was probably less inclined and less likely to do this
than he would have been to accede to some more costly
demand such as were frequently made on his purse.   After a
few such wasteful and pointless sorties, small wonder that
eventually I decided to dispense with most of the démarches
thought to be useful to a virtuoso visiting these shores for the
first time.   It was then that I started devoting long hours to
visiting museums and art galleries, just like a gentleman of
leisure.

This quest for impressions that lay outside the field of my own professional interests must have stemmed from a fear of that narrowing effect that an egocentric preoccupation with a chosen field has on most people. The French have an apt word for this: *déformation professionelle*. I was extremely interested in all aspects of the new life that surrounded me, and registered in my mind and commented—often prematurely, like all new arrivals in America—upon all sorts of trivia.

My habit of gathering revealing sidelights, of looking for unintentional humour in advertisements, in speeches, in newspaper reporting, had developed very early through contact with a vanguard review published in Zurich by some Futurists or Dadaists in the turbulent days of 1917 and the following few years. Its title was *Die Aktion*, and one of its departments was called "*Ich schneide die Zeit aus*"—meaning, roughly, "Scrapbook of Our Times." The editors who culled these fragments were guided by much the same social-critical slant that guided—so it seemed to me later—H. L. Mencken's "Americana" department in the *American Mercury*. And when later I came across some of Margaret Marshall's "Notes by the Way" in the *Nation*, and John Dos Passos' device of "Camera Eye" and of "Newsreel," they struck reminiscent and responsive chords in me.

Thus I did not consider it a waste of time to follow in great detail the "drama" of the launching of Mr. Ford's new "Model A" in 1927; to note the elaborate precautions that surrounded the shipping of matts for full-page advertisements, in sealed packages that were to remain unopened until the deadline; or to make a mental note of the specimen first issue of a new weekly that I found in my dentist's waiting-room. This slim and typographically unprepossessing magazine, which then had no advertising to speak of, seemed so expressive of the big city, so fresh and original in its approach, that I forthwith, with the magnanimity of the amateur observer, put it down as headed for quite a future. I've had the satisfaction of seeing that generous prediction of mine come true. The name of that free-sample "little" magazine was the *New Yorker!*

Rubbernecks generally look up at tall buildings; I looked down when entering them and was for some curious reason quite disproportionately impressed by the indestructibility and handsomeness of the cloisonné-like finish of their floors, with their metal-encased designs. I thought: modern office corridors—cloisonné technique descending from far-off centuries; office corridors—purfling of my Guarnerius; here metal bars let into concrete—there thin ribbons of black wood, bent by candle-flame, let into the contour of my violin.

Or, instead of looking down, I looked ahead of me (in a metaphorical sense, too!) and saw glass signs lit up from within: "Elevators to Floors So-and-So," they said with their soft glow, or "Cashier," or "Transportation." A lavishness of this kind, which was *not* the privilege of the few, was bound to impress me, coming as I did from a Europe impoverished by the inflation of post-war years—where in Central European countries I had travelled in railroad coaches despoiled of their brass handles and metal fixtures of all kinds, the leather straps of the windows cut off and probably used to resole some passenger's boots. I have never compared notes with those contemporaries who, like myself, experienced the scarcity of soap in Germany in 1915 and 1916, but I have an idea that no one who has had to use (sparingly!) *ersatz* sand-soap can ever take for granted the waste in American hotels, where it is *de rigueur* to throw away practically unused cakes of soap after one hand-washing. By the same token, it takes a library full of books and music printed on yellowing, brittle pulp-paper, such as all of us contemporaries of these inflationary years have, to make us fully appreciate what the printing by a daily paper like the *New York Times* of a practically indestructible special edition on rag-paper means. It was *these* signs of lavishness that impressed me, and not Mrs. H.'s collection of jade or her fantastically lighted and scientifically heated aviary behind the thick glass wall in her dining-room.

CHAPTER XXVII

ONE of my visits to Harlem was made in the company of Max Reinhardt and Alexander Moissi, of the unforgettable speaking voice and the lithe, feline movements. We happened upon a Negro wedding party at one of the less tourist-infested night spots where we could take in the Negroes' dancing and music in all their abandoned forgetfulness of self and of the onlooker.

One remark of Moissi's I still remember. He deplored, unexpectedly, their sophistication in dancing *with* each other, instead of—as in the "purer" estate of folk-dancing—*in front of* each other. I forget the examples he cited and exactly how he traced this downward trend, as he understood it, but his reasoning certainly convinced me at the moment.

In the light of what he was telling me, the dancing I had seen not so long ago in Madrid's Teatro Pavon took on a new meaning. There I had seen dancing in its pure forms, without the titillating overtones that we have come to associate with it; some of the dancing done by mistresses of the art who were anything but glamorous—heavy-set women some of them, long past the first bloom of youth, dancing in front of the simplest of backdrops, while some middle-aged guitar-player in a nondescript grey ready-made suit sat on a cane chair on the stage, providing the music. My accompanist and I were about the only foreign visitors in that audience of *aficionados*, whose discrimination was evident in the subtle differences in the applause, and the exclamations that rewarded some particularly outstanding dance or flamenco song.

I was always on the alert for manifestations of this folk-spirit which somehow, as soon as the Bartóks and Pedrells and Cecil Sharps have done their work, seem to lose many of their primary, unspoilt characteristics: they seem fated to undergo a process of dilution and adulteration at the hands of the successors to these pioneer folklorists. As Colin McPhee, on the occasion of his return to the island of Bali in 1932 for an extended stay, expressed it: "It was only too clear this music could not survive much longer. A thousand forces were at work to dissolve it."

When Bartók played for me some records he had made of improvised lamentation songs, or rather orations, it was a gripping revelation. Sorrowing peasant women who had lost some dear one—a child, or a grown son—had been induced somehow to face the (to them) terrifying recording machine, chant into it their names and ages, describe their grievous loss in unrhymed song (or rather *Sprechgesang*); they would sometimes break down, sobbing, in the middle of a record. . . .

When Walter Starkie was roaming Hungary and Rumania, fiddling his way into the uncharted regions and into the intimacy of the real gipsy clans—a journey that resulted in his book *Raggle-Taggle*—he happened to hear a concert I gave in Budapest with Bartók, playing (among other things) the latter's Second Sonata. Later I found this characterization in the Starkie book, a characterization that seems to me singularly apt:

> In Bartok's second sonata there was something barbaric about his [Szigeti's] playing, and the strange melodies resembled the fantastic improvisations on flutes by shepherds. The violin revelled in arabesques, but they were more primitive than the Gipsy ones, as though the basis of the music was a primæval rhapsody of the Magyar race before the invasion of the Gipsies. The varying rhythms, too, gave the same impression of Oriental primitiveness, but without a trace of the usual monotony.

Bartók and I made a point of playing this sonata, admittedly one of his most adventurous and problematic works, at all of the many concerts we gave together—in Budapest, Berlin, London, Paris and Rome—and also in New York when in

February, 1928, he was presented in an all-Bartók programme by Pro Musica at the Gallo Theater. Now that he is no longer among us, it is an eternal regret to me that I failed to record it with him when in the spring of 1940 we recorded *Contrasts* (with Benny Goodman) and the Rhapsody No. 1, dedicated to me.

I took it as a very gratifying sign of Bartók's awareness of my interest in folklore that, during the convalescence from his grave illness in 1943, he devoted a good part of one of his letters to me to matters folkloristic.

Asheville, N. C·
Jan. 30th, 1944.

I've started here a very interesting but, as always, long-drawn-out task—one that I had never tried to do before. Strictly speaking it isn't a musical labour. I am cleaning up and collating Wallachian folk-song texts—2000 of them!

I think many interesting things will emerge from this—pertaining to peasants, I mean. For example, that to be jilted, abandoned, is a bigger *malheur* for the girl than for the lad. Of course we knew this all along but now it can be proven black on white with statistical data. Then, that girls (or women) are so much more vehement, full of fury than men. We knew this too, didn't we? There are ever so many more cursing texts about girls vilifying faithless men than vice versa.

These imprecations, by the way, are extremely curious. What a Shakespearian fantasy is revealed in them! It's quite amazing. Alas, I can't quote to you from the Wallachian because you wouldn't understand that tongue. But we Hungarians also have plenty of this kind. Do you remember:

"*May thirteen shelves of medicine empty themselves in thee!*"
"*May nine cartloads of hay and straw rot in thy bed!*"
"*May thy towel cast off flames and thy washing water turn into blood!*"
"*May the Lord plague thee with bread that's bought,*
With bread that's bought, and with a wife who is a whore!"

Bread bought with money—that is something the urban American wouldn't understand, for don't we all buy our bread over here? Yes, but not so the small-propertied peasant. He raises his wheat himself, bakes his own bread, and if frost has hit his harvest, then he has to buy his bread. But where is he to get the money?

(253)

Similarly, it may be incomprehensible to us that the Wallachian girl wishes for things like these: "May the ague smite thee when thou goest to thy wedding!" And after equally "nice" things: "May God curse thee with nine wives!" But this is a kind wish, some would say. *Varietas delectat, etc.*

Quite remarkable are the "indecent" texts, too. They're not of a disgusting barrack-room swinishness but brimful of the most surprising fancies. A riot of good humour and mockery.

Well, such things occupy me now while I await the end of my exile. . . .

In the same letter‡ Bartók speaks of his violin concerto and, with the humility characteristic of the great man, remarks:

What delighted me most was the fact that I found nothing amiss with the instrumentation; I did not have to change a thing. Whereas, as we all know, orchestral "accompaniment" of the violin is a very ticklish matter. The critics—well, they remained true to form, though they wrote a shade more favourably than usual. I wouldn't even mention them were it not for the fact that one delivered himself of a pearl of wisdom to the effect that *he* doesn't think that this work will "supplant" the concerti of Beethoven, Mendelssohn, and Brahms. . . . How could anybody write such a thing? And where is the madman fit for the insane asylum who would *want* his compositions to "supplant" those works? If the critic had written that he doesn't think that my concerto can be placed *beside* those three—or something like that—then the thing would have been all right. Well. . . .

Bartók then speaks of the "sudden improvement" in his health, of his long walks on the wooded slopes of North Carolina, of his weight, which has increased "from 87 pounds in March to 105 pounds now." He comments: "Perhaps it's thanks to this improvement that I was able to write the work Koussevitzky* commissioned—or vice versa! [This was the Concerto for Orchestra.] I worked at it all through September, practically night and day."

When Bartók's serious illness in 1943 was causing us all such grave concern and I was at last allowed to visit him at Mount Sinai Hospital, I found him poring over some Turkish

* True to his folklore principles, Bartók here uses the Hungarian phonetic spelling of the name: Kusszevicki.

‡ Further extracts from Bartók's letters will be found in the Appendix.

poems with the help of a hand-written Turkish-Hungarian dictionary that he himself had compiled. The poems, scattered about on his bedspread, were also in his hand-writing, together with his attempts at translation. Dissatisfied with the efforts of some philologists on his behalf, he was now having a try at it single-handed.

With such thankless tasks did he occupy himself while awaiting the verdict of the hospital researchers, just as later in Asheville he awaited the end of his "exile" to the lovely North Carolina pine woods for reasons of health by collating those Wallachian texts. Unprofitable, too, was the indignation that some well-meaning admirer's gift of an omnibus of abridged Dickens aroused in him: "The temerity of mutilating, digesting, condensing such prose!" And he went on and on, while I marvelled at the detachment of a man whose frail body and depleted energies could spend themselves on things so remote. All this work, all this expenditure of emotion—how "expensive" they were, when the chief concern of his entourage was whether and how he would survive this physical crisis. Through it all he kept plying us with favourite Turkish poems:

> How should I praise thee, my beloved?
> Thine eyes are worth Roumelia, Bosnia;
> In the universe the like of thy soul is not
> to be found—
> The wailing of those who love thee increases.
> All Kars, Ahiska, Erzerum, Van,
> Balk, Bukhara, are not worth thine eyes.
> Never have I seen such playfulness as with thee.
> Thine eyes equal all Istanbul.
> Should I enumerate one hundred thousand towns,
> it would not explain their value;
> Thine eyes are worth the whole universe.
>
> The daughter is her mother's only one;
> My darling, that thy hands, thy henna be
> vermilion,
> That thy life may be honey!
> I have sown lentils; have they sprouted?
> Has the nightingale sung on the branch?
> My daughter, has thy mother forgotten thee?

Folklore memories that mean much to me are those of long sessions with the Soviet Ethnographic Song and Dance troupe, both in Moscow and in Paris, during its season at the Exposition des Arts Decoratifs in 1930. How unforgettable the ineffable phrasing on that primitive reed flute of the Bashkir or Turkmen player whose playing I compared to Kreisler! My wife had the troupe installed in a small family hotel on the Carrefour Haussmann, a stone's throw from our home on Boulevard Haussmann, so that the singers and dancers, who did not speak a word of any occidental language, would be able to call upon her for help in their many small everyday problems.

That these problems, as in the case of beautiful almond-eyed Nahoum, première dancer of her tribe, involved sundry marital beatings and subsequent recriminations and effusive reconciliations only added to the excitement of our little glimpses into tribal oriental life. Sometimes such a feast of reconciliation would be celebrated right in our home with a succulent *shashlik* prepared by the offending husband, partner of Nahoum and a famous dancer in his own right. We had to get the ritually-slaughtered young lamb from some Oriental butcher in the outskirts of Paris, as none other would do.

After the feast, songs and dances of these supple, soft-eyed children of the East would so transform the customary atmosphere of our quarters that when they had gone back to their hotel we had to pinch ourselves to come back to the Boulevard Haussmann—to Aubusson rugs, Sèvres china, books, pictures, and all the trappings of "civilized" living.

Such contacts got me into the habit of being on the alert for manifestations of the folk-spirit wherever my tours happened to take me. Whether it was the fife-and-drum-accompanied dancing on Pamplona's Plaza del Castillo, or Dinicu's or Boulanger's Roumanian Gipsy bands in Bucharest, or the Teatro Pavon in Madrid, or a session with the erudite Dr. Kunst and his unique ethnographical record collection in the Dutch East Indies, I was always an interested listener and observer. During my first American tours, too, I looked for —and sometimes thought I had found—traces of folkways,

GETI AND IGOR STRAVINSKY RELAXING AFTER RECORDING STRAVINSKY'S *DUO CONCERTANT*, HOLLYWOOD, 1945

SZIGETI AND BRUNO WALTER LISTENING TO A PLAY-BACK OF THEIR RECORDING OF THE BEETHOV
CONCERTO, CARNEGIE HALL, NEW YORK, APRIL, 1947

though not necessarily tied up with music. I ran across these sometimes in the most unexpected places.

For instance, there was that shoeshine I got in Detroit. The lusty young Negro's rhythmic urge and impulse while he was shining my shoes absolutely fascinated me. How he whipped about that strip of flannel, how he snapped it in the air at regular, syncopated intervals, to the rhythm of a tune audible only to his inner ear! In that moment I seemed to be in the presence of something the Negro is born with and to which, I suppose, jazz owes its being; I seemed to sense the irresistible upwelling of music and rhythm better than while listening to many a sophisticated "name" band.

Again, when I checked into my Pullman space on some night trip I was intrigued by something very different—the unintentionally comic solemnity of the duet between the unctuous bass of the Pullman conductor and the baritone of his railroad colleague. "Low-er seven in car two-twenty-nine," one would chant; and the other would respond, in almost liturgical antiphony: "Low-er seven in car two-twenty-nine."

I side with those who believe in the impact of personal experience, however superficial, as a source of information, rather than in the second-hand variety, however exact and vivid. Failing the former, I am not unwilling to rely upon vicarious experience when it comes not from the "proper sources" but paradoxically from someone I trust and respect who is disinterested in the matter, who has no axe to grind. When, for instance, someone not professionally associated with cooking—like a painter or an actor or a writer—tells me of a new dish, I am more inclined to try it out than if I had found it in a cookery book prepared by a practising master of the craft.

It was none other than Leopold Auer who opened my eyes to certain real-estate phenomena peculiar to American shores: the swift changes in the desirability and value of whole blocks, and the radical promotions and town-planning projects carried out in the bold and youthful American way.

Whenever I would meet the venerable master taking his morning walk on the sunny side of Broadway—I was staying then at the Ansonia—I would walk along with him, adapting my step to his slow gait, and our conversations on these occasions by no means touched only on matters violinistic. It was he who gave me my first inkling of the connection between developments like those then in process on Riverside Drive and real-estate operators walking in on him, unannounced and unsolicited, annoying him with offers to buy his recently acquired brownstone house in the West Seventies which he then had no intention of selling. Curious by-product indeed of the meeting of one violinist with an historic practitioner of the craft on Broadway in the middle 'twenties!

When some years later a former pupil of mine, who had become orchestra leader in the huge hotel in Cleveland owned by the Van Sweringen interests, tried to outline the fabulous operations of the Van Sweringen brothers to me, I remembered the vague intimations of Leopold Auer's talk. Even so, of course, I could not fathom the mysteries of such financial empires as the Van Sweringens had created!

Or, again, no amount of reading about the gang wars in Chicago could measure up in eye-opening impact to that casual remark made to me one night at Chicago's Orchestra Hall by a music-loving doctor attached to the Police Department. I had asked him to come along with me to an after-concert party, and he regretted his inability to join us with the words: "I've got to snatch a little sleep between now and the early morning hours; I mean three or four a.m. You see, the gang shootings generally occur about then, and I am routed out of bed at those unearthly hours pretty regularly." It was chance remarks like these that made for more understanding reading of news like that of the "Easter morning" gang shootings some years later.

CHAPTER XXVIII

HOTELS, of course, provided a fertile field of observation for the greenhorn that I was and the "observer" of the American scene that I fancied myself to be.

The impersonality of the American "Grand Hotel" disconcerted me. What struck me first of all was the absence of the all-knowing, all-divining, all-providing, multilingual "concierge" or "portier" of its European counterpart. The Herr Portier—as he used to be called in Central Europe—was usually bespectacled and clad in a brass-buttoned Prince Albert coat; touching his cap whenever you passed his "loge," he handed you your mail (after having scanned the postmarks, observed return addresses on the envelopes and the like, and most certainly drawn some conclusions from them). He it was who also transmitted telephone messages, gave advice to tourists bent on sight-seeing, planned their shopping expeditions, guided them when it came to shows or opera (after making a shrewd analysis of the inquirer's mental and æsthetic level), and was not above monitoring the nocturnal exploits of unattached young males. Thus, after a few days of this, he commonly knew more about the hotel's guest than the latter—sometimes!—desired.

The anonymity of the guest in a big New York hotel, the necessity of spelling one's name again and again in a vain effort to establish one's identity, amazed me. True, there was the "transportation desk," as well as the mail desk. The reception clerk would probably prove willing and able to answer most of one's questions. In some hotels there were also "Ask Mr. X" units placed at strategic points in the rambling lobbies, and these obviously were supposed to supplant the Herr Portier. But what, I asked myself, could ever replace the benevolent omniscience of this bespectacled cicerone, diplomat, (with a dash of the spy in him!) psychologist, and entremetteur?

As I see it now, I just could not get used to all this division of labour, and my admiration for some of the feats of interdepartmental organization remains to this day platonic rather than heartfelt. When I lately chanced upon Thoreau's exclamation about division of labour, it touched a responsive chord. "Where is this division of labour to end?" Thoreau exclaims, "and what object does it finally serve? No doubt another *may* also think for me; but it is not therefore desirable that he should do so to the exclusion of my thinking for myself."

In an effort to grasp the inner workings of hotels I once, with my habit of minding what is none of my business, read the whole of the booklet addressed by a well-known hotel man to his employees, the gist of which could be summed up in the classic sentence: "The customer is always right." The coddling of the customer, the condoning of anything he sees fit to do in a hotel, struck me from the very first. Supposing he carried off his room key, thereby inconveniencing both the hotel and the next occupant of the room: the delinquent client is begged to drop said key into any mail box, without even going to the trouble of wrapping the bulky article or of paying postage on it! No—the hotel will be *glad* to pay the postage, and the United States postal service will transport this key, weighing several ounces, for the price of an ordinary letter of barely half an ounce! I suppose that the slabs of glass on hotel dressers and night table were an afterthought on the part of the hotel corporations—after millions of dressers and night tables showed the scars of cigarette burns. . . . I have never come across any admonishment of the customer, warning him against the "wages" of his schoolboyish little sins.

Musings like these helped me later on to understand many a situation in other fields—for one, the meek and mild attitude of a certain orchestra manager toward the president of the board. It was once again the Prokofiev Concerto that had caused "trouble," and the manager in question simply transmitted to me his president's indignation at my playing such a "revolting" piece of music as the latter judged Prokofiev's Concerto in D to be. I expected that the manager would add a few words of personal, off-the-record protest against this somewhat highhanded bit of music criticism, or rather music censorship "from above," but I waited in vain. . . . The manager evidently regarded the president as the "customer," while we—composer, conductor, soloist, orchestra and manager—were the purveyors who had been found wanting by this customer.

To return to my hotel experiences, unused though I was to American ways I knew enough not to commit the classic blunder of the novice in putting my shoes in front of my door at night for a shine. Nevertheless, I did make some *faux pas*, like the one of wanting to tip the austere Finnish cleaning woman who, unused to being tipped in this huge, impersonal hotel, interpreted my intentions in a manner that could have made me indignant had it not provoked me to good, wholesome laughter.

It must not be assumed, however, that I was incurably addicted to our somewhat anachronistic European ways. I did appreciate the fact that the degree of cleanliness of my room was not dependent on the size of my tip to the chambermaid, and I did not mourn the absence of such obsequious floor-waiters in tails as in Europe handle room service from pantries located on each floor. I liked the easy ways of the personnel, who do not call you the equivalent of "Your Honour" or "Gracious Seigneur" or "Worshipful Sir" (I am translating from Central European usage).

The American waitress who asks, "What will you folks have to drink?" is a refreshing change from these survivals of anachronistic servility. I also rejoiced in the absence of the Parisian *plaçeuse* who at the cinema or the opera, the Salle Pleyel, or the Folies Bergère shows you to your seat and steadfastly waits for her tip while you step on people's toes in the darkened auditorium and fumble for small change.

But such is the force of habit that, while admiring these simplifications of daily life and the smoothly functioning interlocking system in organizations I had dealings with, I still harked back—a little nostalgically—to some of the brilliant "one-man shows" of our antiquated European set-up; not only, that is, to the versatile Herr Portier but also to the old-style impresario, who combined in his person all those functions that here are distributed among a number of departments: talent-discoverer, promoter, publicity engineer, programme counsellor, sales department, railroad routing expert, and what not! When, for instance, I auditioned to one of my first impresarios, Norbert Salter, very early in my career, he himself accompanied me, and expertly too, in the Mendelssohn Concerto. And I often recalled impresario K. or E. S. in Central Europe, or soft-spoken, grey-haired Miss B. in London. It was Miss B. who recurred to me most often, perhaps, and her calm, efficient way; how, after having attended to her principal job, the booking itself, she would thereupon proceed to look after all the details—would look up the most convenient train, arrange for me to be met at the station and entertained after the concert, would make hotel reservations (sometimes, as in Scotland, instructing the hotel to have a blazing fire welcome me in my room), see that the necessary orchestral parts were available, arrange convenient rehearsal times, co-ordinate recording activities and interests with those of the concert field, procure the Home Office authorization required before the foreign artist could apply for a visa, and perhaps—to top it all—help him to cope with some income-tax formalities! Truly an imposing "one-man show"!

I confess that to this day I am gratefully aware of this personal touch whenever I meet with it here in America, too —when I hear of a publisher who writes twenty-page letters of advice to the young author whom he has under contract; when the president of a great corporation shows me the originals of the colour advertising pages destined for *Fortune* or *Time* magazine and holds forth on their respective merits like the true connoisseur he is in private life; when some famous restaurateur doesn't disdain to make his presence felt in the kitchen from time to time. Or, I might add, when a superb conductor like George Szell is able to meet the whole violin section of an orchestra on common ground and suggests ingenious fingerings and bowings that would never have occurred to that body of experts.

I still cling to the old-time notion of the "boss" who does things himself, sometimes unexpected things, like Diaghilev at a ballet rehearsal or the late Mr. Ochs, of the *New York Times*, when he ordered some article, paid for it, read it, and— perhaps discarded it after reading.

CHAPTER XXIX

——————·{◇}·——————

THE miracles of music distribution wrought by the
two nation-wide American audience-organizing associations have amazed me. So have the book clubs. And
right from the time of the inception of the concert-organizing
plans in the 'twenties I fancied I could detect some common
traits in the two "packaging" projects. Both the book and
the music organizations have the obvious and immense
advantage of insuring a steady consumption of cultural
products by an ever-growing audience. The accent on best
sellers in some of the book club plans seems to me to correspond
to a similar trend in the music field; one has only to substitute
the word "sensation" for "best seller" and one has a workable
analogy. But then, I have wondered, how many of the
distributed books remain unread, or are merely skimmed
over? How many musical offerings remain essentially un-
heard, even though the concert subscribers are present in the
body? For, indeed, mere physical presence at a concert does
not necessarily imply *hearing*—listening in an active, collabor-
ative sense.

So in 1926 began my series of annual tours of the United
States, a series that is still in progress and every unit of which
still constitutes a voyage of discovery. How could it be
otherwise? An example: I arrive in a California market
town of no more than a hundred thousand inhabitants, and
there in the hotel lobby are Franz Marc's *Blue Riders* and
copies of other Marc paintings bigger than life—well-painted

copies, too. By what fortuitous circumstances, I ask myself, did these canvases find their way into precisely this hotel lobby? Here I am, in the nineteen-forties, in a fruit-growing section of California, with a substantial sprinkling of Armenians among the population, face to face with the *Blue Riders* at which I used to stare wide-eyed in that gallery window on Berlin's Potsdamerstrasse around 1911 or 1912 when the group headed by Marc and Kandinsky gave its first shows!

Here in the lobby, with its cigarette-vendors and pinball machines, these unexpected canvases set me musing about Kandinsky; about the heroic days of those first *Blue Rider* group shows he used to describe to me, when the first champions of his art had to open court proceedings against art critics who slandered him in the press; about his Dessau Bauhaus days in the 'twenties and our chance meeting in the train speeding from Berlin to Dessau. "You see, I timed my return home so that I wouldn't miss your Beethoven Concerto to-morrow!" he had said, introducing himself. (This Dessau Bauhaus, by the way, has had a potent influence on the newer, more functional trends in architecture, decoration, and furniture.

I thought of those long hours spent in Kandinsky's Paris studio in the late 'thirties, of my mental exhilaration when handling his unframed canvases, of his talk, of the line he drew between "abstract" and "non-objective" art. I remembered the amazing youthfulness of the master, then already over seventy. He had something Toscanini-like in his unimpaired alertness and the thrust of his personality, I always thought.

Then came a swift transition to the present: what did the German occupation of Paris do to such a key personality of a movement the Nazis proscribed as "degenerate art"? How, I wondered, have they taken their revenge on one who during the Munich days had, with a characteristic gesture, relinquished his status of naturalized German citizen to become French? *

While musing on all this, almost forgetting where I was, I started toward my room. And I was brought back to the present by what I saw on the walls everywhere—in my room,

---

* This was written during the war and before news of the passing away of Kandinsky reached me.

along the corridors, in the dining-room: rare California ferns and mountain flowers carefully pressed and framed; a collection probably representing happy years of patient gathering and assembling of these beautiful things.

It is encounters such as these that colour a seemingly endless round of concerts—a round mistakenly supposed to generate a feeling of staleness and routine, at least with respect to the outward circumstances of the virtuoso career. How often, depending on the trouper's *Weltanschauung*, does this element of staleness and routine manage to eat itself into the very core of things, even into the player's attitude toward music itself? . . .

To be able to play Mozart and Beethoven and Stravinsky and César Franck in a little community of fifteen thousand inhabitants is surely something to wonder at. But when, on the next day, one reads on the masthead of the local paper the proud words "Pulitzer Prize Winner"; when one sees pasted on the office windows of this newspaper some seven-week-old issues of the London *Times* and the *Daily Telegraph*; when one realizes that this small-town daily evidently keeps a complete file of these mighty fellow-dailies—one wonders still more. It is then that it dawns on one how peevishly unjust we European artists were when, during our first tours in the United States, we used to hanker for the picturesque and the unexpected that are so characteristic of our European small towns, and repeated endless clichés about the monotony of touring in this country. If we failed to glean worth-while experiences, meet with "profiles," in the course of these trips, the fault was probably our own.

That wiry old man whom I seem to see and hear still, talking about his particular field and interests and creative urges. . . . It was a thirty-mile ride, and I started him talking and kept prodding him. With a less willing listener by his side he might have remained silent; or the roles might have been reversed and *he* become the questioner (and I the loser in the process). As it happened, I was listening to a man who clearly belonged to the race of industrial empire builders and who gave me fleeting glimpses of the America I had read about in Lincoln Steffens, Dreiser and Mencken. I listened to him with growing sympathy and respect, both of which are invariably aroused in me by any ardent and sincere inside story told by a man about his life-work. He was all of a piece and I liked him.

His field was the telephone. Besides having built up an organization that reached into many States from coast to coast, he had made several inventions, some of which, involving automatic dialling and accounting of long-distance calls, he succeeded in explaining even to my congenitally non-technical mind. The "buying up of town," as he called his typical negotiation when enlarging his telephone network, the subtle way he had of evaluating a town's potentialities, his tactics of waiting for independent operators to go nearly bankrupt and then buying them out, his adamant anti-union attitude, his unshakable conviction that any government operation of a public utility is "nefarious"—all this and much more came out during that thirty-mile ride.

There were also some unexpected glimpses of the man—unexpected, though once you integrated them with his dominant traits they made sense; they belonged; they helped to cut the single cloth of him that made him so unequivocally all of a piece.

I asked him about certain licence fees that came to him from some of his devices.

"Oh, those revenues," he said casually. "I just turn them over to one or the other of my churches around here. They help pay for repairs. You know—windows, pipe organs, and so on. It's my idea of having a good time, seeing what these unexpected windfalls do to them."

What he had said about the "nefariousness" of all government operation was very interesting to one who had travelled as extensively in the Soviet Union as I had done; I had seen the opposite school of thought in operation. I had also observed at rather close range the workings of the British postal and telegraph systems, especially their non-profit-making cultural and artistic offshoots like the British Broadcasting Corporation and the G.P.O. (Documentary) Film Unit, in which my friend Alberto Cavalcanti had been one of the principal artisans.

We continued toward our destination, the railroad junction, and as he went on talking of the telephone—not as a business nor as a source of dividends, but as the "telephone art," of which a non-initiate like myself could, of course, have no inkling—I felt an ever closer kinship with this shyly self-revealed fellow "art-worker." His attitude touched me; there was a hint of the mystic in him as he spoke of the never-ending research, of the creative satisfaction that sometimes is his, of the comparative anonymity of the builders of the big edifice, among whom he counted himself; in the last I thought I sensed a note of resignation.

This concept of the building of a big edifice by anonymous workers struck a responsive chord in me. I recalled the builders of the medieval cathedrals, cathedrals that in some cases took centuries to build and then were still not considered finished. The body of technological achievement called the telephone, the synthesis of innumerable partial inventions, of improvements, seemed just so much unfinished business to my companion. There was still a lot of work to be done, just as there is in any art, and I felt that men of his stamp would do it.

Even his avocations were along the line of research. During our trip he showed me from afar a little island to which he retires to think out problems and to make experiments connected with the conservation of food by freezing. In this connection he spoke of the not at all remote possibility of freezing foodstuffs, say the meat of a watermelon, for the fantastic period of twenty-five years—and as casually as I should speak of twenty-five minutes. His singling out the meat of a watermelon struck me with particular impact. It brought back memories of my refrigeratorless childhood in Máramaros-Sziget when watermelons had to be lowered on a string into our deep well whenever we wanted a cool slice for our midday meal on a hot August day. . . .

This typically American pioneer type brings to my mind a rather different portrait of a self-made man, a portly old banker of German extraction who also had become a leader in his field. Since each of these two men headed a concert group as a part of his civic duty, they seem to me to typify the widely differing ways in which music can be served by civic-minded Americans. The telephone magnate did it, indeed, entirely from a sense of duty, acting as a sort of figure-head because (as he explained apologetically) he couldn't "carry a tune"; whereas the banker was intensely musical and sang in the male choir over which he presided. I suppose it is not far-fetched to attribute to his nostalgia for the land of his birth his endowing, building up, and presiding over this musical unit, which was patterned after the German model familiar in the end of the nineteenth century. It managed to fuse into one indivisible whole many heterogeneous elements that he must have identified with his German homeland: the finest type of chamber music; *gutbürgerlich Männerchor* singing by amateurs, and companionable Sunday afternoon beer-drinking in dark-brown-stained "Gothic" clubrooms, their walls covered with framed funny postcards, mementos of European trips, and with group photographs of the choir on its excursions. Bartenders with rolled-up shirt-sleeves, whom the members called by name, completed the picture of an active musical interest.

Season after season I returned to play in the city in which this banker was the benevolent musical autocrat. With no committee to influence his choice of soloists, he could indulge year after year in his favourite string quartet (the Flonzaley group), his favourite pianist or violinist or Lieder singer, with perhaps a 'cellist for a change.

The contracts he signed had a curious clause, written in by his hand: "The artist agrees to arrive in the city the evening preceding the Sunday afternoon matinée"; this meant nothing less than that "his artists" were not to be booked anywhere near by the night before their appearance—a sacrifice which the old gentleman's liberality in the matter of fees made well worth while to artist and management alike. Thus he could assure himself (by telephoning to the hotel on Saturday evening) that the guest artist would spend a restful night before the matinée and would not arrive at the last moment, panting, perhaps to change into concert clothes backstage. (Some such incident must have caused the "paternal employer" to write in this odd contract clause.) Although not specified in the contract, it was understood that he would "partake" of beer and cold cuts in the Bierstube after the matinée; and, whenever my railroad schedule would not permit a sufficiently leisurely and *gemütlich* session at the president's table, he would call to Hans or Fritz to wrap up some slices of liverwurst and salami for the departing virtuoso.

Such picturesque reminders of the Old World and of habits that we no longer associate with touring are of course no more than interludes, and I took—and continue to take—them for pleasant enough survivals of the past, and as no more than that.

The encounters and patterns that have a real meaning to me are those that point to the future and which are to my mind unmistakable American in their implications. There is, for instance, that intensely musical and discriminatingly perceptive young man who owns a record shop and who with a bold gesture branches into concert promotion in his city, taking in his stride rebuffs, discouragements, inimical moves against his ventures. He is out to create a counterblast to the inert star system which the old-established concert purveyor of his city follows as the line of least resistance, and the young crusader seems to be having his way after all, gloomy prognostications to the contrary notwithstanding. Seeing this enthusiast among his private collection of records and scores, and hearing him discuss Scarlatti sonatas, the *Goldberg* Variations, the differences between Tovey's and Schnabel's editorial views on Beethoven sonatas, it is difficult to realize that the record shop and concert management he runs are his *business* and not an avocation. One is reminded of the youngster who dreamed he was employed in a candy factory —and then had his dream come true.

Then there is the boy, born to luxury (his mother is one of the highest-paid creative workers in the moving-picture industry), who does usher work during the summer symphony series, spending all his earnings on a library of record albums, on scores, on lessons.

And how touching the expression of a typically American civic pride in those two high-school kids I met in Mississippi!

Their music enthusiasm found an outlet first in a little music magazine that they themselves wrote, edited, and mimeographed, which later advanced to the dignity of an eight-by-five-inch printed publication. I have a copy before me as I write. In their editorials they admonish their elders and crusade for their home town's place in the sun, musically speaking: Why no local opera this season? Why are our better teachers moving away from here? Why has the local orchestra been disbanded? Then after these S O S calls come some constructive suggestions: Send more and more postal cards and telephone calls to the local radio station, asking for music contests and the like. And there are quotations about music from as diverse sources as Luther Burbank and Confucius, topped by Sydney Smith's definition of music as "the only cheap and unpunished rapture upon earth." What a heartwarming answer to that hoary old cliché about the inescapable commercialization of the American music scene! And the popular band leader whose initiative and prosperity provided the start for that brilliant young conductor and his choral group—so much more important to the cause of music than yet another sensational virtuoso . . . that son of one of the patrician families of New York whose work on behalf of the social betterment of the Negro musician, whose critical writings on jazz and whose talent-scout activities are all expressions of the same healthy, restless dissatisfaction with "things as they are" . . . these typify essential Americanism for me.

This is the spirit that put untried young organists, and conductors at Broadway movie theatres, at the helm of great orchestras and with results that have made and are making musical history. This is the adventurousness that guides young radio departmental heads and conductors who plan some pioneering "sustaining" series, as opposed to the commercially sponsored music, do their planning over the heads of their superiors, and somehow or other manage to make both ends meet when it comes to budgeting. It is the spirit that prompted one young society woman to create and finance out of her private means a little rallying point for devotees of progressive art in one American city of coal and steel. Housed in one room of the "Little Theatre" building of that city, it contained a well-stocked art reference library, a gramophone, with a substantial collection of records, travelling exhibits from the New York Museum of Modern Art, and showings of films from the film library of the same institution. After the sombre marble and bronze and gilt of some of the public building interiors of her city, it was refreshing indeed to go there and see some Calder mobiles and assist in the evening at the projection of the silent film *Jeanne d'Arc* with Falconetti in the role of Joan—a film I had not seen since 1928 when it created so much discussion in Paris.

It is no doubt easy to quote the delectable inanities of the Helen Hokinson type of music-club woman, to smile at musical quizzes—in a word, to summarize the musical scene in the superior and debunking way we all know. So easy that I offer my own Hokinson favourite. The cartoon shows two rotund, fur-bedecked, chinless clubwomen, with perky little hats perilously perched on their jaunty coiffures, chatting in the streamlined reception lounge of a Fifth Avenue beauty salon. The caption reads: "I don't know, I sort of hate to waste a facial on the New Friends of Music."

As for friends of music without a capital F or M, I don't think I have ever met more refreshingly fervent ones than during a visit to the High School of Music and Art in New York City. To be surrounded by those eager, young, up-turned faces while I was listening to and commenting upon the playing of their star pupil blotted out distasteful memories —like a certain incident in Carnegie Hall. It was a sold-out concert and I was standing in a group of rapt devotees listening to music that was ineffably Toscanini when I was shocked out of absorption by a lady who, leaving her orchestra seat, walked by and calmly asked one of us if he would like to take her seat for the Beethoven symphony that was to conclude the programme. I imagine he was glad to listen to this, sitting down, but I have wondered since (as I did then) what *could* have been important enough—what tea-party or shopping expedition—to that worthy season-ticket holder to make her leave Carnegie Hall just before Toscanini and Beethoven.

It is the two youngsters who broke in on my hammock

siesta one warm summer afternoon not long ago whom I prefer to think of as representing the future clubwoman and the future executive member of some symphony board—not the Hokinson ladies. This boy and girl, about fifteen or sixteen years old, came into our California garden unannounced and asked my wife in a disarmingly uninhibited way if they might talk to me for a little while.

To my surprise they talked of the Alban Berg Concerto which I was then studying, of orange-growing, of their parents' experiences with avocado trees, of the young girl's experiments in interpretative dancing to Shostakovich symphonies (a practice I was quick to deplore), of her plans to study in the sculpture studios of Puccinelli and Carl Milles, and of the boy's journalistic publishing ventures (accomplished with portable typewriter and plenty of carbon paper).

Next day, on returning from an evening ride, we found at the entrance of our home a case of oranges and a copy of the volume of collected verse we had been discussing. The two youngsters had left them for us.

An encounter like this more than evens out the more conventional ones—the stereotyped questions asked by school paper reporters. "What do you think of jazz?" "Do you find a great difference in audiences?" "Who is your favourite composer?" It also makes up for the stagnant atmosphere of most club teas and the obligatory visiting of local points of interest.

I like to think of this boy and girl as symbolic: symbolic of the stimulation they bring to the more or less tired European. They are like the sturdy American grapevine stock that was used to rejuvenate the worn-out classic vineyards of Bordeaux, after uninterrupted harvesting and the ravages of phylloxera had for decades weakened their vines. Isn't this in a sense what America will be called upon to do in every domain of depleted Europe?

CHAPTER XXX

—··{{❀}}··—

IN the spring of 1931 I made my first tour of the Far East,
going there by way of the Trans-Siberian railway. Two
concerts in Honolulu linked this trip to my sixth round of
concerts in the United States, thus making it a round-the-
world tour. In the spring of 1932 I set out—after the usual
European concert schedule which always preceded and
followed my American tours—for Australia and New Zealand
and made a return tour of the Far East, this time returning
to Europe before starting my American season for 1932–33.
Thus almost two round-the-world tours were crammed into
less than two years, making such a total of concerts that I was
somewhat taken aback on seeing the exact number in print
after my American management chalked up the count for
press release. My second Australian tour was to have been in
the spring of 1941, under the auspices of the Australian
Broadcasting Commission, but the difficulties of insuring my
return to the States obliged me to give up this contract.

A travelogue of trips that covered so much ground in so
little time? And all within the limitations of these pages?
The question is rhetorical. When I seek the reasons for my
reluctance to present "picturesque" accounts—studded, of
course, with the obligatory anecdotes—I suspect that it has
something to do with my being constantly interviewed on
such tours. Giving out unconsidered and superficial impressions, "Chamber of Commerce" enthusiasms, while the tour
is in progress, using up everything usable as one goes along,
for newsprint, in conversation, for impromptu after-supper

speeches (as in Australia), spending everything as if it were small change: all this does something to one. It accounts to a great extent for the reticence that my family and intimate friends used to chide me about. The halting and disconnected impressions I used to retail at the family dinner table on the lighted terrace of our Riviera summer home did not make a brave showing; I had to admit as much to myself. However, I think that my letters to my wife, my "front-line" dispatches as we used to call them, had conveyed the essential features and thus somewhat compensated for my shortcomings as a raconteur.

Bits of opals in their matrices that I brought from Australia; rare ferns from New Zealand, pressed between the pages of an album; jewel-like butterflies and scorpions under glass from Java; tapa cloths from the Fijis, and so on—such souvenirs came to my rescue to some extent in these efforts to relive my travels. Writing as I do now in our new home in California, without any such aids, without even so much as one of my diaries with their meagre jottings, I shall not attempt to outline certain of my other tours: the one to Palestine in 1935, for instance, or the South American tour of 1936, or the South African one in 1938.

When I decided to include in this chapter my letter to a friend of mine who had published it in the Hungarian vanguard revue *Nyugat*, and when I began to translate it into English, I was at first somewhat discouraged to see it revealing that I have the same flaws as a letter-writer that I have as a raconteur. But since it is the only on-the-spot account of this trip available to me, I give it for what it is worth.

Dear Friend: July 12, 1931.

"Circumstances, and my own peculiar inner organization, prevented my keeping the promise (which seemed so easy to make at the time!) that I should take notes about my journey and write to you occasionally. The fact is that to attempt to review one's experiences (and so many of them) while they are still being experienced is not only difficult, but may even result in the lack of truth that inevitably springs from lack of perspective.

How should I begin? How can I sift the important from the unimportant in order to comply with what you expect of me?

Thus far, I have 'escaped' my problem by writing to no one but my wife, and in my letters to her, of course, I have been able to throw everything together pell-mell—abbreviated impressions of Nikko, the 'inside story' of my five concerts in Tokyo, a stomach-ache or the loss of an eraser or some other trivial thing that seemed important on the day when I wrote her. Everything went into these letters; a chat with an American writer of pulp stories; the swim in Repulse Bay at Hong Kong; Yoshiwara; the singing groans of Chinese coolies carrying a heavy load; an unforgettable day in Peiping; a picnic luncheon with several diplomats stationed in Tokyo, where, listening to the conversation and observing the group, I had the feeling that they were acting out a Proustian dialogue in a typical Proust setting, magically transported to the Far East. . . . I went about it in this fragmentary way, getting things out of my system, letting her distil some sort of unity out of it all.

You can well imagine how abnormal travelling in this way is —how much there is to see and experience. Yet one is always up against the one inexorable fact of a touring virtuoso's existence: it is not the day or night or the sights and pleasures that are important, but always those same two hours between seven and nine, with the old repertoire, which is played at hundreds of concerts but which one must experience and confront every time as if it were a first time. In addition to this, there are the innumerable demands made on one during the day. . . .

You know that I happen to be a 'collector of experiences.' As chance would have it, I can now add to them—an earthquake! It occurred on the night of my concert in Tokyo, just after I had played the Beethoven Concerto. I manifested my panic by grabbing the arm of an unknown woman (who unfortunately was not even good-looking), and without rhyme or reason began to kiss her hand, moaning like a baby and dragging her toward the exit.

But I suppose you want to know about the Hungarians I have been meeting or hearing from while here. Telegrams have been sent to me by unknown countrymen from Mukden, Cambodia, etc. The receptions by the Hungarians in Tsien Tsin, Peiping, and Shanghai were really touching. In Shanghai I was given a bouquet by Captain John Risztics of the Hungarian Air Force, who represents the German Junkers firm here. I did not meet Hungarians in Japan, but, strange to say, I was greeted in Hungarian by the first interpreter of the Italian Legation. Fiume is his home town. He greeted me with a Fascist salute, of all things. The attaché of the Czech Legation was with him, and he, too, spoke excellent Hungarian.

Of my six concerts in Tokyo, five were attended by Prince

Kuni (of the Imperial family) and his wife. I was very much impressed with the puppet theatre, *bundaki*, with the performance of the No-play, and with the Kabuki theatre.

I also saw many things not listed in a Cook's tour. I roamed about at night, visited bars where well-bred, pleasant-mannered girls, working as entertainers, discussed Renoir in halting English and were well acquainted with good gramophone records. But I also 'happened' into bars where girl entertainers got drunk long before midnight, though even at such places the unwritten law seems to be not to go too far. The company of these women and a minor flirtation are ostensibly sufficient for the Japanese guests who do not have enough money to be regaled in the tradition of the expensive Geishas. The Japanese visitor appears to be satisfied when a pretty girl touches his coat, looks at him with kittenish playfulness, handles and examines whatever he may have with him—briefcase, packages, or the like—or sips from his glass; in other words, is close to him. This seems to be the modern version of the Geisha tradition. At a 'formal' Geisha dinner the ritual recalls some of those rigidly stylized elements one associates with elocution classes at the Paris Conservatoire or with the excessive traditionalism of the Comédie Française; whereas in these bars you will find an impersonal, stiff, non-sensual femininity, ingratiating mannerisms, stylized childishness.

'Form is important in everything, even in everyday relationships. The people are polite (you are expected to bow three times when introduced, and you inhale noisily to imply that you are 'happy to breathe the same air'). The almost universal fetishism is expressed, in the case of the visiting virtuoso, by incessant demands for autographs, by constant photographing on your arrival, when someone hands you a bouquet, on the platform, at receptions, etc. Once I had to autograph five hundred gramophone records for students, businessmen, housewives, and office girls. As this cross-section of my audience passed in front of me at close range, I was sharply conscious of that fetishism: what puerile happiness they showed at being near the artist, as they bowed formally in his presence and whispered *Aritago* (Thank you)!

What queer superstitions they have in Japan, or rather what senseless aping of things seen in the West (though in a different context)! For instance, there are gauze masks everywhere—on soldiers, messengers, railroad employees, grocery clerks—which give an odd simian look to their noses and mouths. They breathe through this 'disinfected gauze' and feel secure from contamination! The thought of gas attacks flits through one's mind. . . .

In the huge dance halls, one sees taxi dancers who receive ten or twenty sen (a few pence) for every short dance. When they

(277)

leave after closing hours, their tickets are stamped to control unauthorized 'stop-offs' on the way home. This is not by any means for moral reasons, but rather for the protection of state-controlled prostitution against unfair competition!

I remember the churches in Kyoto, with their fairy gardens, and the floors of the 'cheeping corridor,' where the parquet is so artfully joined together that at each step the floor gives forth sounds like the cheeping of birds—so that the enemy in those far-off days could not enter the church at night undiscovered, no matter how stealthy his step! Then there was the line of the faithful in front of the holy well near the church. I could see them from a hill, and while the water spout gushed at them, the priests chanted and thus guaranteed them their 'blessing'; for a down payment, of course!

The anachronism of all this—what contrasts everywhere!—is startlingly apparent when suddenly, on the boulevard in Kyoto, one is confronted with the 'Café Élan-Vital' (testifying, probably, to some undigested Bergson).

At the Kyoto railroad station they sell small baskets of strawberries. With the basket comes a small envelope of sugar and a tiny chopstick, covered with transparent paper. Everything is done in such good taste that it might have been packaged by Rumpelmayer or Sherry. Ten cents.

The Japanese ritual of eating is something I can't even begin to tell you about in this letter! They make a cult out of it. This preoccupation with externals permeates much of their existence. A gift, for instance, must have a ribbon of a certain colour and width; the colour must be white and red and the ribbon must be tied in a particular way.

In the people's park in Tokyo, I mingled with the crowd that stood around gaping, enthralled at the antics of judo and ju-jutsu athletes. The victims were selected from the audience. With an unforgettable and irresistible smile, and with the magnetism with which these troupers all seem to be endowed, the victims were coaxed on to the stage, only to be 'disposed of,' to the great glee of the onlookers. As I stood there, I felt: the same crowd and the same mountebanks as generations and generations ago, as if they had stepped out of an eighteenth-century woodcut—a ritual almost immutable in its rigid formalism, with the sole difference that these survivals of a bygone age are probably content with less money than their predecessors.

I won't even attempt to write about those wonderful impressions of Peiping; I feel rather like merely jotting down a few things, such as the unexpected sight of armoured trains suggesting war activities. I saw youngsters of from fourteen to eighteen years, savage-looking boys in knickers, not even in uniform, exercising, cooking, washing their clothes. Their sleeping tents were decorated with small flags and pin-up photographs of generals. On the station platform were portable guardhouses and soldiers with bayonets. (By the way, passport examination at Harbin was accomplished by seven examiners, no less; in front and behind were soldiers with fixed bayonets.) I saw camouflaged trains, with bits of landscape daubed on them; they were transporting the debris of a blown-up steel bridge. Naturally no one was willing to give me the why and wherefore of all this.*

As for the rest of Peiping, faced with the wonders of the 'Forbidden City,' with the immense conceptions that are almost overdimensional and yet still retain their harmony, never degenerating into the merely 'colossal'; faced with these courtyards, stairways, throne-chambers, I had to smile when certain European clichés came to my mind—like the one about the essentially 'Latin feeling' for equilibrium, for harmony and proportion. I wonder what I shall think of the Place de la Concorde—now! I believe that I shall from now on see everything, even the Acropolis, through different eyes.

They sell postcards in the Forbidden City, but only the cards on top show the city itself; underneath are pornographic pictures. What a reflection on the general run of tourists, rather than on the vendors! Everywhere, on monumental terraces, between splendid columns, one finds incongruous little cloth-covered tables where liquor, lemonade, and sweets are sold during the summer months.

On the Shanghai streets there are always inoculation trucks, for cholera is an ever-present menace. At night, in the heat, hundreds of Chinese sleep on the sidewalks and on the little 'islands' near the roads. It is considered a luxury to sleep in a rocking chair. And near by one may encounter a sign on the window of some dive, like this one: '*Hallo, Hamburg in Sicht!*' (Hello, Hamburg in sight!)

On the boat coming here there was a cage with a small tiger in it, which the sportsman owner was taking to America. Sometimes, on deck, he would wrestle with the tiger as if it were an oversized, playful dog. For three days I saw dolphins playing, chasing one another, shooting out of the water in graceful arcs.

Close to Mukden there is a mausoleum. I was amazed at the subtle psychological build-up with which the Chinese drove home the meaning of such a memorial. This is the mise-en-scene: While the pilgrim slowly walks he is surrounded on both sides by colossal statues of horses, camels, and elephants (signs of the Emperor's

* To-day, of course, I know that these were the first stirrings resulting from those Japanese acts of aggression which culminated in the Mukden Incident of September, 1931.

wealth); then the pilgrim comes upon the towers, the courts, the chapels, and finally, at his destination, a large hill, topped by a solitary tree. Under the tree are the bones of the Emperor, and nothing else. And what a warbling of birds on that late afternoon!

Apropos of trees, in Saigon the small fires of the peasants who sell fruit by the wayside have an incense fragrance like the boudoir of a movie star; it is probably sandalwood. Gardenias here are very common; one can see them on the tables in every tavern.

To my regret I had hardly any Chinese audience in China; mostly Europeans. The concert hall in Peiping was filled with diplomats, with local Europeans, and globe-trotters. As there was no artists' room (the concert was given in the Grand Hotel) I had to go to the kitchen where the Chinese servants were cleaning silverware, and 'warm up' before them. I enjoyed this little interlude and I hope the pleasure was mutual. What added spice to the incident was the knowledge that a few minutes after this little improvised recital for the underprivileged I would be playing for that monocled, dressed-up crowd. . . .

At the beginning of my letter I wrote that the coolies, while unloading, sing. Twelve or fourteen coolies, while carrying heavy rails, sing thus:

or, while carrying their heavy load, two coolies help each other with a duet like this:

In Shanshung a white (Russian) *nassiltchik* took over my luggage—that is, I paid *him*, whereas the yellow coolies were the ones who *carried* the bags.

On the boat for Saigon I had a long conversation with an American writer of best sellers—'nature,' 'hunting,' and 'adventure' stories. He was on his way to Indo-China for a tiger hunt (with the unavowed aim of manufacturing some more pulp stories). With what disdain he talked about Sinclair Lewis, Dreiser, Dos Passos! In Singapore I was the guest of honour of the Rotary Club. By some strange coincidence the speaker was another such 'travel writer,' whose income was said to be considerable.

He does his 'exploring' on a camel or motor-cycle, and in his speech (spiced with so-called 'humour'), he too, very much in the vein of the other writer, attacked 'un-American' men of letters like Sinclair Lewis and Dreiser, who he said 'discredit' America. How instructive, an experience like this . . . this conspiracy against writers who deal in unadorned truth ! . . .

It is now getting late and there is much packing to do to-morrow, so I shall close this interminable letter without rounding it off. I look forward with real pleasure to long talks with you. Talks, yes—for one can then stammer a bit. It is difficult to stammer in writing, perhaps impossible. Yet . . .

A thousand and one warm greetings to both of you. . . ."

CHAPTER XXXI

EVEN though we touring virtuosi, by the very nature of our profession, have little leisure to observe and discuss changing political trends, I couldn't help taking mental note during my visits to Germany (there were two or three of these every season) of the mounting crescendo in those symptoms one could observe in daily life; to name only one example, in the more and more virulent note of political campaigning which culminated in Hitler's seizure of power. Physical and mental changes in human beings are more clearly perceived when substantial intervals elapse between the contacts of observer and observed. In this way my concerts in Germany before and after my midwinter tours in America gave me the "feel" of the changing trends, despite the necessarily superficial nature of one's impressions on such flying visits. Each of these visits would include perhaps half a dozen engagements within barely a fortnight; sometimes I would merely dart through Germany playing a couple of concerts there en route from, say, Brussels to Stockholm.

But the virtuoso's *déformation professionelle*, his vanity and egocentric slant, make him a voracious newspaper reader, especially on tour, when he wants to "size up" at a glance the new territory he has just entered, and this voraciousness helps somewhat. Then, too, the flitting about on the surface of large territories offsets the absence of *inten*siveness—the impossibility of leisurely inquiry, discussion, observation— by a certain *exten*siveness. Besides, he has the advantage of knowing the by-ways of a country and not only the international centres with their stereotyped characteristics. I found, for instance, that merely glancing over the headlines of obscure regional sheets and leafing through pamphlets at a railway station news-stand, say, somewhere in Schleswig-Holstein or in Thuringia, was more revealing than was the corresponding cross-section of the Press that could be gleaned in some important railroad centre. To borrow a simile from the world of the theatre, it seemed as if the Nazis were trying out their new play on some circuit off the beaten track before confronting metropolitan audiences and critics. In places like Eisenach or Erfurt I was sometimes amazed to see pasted up in the windows of bookstores (which were at the same time regional subscription and advertising agencies for all the Nazi dailies and magazines) all those *Beobachters* and *Volkswachts* and *National* something-or-others, with their lists of the "national" minded citizens of the town who had subscribed to this or that sheet, and others naming those who had given up their subscriptions or had failed to subscribe! Some of the latter lists were adorned with scurrilous invectives addressed to the "*undeutsch*" citizens. Such a placard, displayed conspicuously in a town where almost everyone knew everyone else, virtually amounted to a blacklisting (or worse) of the courageous "conscientious objector" or resistor to the rising tide of Nazism. Even though these crude *agent provocateur* methods were only an infinitesimally small detail in the vast master plan, they were the handwriting on the wall, for those who wished to see. . . .

The more or less open boycotting of the powerful Wolff & Sachs concert management in Berlin, my personal representatives, had not by any means started with Hitler's rise to power; it was something that both they and I had noticed and that I had occasionally discussed with my manager since the late 1920s, in the course of our usual professional surveying of my current season and the forecasting of the next—discussed at first almost incredulously, then with an ironic shrug of the shoulders, and only gradually with the concern that these omens should have rated from the beginning.

Even a casual observer like myself could not fail to note the growing emphasis in music criticism—especially in the provincial strongholds of "the movement"—on what constituted "*deutsch*" in art and what it was that merited the opprobrium of "*undeutsch*"—the most devastating critical indictment of all! It was easy to shrug shoulders at a political build-up that did not disdain to use either such petty methods or the more spectacular (and odoriferous) one of throwing stink-bombs in order to break up performances of so-called decadent, "*entartet*" music. One can, of course, regard these things as hardly worth mentioning in comparison with the enormity of the crime they were leading up to, the crime against all that our ethical code and civilization stand for; but I am trying here to recapture the reactions I had at the time instead of reminiscing "synthetically" by hindsight.

Nicolas Slonimsky, in his *Music since* 1900,* finds it worth while to list quite a number of these bomb-throwings. I quote at random:

21 March 1928: A group of conscientious objectors to modern music and jazz throw a stink-bomb in the Budapest Opera Theatre during the Hungarian première of KRENEK'S *Jonny Spielt Auf.*

20 October 1930: Hitlerite students throw stink-bombs at the Frankfort Opera House in protest against the "immoral" opera, *Mahagonny,* by Kurt WEILL, and one Communist is killed by a beer stein during a post-theatrical argument.

Slonimsky also lists these historic dates:

11 March 1928: *Lied der Sturmkolonnen,* Hitlerite hymn to the tune of the *Internationale,* is sung for the first time at Bernau. . . .

14 May 1931: An unruly Fascist strikes TOSCANINI at his concert at Bologna for refusal to lead the orchestra in a performance of the Fascist hymn, *Giovinezza.* . . .

Some of my concerts in Germany coincided with the frenzy of excitement that accompanied Hindenburg's election campaign. I played in Weimar the day he was elected and it was disheartening to see, from the windows of Goethe's house which I was just then visiting, the beflagged square with its milling crowd of rowdies, groups surrounding a truck carrying a loudspeaker or another from which someone was haranguing

* *Music Since* 1900, pp. 298, 328, 333.

the people. At the time this discrepancy between Goethe's world and the one the Nazis were building seemed to me the *non plus ultra* of saddening contrasts. Who could then have imagined the horror of the contrast between Goethe's concept of the "good European" and the nameless atrocities that within the decade were to be committed only a few miles from his house, at Buchenwald.

One of my appearances at the famous old *Museums-Gesellschaft* of Frankfurt-am-Main, where I played Bartók's First Rhapsody for violin and orchestra, occurred on the evening of one of Hitler's election rallies—in the huge Frankfurt Sportpalast, I think. I remember my amused and scornful comments on the fact that on that particular night the traditionally completely filled *Museums Konzert* showed unwonted empty rows of seats because of this "counter-attraction," as I disdainfully called it. And I remember too the half-imploring, half-reproachful look and gesture of the young woman to whom I was talking in this vein, and how she tried to put a stop to my "irreverence" by a sort of apologia for Hitler. It was at this concert, in the midst of the applause that greeted the Bartók work, that a shrill whistle pierced the air. Apparently it came from the gallery, and instinctively I looked up as if searching for the lone demonstrator—a most irrational gesture, by the way. But I followed it with a more rational one: lifting the violin to my chin I struck the exact "double" of the whistled note and "whistled" it back at him with my harmonic; this repartee evoked an outburst of applause which—as often happens in such cases—even surpassed the initial salvos.

Another incident of this kind that I had quite forgotten came back to me when I read a letter from my former manager in Vienna, printed in the *New York Times* of February 22nd, 1942:

To the Music Editor:

On seeing the Ravel sonata for violin and piano programmed by Szigeti in his Carnegie Hall recital on Feb. 25, it brought back some very vivid memories of its performance by Szigeti in Vienna.

It must have been in 1932 or 1933, before Vienna had awakened to the acuteness of the Nazi menace; Josephine Baker, the Negro star from Paris, was drawing packed houses at the premier night club of the capital; the Social-Democratic Arbeiter Sinfonie Konzerte were playing all the advanced symphonic works which later were labelled "Entartete Kunst" (Degenerate Art) by the Nazis; Szigeti gave a recital under my management featuring this then much-discussed work with the famous "Blues" movement.

In all my long managerial experience, this was the first time that such a "bagarre" developed at a recital in venerable Musikvereins-Saal! After the Blues, hoots and cries of "Neger-musik!" and "Pfui!" from the few Nazi provocateurs back of the orchestra stalls soon developed into a free fight, in the course of which the rowdies were ejected. Little did we realize that incidents like these, which we minimized then—they were repeated nightly at Josephine Baker's performances too—were all part of the Nazi master plan: to lump all exotic, advanced art—Stravinsky, Picasso, Schoenberg, Alban Berg, Kandinsky, Marian Anderson, whatever it might be—together as "Negroid" and discredit it as unworthy of the Aryan.

GEORGE KUGEL

New York, Feb. 16, 1942.

When I recently gave the first American broadcast performance of Alban Berg's Violin Concerto (on the General Motors programme under Dimitri Mitropoulos, December 30th, 1945), the composer Jacques de Menasce, a friend of Berg's, told me of a similar *bagarre* that occurred at the same hall at the first concert performance of excerpts from Berg's opera *Lulu* around 1935. There had been quite a commotion during the concert, the already powerful Nazi Party having dispatched some of their roughnecks to demonstrate against this, yet another of those modern "degenerate" musical concoctions. Among other things, they had shouted, "Long live Tchaikovsky!" Berg's reaction was quite typical of his philosophical detachment—a sad, indulgent smile, and just these words: "Why, the poor boys! If they only knew that their grandfathers did exactly the same when Tchaikovsky's Fifth was played in that same hall forty years ago! Only *then* they shouted for some Schubert. . . ."

I am trying hard to avoid interpreting incidents connected with Germany with that brand of hindsight in which one tends to indulge nowadays. But even at the time I seem to have instinctively pigeon-holed my experiences in Germany—in a reflex-like, subconscious manner—in (roughly speaking) two categories, the one labelled "Weimar Republic," the other sensed (uneasily) as having "the shape of things to come." I felt that to the former belonged Hindemith's sunny, modern apartment in the Altstadt of Frankfurt-am-Main, one of a group of such apartments reserved by the municipality—at a token rental, I believe—for distinguished art-workers, men of letters, and the like. It was in some forbidding-looking old building or cloister—"Kuhturm," I think Hindemith's domicile was called—with fortress-like walls and courtyards that made the contrast with the cheerful, "functional" interior all the more striking. A municipality with sufficient artistic clairvoyance to offer inducements to men of the Hindemith stamp was something that at the time seemed to me to more than offset those stink-bomb-throwing students and other disquieting symptoms one heard or saw.

What Kandinsky told me about the Dessau Bauhaus idea —and what I happened to read about it—also belonged to these more reassuring signs of the Weimar Republic interlude, as did the fact that it was the Berlin State Opera which on May 6th, 1930, gave the world première of Darius Milhaud and Paul Claudel's opera, *Christopher Columbus*, under Erich Kleiber's baton. What a lavish production this was, brought about by what unsparing efforts on the part of all concerned! Milhaud, in whose box I sat with André Gide, gave me some statistical data on the almost incredible number of rehearsals that went into the extremely complex task; he spoke with the mingled pride and gratitude composers often show: a slightly perverse pride in the sometimes all but unsurmountable difficulties of their scores, but a corresponding gratitude when the challenges are fully met. . . .

I, too, almost came to settle in the Berlin counterpart of these civic apartments like the one Hindemith was living in, and which seemed to me typical of the Weimar Republic spirit. Two tempting offers to teach were extended to me during these last years of the republic. One was to head the violin master classes at the State Hochschule in Berlin, a position to which Joachim's immense prestige still seemed to cling even a quarter of a century after his passing. Professor Leo Kestenberg, a former Busoni disciple and a great international figure in music education, approached me on behalf of the Prussian Ministry of Fine Arts, where he directed the section for music. When I entered the portals of the Hochschule for my appointment with the director, Franz Schreker, another visit to this same Hochschule a quarter of a century before passed lightning-like before my mind's eye; I had at that time come to assist at one of the venerable Joachim's lessons, a visit I mentioned in an earlier chapter.

During my interview with Schreker I showed no inclination to transfer our home from Paris to Berlin, but I toyed with the idea of compromising for a special class of two or three months' duration. This was not feasible for the Hochschule, though surprisingly enough Schreker would have consented to a five-month teaching period, and to my keeping my home in Paris for the rest of the year; in which case I would have lived during my Berlin tenure in one of the villas the state or the municipality (I don't remember which) set aside for artists, scientists, and the like; I know that Schönberg was one of these. The fates, however, watched over me— as so often—and nothing came of this project.

The other pedagogical offer—which also did not materialize —forms a neat contrast to the preceding and fits well into my formula of the two divergent "categories" of my German experiences. It was to join Furtwängler, Gieseking, and Feuermann in the summer master classes that the newly founded German Music Institute for Foreigners proposed giving in the former Royal Palace of Charlottenburg. A German counterpart to the Fontainebleau Summer Academy must have been visualized by the sponsors and, as I see it now, it had many of the earmarks of the typically German "cultural penetration" concept of which the *Deutscher Schulverein* (sponsoring German-language schools in foreign lands) was but one example. The moving spirit and financial backer was said to be Dr. Roselius, the Hanseatic coffee tycoon whose "Kaffee-Hag" has become a staple in America, as well as on the Continent.

The whole plan seemed somewhat puzzling to me, and still more so the financial underwriting of such a scheme by a Hanseatic merchant prince. However, it was pointed out to me that "Kaffee Hag" was sponsoring other cultural projects too, such as a lavishly produced literary-artistic monthly with exquisite colour plates, and literary contributions by the highest-paid authors both German and foreign, which was—if I am not mistaken—mailed free to a selected list of persons all over the world. (Though, even if there *were* some paid subscriptions, these could never have made the project a profitable one, any more than the Summer School at Schloss Charlottenburg, no matter how large its enrollment, could ever have paid its way.) It is well known now that cultural infiltration was an instrument of pan-German planning for a longer time than one would guess. During World War I, when I was living in Switzerland, I was struck by the initiative of Germany and Austria in sending their great orchestras and theatrical troupes (the Burgtheater, the Reinhardt Theater, and so on) into neutral countries, an initiative they seemed to retain right up to the end of the war. Even when France countered with tours made by the Comédie Française, the Paris Opéra, and the Paris Conservatoire Orchestra under Messager, its "offensive" seems to have been outmanœuvred by that of the Central Powers. An article from Switzerland published in *Modern Music* for February, 1945, describes the World War II version of these same tactics in these words:

> The subjugation of Europe, a military fact for almost four years, was intensified by the strenuous effort of the Germans to take total possession of its spiritual life. The farther back the armies of the Reich have been pressed, the more frantic has been their cultural offensive, both on the ground and over the air waves.

After surveying music inside the Reich and in France, the article describes the case of Switzerland with this significant preamble: "The most coveted neutral battleground has been and still is Switzerland." Then come examples of how well-known Swiss critics have vigorously protested against this "invasion" and propaganda carried on by "musicians, lecturers, and Nazi scholars" who aim at the "progressive indoctrination of the country in the whole intellectual sphere."

In Czechoslovakia the Nazis did not hesitate to insult the national cultural pride of the oppressed Czechs by issuing

K (289)

postage stamps commemorating the Dvořák Centenary and the bicentennial of the Prague première of Mozart's *Don Giovanni*.

That this "cultural offensive" did not wait until 1939 to reopen, but was going full blast in the middle thirties, was affirmed to me by my personal representative, the late Dr. Schiff, who in 1933 transferred his managerial activities from Germany to Paris (and later New York). He used to give me concrete examples of "underbidding" by Nazi managerial firms when booking famous German conductors, virtuosi, and singers for symphony and opera engagements in neutral countries, and told me how the Nazi Propaganda Ministry was footing the bill. It was obviously a system of supplementing the moderate fees the neutral "talent-buyers" were paying to these German artists—in other words, a system of "export" subsidies handed out more or less openly by the Goebbels machine!

After these examples of German high-pressure methods it is refreshing to turn to Sir Thomas Beecham's autobiography for a glimpse of musical propaganda as practised by the British during World War I, and apparently practised with an engaging nonchalance. He tells how it had been "suggested by a member of the Government" that he organize a series of concerts, to be conducted by him (in Italy, I believe); a series that was to be "a composite affair, an odd mixture of the social, political, and artistic in one." This member of the Government, continues Sir Thomas, thought that it might "help at this juncture if some Englishman would go out there, make himself as agreeable as possible, give parties and throw in a few orchestral concerts as well."

A far cry indeed from the methods of the Prussian Ministry of Culture, which appears always to have devoted a good deal of attention to the filling of foreign university chairs, conductorial positions in foreign opera houses, and the like; filling them with men who were *personæ gratæ* with the party then in power; and to this end they were sometimes not above acting the role of educational or theatrical agency. A German conductor who had been "placed" in an important position in Tokyo by Goebbels told me some illuminating

things about the procedure that was followed. This conductor, by the way, outwitted Goebbels in a way that warms
the cockles of the heart. Being an Aryan married to a lady of
Jewish birth, he was given to understand that he could not
continue to hold his position in Germany unless he divorced
her. It was then that this offer to go to Tokyo, which
represented a considerable advance in salary, prestige, and
(one should add) freedom, was made to him. The conductor
accepted, divorced his wife, and went to Tokyo—only to
leave that position after a relatively short term of activity to
come to the United States. In the meanwhile he arranged for
his divorced wife to leave Germany and meet him in the
States, where they remarried and have lived ever since.

On April 1st, 1933, Goebbels took over the German Radio,
and on May 7th, 1933, was the celebration of the centenary of
the birth of Johannes Brahms. The reason these two dates
are thus incongruously linked together in my memory is
that I had been chosen by the German Radio to give the
centenary broadcast of the Brahms Violin Concerto on May
7th. I did not fulfil this assignment, and thus came to an
end over a quarter of a century of almost uninterrupted
playing in a country which, especially in the first years of
our century, functioned, rightly or wrongly, as the supreme
arbiter of musical values.

With Germany non-existent from my point of view—as far
as concerts went—it was interesting to see how intensified
touring of other countries automatically took the place of
this "lost" territory (lost also in a larger sense). South
America, South Africa, Egypt, Palestine, and more frequent
visits to Scandinavia filled out the years between 1933 and
1939. Ever since my boyhood I had played in England
regularly, and it was only natural that those years should
have marked a peak in the number of my appearances there.
The pages I devoted to the carefree years of adolescence that
I spent in England must have made it clear that crossing the
Channel to England would always seem something like a
homecoming for me.

Viewed across the chasm of six years, some of my London

K*   (291)

appearances of the last seasons before World War II are particularly full of meaning to me now. A folder of the 1939 London Music Festival (April 23rd—May 28th), at which I played the Beethoven Concerto, evokes nostalgic memories. The diversity and richness of these musical offerings will be difficult if not impossible to duplicate in years to come. Toscanini conducting the *Missa Solemnis*, Mozart operas at Glyndebourne, Shakespeare at Stratford-on-Avon, Handel's *Fireworks* Music in the open air accompanied by actual fireworks in Regent's Park, Covent Garden opera, the "Old Vic" theatre, Beecham, Bruno Walter, Sir Henry Wood, ballet, and chamber music at Burlington House, at Hampton Court Palace, at the London Museum, the National Gallery, and the Wallace Collection (where I played a Mozart Divertimento with chamber orchestra)—read in 1945 this folder take on a slightly fabulous quality and makes one somewhat dizzy!

For me Sir John Lavery's picture (reproduced in this volume) of one of the musicales at the Viscountess Wimborne's, in the lovely music room at Arlington House (I played there in 1937 or 1938) has a finality about it; it is like a good-bye to a section of one's life and also a good-bye to a period in the life of a great city. The Viscountess's words, on October 6th, 1943, in a letter accompanying the reproduction of the picture, are poignant in their discreet melancholy (one can see her in the right-hand corner of the painting):

> What pleasant days these were! When we all met on those evenings at home. The house has been badly bombed but the concert room itself is quite intact.

(I see the Sitwells, and Siegfried Sassoon talking to William Walton, who was the guiding spirit of these unique gatherings; the night I played the late Paul Cravath was sitting in the front row, not far from—the German Ambassador, Freiherr von Schoen.)

These last years had even then an aura of leave-taking about them, which I, of course, did not admit to myself in so many words. This became especially pronounced after the Munich days of 1938.

CHAPTER XXXII

WHAT had been, until September, 1938, an aura of leave-taking took on suddenly a concrete and disrupting quality immediately after that "Munich" period. To make clear what the war-or-no-war tension of that autumn meant to me would lead me too far afield, but I can at least indicate one small technical aspect those anxious days had for me.

My usual accumulated American contracts for the midwinter season 1938–39 made imperative some quick thinking and quicker action. I couldn't risk being stranded in France with no boat connection to the United States. The probability of war prompted me to pack up my most necessary belongings post-haste, run around for days to obtain Belgian and Scandinavian visas, and make for the port of Antwerp, there to await the results of the Chamberlain-Hitler conferences. If it came to the worst, I was to take a boat to one of the Scandinavian countries, which I could assume would remain neutral or friendly, and from there I could still hope to get passage on a Scandinavian-American liner.

In October, 1938, when the release came—or what we took for release but was only a reprieve—I went back to Paris with all my unused Scandinavian visas. It seemed that I was always "going back to Paris"—going to or coming from. At this time particularly I regretted that I had never had enough leisure there at any one time to meet the painters and writers I wanted to—to explore the *atelier* part of *la vie parisienne*. My trips there were always for short interludes of privacy, of gathering my resources for the next tour. Even when I had the chance to meet one of the Parisians I admired, shyness on both our parts prevented it. On a west-bound Atlantic steamer Julian Green and I had sat together at a captain's luncheon without talking, unaware of each other's identity. Probably misgivings about the purser's perspicacity in selecting "personalities" made us tongue-tied. To think that I had read him and that he—just as certainly—had heard me (for my sonata partner was greatly admired by him and he must have heard us together), and here we sat side by side barely talking to each other!

Back in Paris I breathed again and had the irresistible impulse to revisit all the old haunts—the Louvre, the Musée Guimet, the Bibliothèque Nationale—before starting out on my tour: a sentimental pilgrimage prompted by my premonition of the inevitability of war. I found most of these places still closed, sandbags at the entrances, their principal treasures either transported to various havens of "security" in central France or packed in cases and deposited in the bombproof cellars of the institutions themselves.

This feeling of leave-taking persisted right into 1939. Rereading one of my letters to my wife that she happened to find among her papers made disturbingly real to me the forebodings which plagued so many of us Europeans during what we later found to be only a stay of execution—from the autumn of 1938 to September 1st, 1939. It was written after my 1938–39 tour, one that included as usual the United States as well as the Continent. I was on one of my short spring vacations, preliminary to settling down for our regular summer holidays together.

May 15th, 1939

... As you may have guessed, I couldn't resist that impulse I wrote to you about Wednesday from Plombières: I *did* make the pilgrimage to the Isenheim Altarpiece—by slow and uncomfortable stages, most of the time by those dreadful "regional" buses.

Impulse isn't really the right word. What drew me there just at this time was the gnawing fear that this was perhaps the last chance I might have to see it in its native Alsace. What Jean and Maria told me last month in Strasbourg settled the matter for me. I didn't want it to be another item in the catalogue of unfulfilled promises we make to each other and to ourselves: you know, Corsica, the Fjords, the Puszta . . .

But it was worth it! I forgot all the jolting by the buses when I reached Gérardmer, which is quite beautiful, especially before the tourists descend on it. Then a grand walk to "La Schlucht" on the German-Alsatian border, where I found the walls of the inn where I lunched covered with framed "Franco-German fraternization" mementos, clippings, snapshots (Wilhelm II and so on). . . . Next day to Colmar and to the Altarpiece. . . .

I can't and won't write about that! How could I describe it in a word or two? Its crushing impact on anyone who stands before it? . . . Rather let me tell you of a chance meeting there in front of it. Imagine—all of a sudden I am aware of vaguely familiar faces, foreign accents, foreign accoutrements; there stands Honegger with his wife—Paul Sacher (the Basle conductor, you remember—Bartók's friend who commissioned his "Celesta Music")—Kenneth Wright from the B.B.C.—and one or two others. *Qu'en dis-tu?*

Honegger explained that there had been a première of his at the Sacher concert in Basle the night before and that the B.B.C. had sent Wright over to cover it. How nice of the B.B.C.! How characteristic of them!* They all decided on the spur of the moment to hire a car and come over from Basle to see the Altar! All very well—but that our two independent impulses should have coincided in this way. . . !

Also visited the Museum of the World War of which Hansi (you know "Professor Knatschke" !) is curator. At lunch at the *auberge* (the one in our culinary guide) Hansi was at the table next to mine, being served with visible *empressement* by the *maître d'hôtel* and everybody! Very picturesque in wide-brimmed Quartier Latin hat. Much older and heavier than in his pictures —especially than the photographs on the Warrants for his arrest —"Dead or alive . . . 10,000 or 20,000 marks reward . . ." and so on that the German *Kommandantur* issued in 1915 and 1916 and that are framed in the museum of which the "condemned to death" *in absentia* is now curator. He was eating *foie gras* and trout . . . so was I.

I wonder what the price on Hansi's head was this time, and whether he evaded the Gestapo as successfully as he had

* By "characteristic of them" I was alluding to the gestures the B.B.C. were wont to make toward foreign composers; for instance, when on the death of King George V, January 20th, 1936, they commissioned Hindemith (a German) to compose a *Funeral Music* for viola and orchestra, first played at Queen's Hall on January 22nd—two days later!

the *Kommandantur*. The Alsatian patriot who created the devasting caricature of the bespectacled, knapsack-carrying German tourist called "*Le Professeur Knatschke*," and whose vitriolic wit disquieted the humourless Germans before 1914, must have been one of their prize quarry. Germans are notoriously vulnerable to ridicule: men like Hansi or David Low are their natural enemies and therefore their first targets.

As for the Altar, we know now that Matthias Grünewald's masterpiece, given back to France in 1918 by virtue of the Versailles treaty, had again been carried off by the Germans during World War II. By this time it is back in liberated France. Hindemith's opera *Mathis der Maler* is of course based on the life of this master.

It is the concertless periods in the spring and summer that are set aside in a virtuoso's life for letting up, for vegetating. Once the first fatigue is washed away by relaxation, however, this always seems to lead into a period of taking stock, of planning one's work, of thinking backwards and forwards.

Short cure periods which I sometimes spent at Badgastein or at the Italian spa Montecatini were still more conducive to this kind of day-dreaming and monologuing. Sometimes at these health resorts I made notations on the backs of my menus and sent them to my wife—more for the dietetic wisdom contained on the front of the cards than for the scribblings that replaced regular letter-writing between us.

Most of these I have thrown away; others, from Montecatini, have now—with the passage of time, and with the newsreel picture of the dead Mussolini on the Milan streets still fresh in my mind—acquired a new interest for me. Here are a few of these:

August, 1938

On the walls of a pompous cemetery near Genoa, cluttered up with funeral and æsthetically funereal statuary ("pompous" isn't so far-fetched . . . isn't *Entreprise des Pompes Funèbres* the French designation for funeral parlours?), I see the legend: *Evviva la Casa di Savoia!* Whereas everywhere else, on factory walls, on roofs, it is *Duce* this, *Duce* that, *Duce a Noi*, *Evviva*, the founder of the empire, and so on. Is the cemetery the only remaining sphere of influence of the royalist bill-stickers?

In a telegraph office a notice ordering the public to abandon the use of the antiquated indirect form of address, *Lei*, in favour of *Voi* or *Tu*. Thank God they don't pretend to the equivalent of "citoyen" or "Tovarish"!

Razza, razza . . . everywhere nowadays. How phoney and translated from the German the word sounds. Not even freely translated—anything but. Apparently it is the new toy the Duce throws them from time to time. The toy *Sanzione* already cast off. Though only this morning I came across a marble plaque on some public building exhorting Fascisti never to forget the "ignominy" thrust upon them by the sanctionist bloc in Geneva.

Now that the Duce has imposed a diplomatic uniform on Italian diplomats, eliminating full dress entirely, he evidently is out to do the same to opera conductors: to demonstrate their complete absorption into his "new order" they are to wear a sort of special opera conductors' uniform—whether appearing in Italy or abroad! No more of the internationalism of white tie and tails. Let the plutodemocrats in the Teatro Colón in Buenos Aires or at Covent Garden in London sit up and take notice!

There is a Scuola Communale Giacomo Puccini near Viareggio. On Puccini's table in his drawing-room, a score of *Rimsky-Korsakov's Capriccio espagnol* and a volume of American folk-lore. In a frame two pictures of Puccini cut out from pre-war sixpenny London illustrated newspapers with captions like "Legitimate Successor of Verdi" and "Supplanted Wagner at Covent Garden." Framed, mind you!

A shrug of the shoulders of the newsboy at Genoa when I protested against the penny *Daily Telegraph* costing two lire, whereas the tuppenny *Times* was marked one lire fifty. Who decides what here?

The tiny German professor, not more than five-feet-nothing, approaching the postcard and catalogue stand at the Palazzo Vecchio in Florence—where there is just now an exhibition of arms, shields, swords, and sundry other war implements from Roman times to the nineteenth century—giving the Fascist salute and saying in his best Saxon accent: "*Heil Moozeleeny!*"

To my surprise I meet at the drinking pavilion Maestro P., conductor of the municipal symphony orchestra in Shanghai—

here for the cure same as I. The same ebullient little P. I knew in China in 1931 except that here he is flanked by his wife and daughter who never joined him at his post there. What a hold that world has on anyone who has tasted of life in those climes! When I ask P. whether he is returning to his job in spite of the war, in spite of all that his city is enduring, his eyes light up. Of course he is going back. It is amazing how not only the Chinese but also the foreign settlements can take it, what quality of tenaciousness life has over there. . . .

Got to talking in the train with group of English dancers touring the summer resorts with an Italian troupe called the "Spada Revue" —a seedy, down-at-the-heels girl show. In conversation with one of them, Beryl C., I tried to fathom the mystery of why a perfectly respectable suburban London girl should choose to knock about in discomfort, satisfied with modest pay in inflated lire, without an earthly chance of advancement in her so-called career.

Apparently a combination of reasons: escape from the drabness of lower-middle-class life around Clapham, the lure of travel, the physical exhilaration in her gaudy trappings, and footlights. So she admitted. Also the pitifully small "successes" that these girls record: how this or that young man from Parma or Lucca kept following the troupe for the sake of Myrtle—how another kept calling up long distance that girl "you see over there." They are simply out for the equivalent of the modest opportunities which girls of the well-to-do middle class get automatically through vacations at resort hotels, grand tours on the European continent, and the like—all of which are denied to the small tradesman's or railway official's daughter. These girls' lack of talent—their lack of glamour—the unavoidable mediocrity of the fate they seem to be running away from!

Met Baron Villani at the cure pavilion this morning. He and his Viennese wife full of stories about the recent marriage of King Zog of Albania to Countess Geraldine Apponyi. As Hungarian minister to Rome he attended the wedding and gave away the bride, who is half Hungarian, half American. What a carefully wrought mosaic and how transparent the worthy Baron's pride in his diplomatic artisanship! How difficult it seems to get rid of the traditions of planning, of scheming, of intriguing that this so-called cementing of the "bonds between countries" involves. The end of secret diplomacy indeed!

My Vienna manager having unwittingly tipped them off as to my present whereabouts, who should appear to-day, unannounced, in the typically Japanese fetishist tradition, but the young violin student Masao Araya, camera strapped over his shoulder, accompanied demurely by his equally young wife. An hour lost in listening to him report on his studies in Vienna, advising him academically as to the continuation of said studies ("Pelhaps in Paris with Mister Enesco?"), getting photographed by and with him—and getting rid of them with a courtesy difficult to muster on this hot August day. . . .

Those summers of 1938 and 1939, how they seem to merge into one! . . . How the outbreak of the war, which found us once again in the peaceful Jura mountain retreat of Prémanon, plumb on the Franco-Swiss frontier, struck us as the inevitable conclusion of the "alarums and excursions" of the preceding summer and the Munich crisis of September! The long season of 1938–39, with its far-flung tours, now seems like nothing so much as the mere minutes between prologue and play. These months were like the moments the hushed audience spends under dimming lights in the theatre tensely awaiting the parting of the curtains.

The musical implications of diary entries like: "1938, Dec. 15–17: Cleveland, world première of Bloch Concerto," or "1939, Jan. 9: Carnegie Hall recital with Benny Goodman: world première of Bartók's *Contrasts* for clarinet, violin and piano"—these pale beside the drama inherent in that four weeks' tour which I carried out in November, 1939. Instead of obeying the injunctions of my American managers and heeding the advice of my many virtuoso friends who—most of them—had left Europe in September or October (while the going was still good), I stayed on and played a curious assortment of engagements, spending most of my energies not on the music but on the overcoming of sometimes insuperable obstacles which surrounded the getting of visas in those panicky November days when the German invasion of the Lowlands was being expected by those in the know.

These concerts were: Dublin, with both the French and the German ministers sitting in my audience at the two programmes I gave at the Royal Dublin Society; from there in a blacked-out plane from Brighton to Amsterdam, where I played under Mengelberg the day following the Munich Hofbräu attempt on Hitler's life (Nov. 8th, 1939)—the failure of which, by the way, elicited from the veteran conductor and myself notably divergent reactions; then came Geneva and Lausanne, a pair of engagements that brought me my first and—up to the present (1945)—last visit at the Lake Geneva home of my daughter, who had married Nikita Magaloff early in 1939; my farewell concert in Budapest, with Bartók listening to his *Portrait* for violin and orchestra, a thirty-five-year-old work of his which was fêted like a virtual première; recitals in Zagreb, Novisad, and Belgrade; from there a last glimpse of Venice, and on to Florence, where I had arranged to meet the Bartóks, who were playing a duo-piano recital at the Pitti Palace; visits with them to the Uffizi Galleries and to the incomparable Fra Angelicos in the Museum of St. Mark, and then off to Genoa to board the boat that was to take us to America—for good.

When, walking my dogs in the company of some friend on the golf links adjoining our home, I catch myself making that widely sweeping, slightly comic gesture toward the almost Neapolitan blue of "our" bay (a gesture implying that I have proprietary rights in all this beauty surrounding us), I have to smile inwardly. Barely five years ago the whole region was unknown to us, and now this feeling of having our roots here. . . . A summer vacation that perpetuated itself. A California interlude between a spring and a fall tour that became a thing of permanence. A thing of permanence in which, now, the tours have become the interludes in the real business of living.

That proprietary gesture of mine would be so much more fitting coming from my wife. For she, giving so much of herself to the soil surrounding our house—planning, digging, planting our garden by the sweat of her brow—can rightfully have a feeling of earth-nearness and of root-taking. Indeed, I myself never saw this home of ours (which my wife had bought and furnished while I was on tour) until one memorable day in January, 1942—memorable because, only five hours before my arrival, I had left the plane at Albuquerque in order to make room for some ferrying pilots; and *that* was the plane that crashed shortly afterward, carrying Carole Lombard and all those young pilots to their deaths! Rodzinski, in his telegram of congratulation, called this day my "rebirthday"—as indeed it was. Inevitably the coincidence made a deep mark on me and created an additional bond between the soil and myself.

Anything that helped one to overcome the depression that followed and persisted after May, 1940, that helped one to bear the torturing uncertainty about one's kin in Europe, about one's home and belongings, all at the mercy of the invading oppressor, becomes a part of oneself in a very special way. Settling down somewhere in happier days, with the choice of the whole world spread out before one's greed, could never have this quality of inevitableness that persists even after one is free to roam the world again.

CHAPTER XXXIII

—————·{◇}·—————

B
UT I am rambling on and on, and I see that I still owe
my reader something resembling a conclusion. When
I showed parts of this manuscript to a Hungarian I know
and asked him for comments and suggestions, he said: "Yes,
all well and good, but—where is the mess-edge?" I looked
at him blankly, whereupon he asked me with a deeply concerned expression whether I realized that every book, every
article, every lecture that wants itself to be respected in this
country must have a clearly formulated *message*; urged that
what might perhaps satisfy the well-intentioned reader who is
willing to draw his own conclusions would not be sufficient
for the more superficial one who prefers to have ideas completely "digested" for him. He added, "*You* should know
the type, the concert-goer who reads the programme
annotations *while* you are playing!"

"Message" there shall be none, however, if I can help it.
But I do concede to my Hungarian friend that a final chapter
is possibly the best place (or pretext) for a summary and
generalization on the why and wherefores of the virtuoso
career. What is it exactly that makes for this ever-present and
ever-renewed zest in our profession even after decades of
trouping? It cannot be the love of music pure and simple, for
we share this with multitudes who either are on the receiving
end alone or, not content with this, also aspire to the satisfaction
of making music themselves. There must be other reasons why
we endure the many ordeals and distractions inseparable from

any public and competitive career—for example, the inescapable necessity of constantly polishing one's technique; and others have been implied in these pages. So many of these have little or no connection with the love of music; indeed, this love would be enhanced by their absence. The answer may be in the physical exhilaration that goes with the reputedly intellectual and emotional pursuit of giving public performances of music; but it is only a partial answer, like other explanations that come to mind. One could stress this or that less publicized component of the public performer's make-up: inordinate personal ambition, perhaps a touch of exhibitionism, the didactic urge, perhaps even the sporting or gambling instinct that can be aroused by the palpable rewards of a virtuoso career. Any such generalization is of course a half-truth, to be qualified like all generalizations.

I can speak only for myself, but I think that one thing I have mentioned casually in these pages may well help to answer the question what makes the virtuoso keep going. It was a trilingual poster of a Paris theatre that I saw on a *colonne d'affiches* 'way back in 1908 or thereabouts that gives me the clue. I remember a feeling of contentment which at the time I did not try to account for, and it was only many years later that its source dawned on me. It must have been the simple fact that a performance in a capital city reaches out beyond the linguistic and national limits of its locale. I could add other related fragments to this one, and were I to lump them together I should probably find that they all had something in common—something that, for want of a better and more inclusive description, I would call the irrational pleasure that *communication* gives: communication that transcends the barriers of language, of nationality, of race and that has never ceased, during these four decades of my playing in public, to give *me*, at least, this irrational pleasure.

I seem always, though without formulating it to myself in so many words, to have been more than normally conscious of the factors that make for communication, for understanding, and also of those that work against them. Felix Moscheles, with his Esperanto propaganda; my consumptive Hungarian impresario Joseph Teleki, whose self-taught English (learnt from a Hungarian-English dictionary) enabled him later to translate plays for the English and central·European theatre markets—such men must have left their mark on me.

My mother tongue, Hungarian, with its limited international usefulness, may also have contributed toward this striving to overcome the feeling of isolation imposed by the barrier of language. When one's mother tongue is Hungarian, translating somehow becomes second nature. I mean the unconscious, automatic *mental* translating into some other language of one's random thoughts—of those imaginary dialogues, those drafted, unwritten letters that crowd in on one during walks, journeys, or siestas on ocean trips.

But it is not only in this day-dreaming fashion that "translating" becomes a habit of those born into the cramped language areas of a small country. It seems to me typical of this more than usual adaptability of the Hungarian for other language outlets that the first German daily to be published in Allied-occupied territory in the Rhineland during World War II, the *Kölnischer Kurier*, should have a Hungarian writer and journalist for its editor: Captain Hans Habe, working for the Psychological Warfare Branch of the Army of the United States, author of *A Thousand Shall Fall* and other widely read books, whose name (before he adopted the pen-name of Habe) was Janos Bekessy. Habe also took over supervision of all German-language papers published in Anglo-American-occupied Germany, and issued in Frankfurt a paper put out by many of the people who once were connected with the famed *Frankfurter Zeitung* in its pre-Nazi days. Two of the greatest German publishing houses before the war, S. Fischer and Paul Zsolnay, were founded by men of Hungarian birth; Vertès,, the virtuoso draftsman with the exquisite "Latin" touch, interpreter of the Parisienne's innate elegance, is a Hungarian; both Max Reinhardt and Leslie Howard were of Hungarian descent. These few names will perhaps bear out what I said of the intellectual *Wanderlust* which small countries like ours seem to foster. I find it rather significant when Virgil Thomson says in an evaluation of Bartók early in 1946, "He thought of himself, I am sure, as always and predominantly a Hungarian; but he was in effect an internationalist and the inventor of one of the most widely practised international styles of the period between the two wars."

The fact that my profession happens to be one of translating into sound (and into *sense*, or—if you like—into *sound sense*) the symbols of the music page—this is not negligible either.

On my first acquaintance with Switzerland, its three-language system was one of the things that most impressed me. I rejoiced in its smooth working, in the way in which every official communication spoke equally to the German, the French, or the Italian language groups of the Confederation. Even the Romansch-speaking minority in the cantons of Grisons and Engadine got its linguistic due. Later, the liberality with which New York treated its not yet assimilated immigrant population struck me when I landed in the States in 1925. The notice boards in Central Park repeating the texts in Italian, Yiddish and German proved this attitude eloquently.*

On my successive visits to the Soviet Union I could follow the ever-greater recognition and freedom given by the Central Government to the numerous languages and literatures other than Russian. To cite only one small instance: when I first played in Kharkov in the middle 'twenties, my posters were in Russian only. On my subsequent annual visits, the Russian and the Ukrainian texts were printed side by side. The name of the theatre in which I had played had, meanwhile, also been changed; it now bore the name of a great Ukrainian national poet, Chevchenko.

My awareness of these signs of fair play and give-and-take became more and more pronounced through my travels, and I naturally was always on the look-out for examples of the contrary spirit, too. The almost universal use of old-style Gothic lettering in Germany seemed to me symbolic of an insular, barrier-creating, backward mentality. And, although reading this lettering never gave me any trouble, I felt happier when more and more important German publishers and

---

* How touching (and, one should perhaps add, daring) when Anne O'Hare McCormick speaks—apropos of the UNO's coming to these shores —of New York as "this towering cosmopolis, the magnificent mongrel bred of the blood and energy of all the races of the earth"!

papers began adopting the Latin alphabet during the hopeful and short-lived days of the Weimar Republic. *Insular* has always held for me a meaning of negation—though, oddly enough, this word (or rather *Islander*) happens to be precisely the literal meaning of the Hungarian word Szigeti!

The absence of this insular attitude and the degree of the artist's *Einfühlungsvermögen* (inadequately translated as "capacity for identification") always seemed to me the hallmark of an artist's worth, the yardstick of his stature. It was my explanation of his constantly reaching out for challenges ever farther from his original field or medium, or what we are pleased to call his congenial genre. The great painters who in all times have tried their hand on unsaleable subjects remote from their accredited genre were only striving to prove their mettle to themselves. Such great examples of artistic discipline looked down on me from every gallery wall. Yet beyond this subjective approach, when we turn to the concept of communication—the artist's communication with his audience —I think we find a similar urge, an urge to reach out for an ever wider and more universal audience than our performance was originally destined for, an urge to put our performances to the test in environments other than those in which, by the nature of things, they would be most certain of acceptance. Why otherwise would the number of languages into which an author is translated be so inordinately satisfying to him— so much more satisfying than the fact of going into more and more printings in the original language can ever be?

During the stir created by Kreisler's first performance of Elgar's Violin Concerto in London, in November, 1910 (a furore comparable to a Shostakovich première in our days though minus plane-transported microfilm and five-figure broadcast fees!), I was impressed chiefly by the fact that it was a *Viennese* who transmitted the Englishness of Elgar to England and to the rest of the world; this angle seemed to me to enhance the achievement. Likewise it pleased me to recall that it was the Hungarian (or, if you like, the Central European) Nikisch, who first brought fame to a symphonic work as English as Elgar's *Enigma* Variations and who revealed

Tchaikovsky's *Pathétique* not only to the whole of Europe but also to the Russians themselves, who had remained sceptical of the symphony after its unsuccessful première under the composer's baton.

Édouard Risler and Lucien Capet the Frenchmen, Toscanini the Italian, bringing Beethoven in its purest form to Germany; the miracles that the non-Latin Koussevitzky works with a score like Ravel's *Daphnis et Chloe*; a purebred New Englander like George Copeland or the German Gieseking capturing the very essence of Debussy's impressionism; Bruno Walter re-creating for us the devout Catholic mysticism of Bruckner—all these men proved to me that, especially in our domain, racial and national theories and prejudices that proclaim the predisposition of any one race or nation toward a given realm of art are completely invalidated. Křenek, writing of Gustav Mahler, draws a parallel between Mahler's activities in various parts of the "polyglot Empire" and his enhanced sense of *"universality* which is so characteristic of Mahler's music as well as of all truly symphonic music since Beethoven." When Henry Cowell asked me to record Charles Ives's Fourth Sonata, *Children's Day at a Camp Meeting*, and when the aged composer expressed his approval of my playing of this typical bit of "Americana," it meant more to me than, say, corresponding praise from my great countryman, Bartók.

I thought of how the intuitiveness of artists like Tairov and Alice Koonen revealed to me—over the barrier of a language I did not understand—the essential Americanism of Eugene O'Neill's *Desire Under the Elms* when they gave a Russian version of it in Moscow in the late 1920s. And I had to smile as I recalled an incident at a Kreisler rehearsal in the Paris Opéra one morning in the middle 1930's, which revealed the exact antithesis of this global thinking in literature, art, the theatre, and music. Kreisler was playing a concerto by Mozart (that "supreme internationalist and equalitarian in art," as Olin Downes felicitously put it)—playing with that intense, human mellowness of his which speaks to all peoples, to all classes, to all ages. The conductor was Philippe Gaubert, and his face, as well as those of the musicians, reflected the joy of participating in an ineffably beautiful musical moment. At last Gaubert could not contain himself any longer, and—even while conducting—blurted out: "How that man plays! How beautifully . . . *comme s'* . . . *il était français!*"

The insularity of that praise—which was intended to be all-encompassing—shattered the enchantment of the moment, for me at least. But I quickly recovered what the well-meaning Frenchman had made me lose. Kreisler was still playing, and I silently corrected Gaubert's *"comme s'il était français"* by going beyond that, beyond even Goethe's "Good European," to the highest rung of praise: "He plays like . . . a citizen of the world!"

APPENDIX

WHILE proof-reading these pages I received the first volume of Bela Bartók's letters ever to have been published (Hungarian Arts Council, Budapest, 1948, edited by Dr. James Demény), and almost the first page that catches my eye—on excitedly thumbing through the volume—is this excerpt from a letter to his mother dated December 30th, 1930: "The success in London was, it is true, rather big, but just a little *belated*—by some twenty-four years. . . ."

Which sets me wondering: by just how many years belated he would have found the present vogue of his works, the posthumous honours, the cyclical performances of his six quartets, the recent belated broadcast of *The Miraculous Mandarin* by Antal Dorati, the inscription of his name on one of the pillars of the balcony of the Amsterdam Concertgebouw, and one could go on.

The above excerpt, however, is one of the very rare instances when a glimpse of bitterness mingles with his philosophical resignation. He seemed to be always expecting the minimum, anticipating reserve, accepting lack of whole-hearted appreciation. Of bitterness there are few traces; when his assignment at Columbia University (an assignment to transcribe into musical notation hundreds of South Slav chanted epic poems assembled on thousands of phonograph records by Professor Parry of Harvard) was not renewed, he wrote to his son (October 17th, 1941):

> My activity at Columbia University will probably not be continued, which is more than aggravating because thus I will have to leave this very interesting work in July, 1942, in an unfinished state. Concerts are few and far between; if we had to live on these we would really be at the end of our tether.

This "very interesting work" was described in Bartók's letter as "that South Slavic material which I mentioned the other day (1600 and even many more heroic folk poems await their musical notation; a Harvard University Professor assembled this material on several thousand discs some five or six years ago)". For his work on this—as he calls it—"peerless" material he was "paid fifteen hundred dollars for half a year" and he adds, "Such material can only be found here, nowhere else in the world—and the Bulgarian material apart—*this* is what I missed so much on the other side, in Europe."

I cannot resist giving some other excerpts from this volume, especially as considerable time may elapse before its contents will be available in English.

The question of adequate rehearsal time, adequate preparation of his work always seemed to harass him. It was either that his work could not be given for lack of adequate rehearsal time, or that it *would* be given in spite of this lack!

So when the Italian conductor Egisto Tango (active in the Budapest Opera House) refused to produce the *Fából Faragott Királyfi* ("The Prince Carved of Wood") and the *Bluebeard's Castle* without first obtaining the promise of thirty rehearsals from the authorities, Bartók is full of praise and gratitude for him for his artistic integrity. "Imagine some other conductor—with less talent and less preparation than Tango—who would have slapped it together in five or six rehearsals! But how! May the Lord save us from such!" He mentions the fact as something extraordinary that Tango will "study the score for three weeks, whereas the former Budapest conductor used not even to glance at such scores, relying on the rehearsals to put *him* wise."

A letter dated August, 1905, from Paris, gives his mother the story of that Anton Rubinstein Composers' Contest in which Bartók lost to—a certain Brugnoli. True, neither the first nor the second prizes were given to any of the contestants, but still the "honorary diploma" was awarded to Brugnoli whose compositions young Bartók calls "completely worthless conglomerates, gathered together from everywhere. That the jury did not realize how much better my works were, *that* is the most scandalous aspect of the affair." (Chairman of the contest was Leopold Auer, who said: "Yes, this is the new trend, we are already too old for it." There were twelve jurors, among them the Paris conductor, Chevillard, and Hollander from Berlin.)

Although a slim volume of 140 pages of selected letters cannot attempt to cover forty-five years of a life such as Bartók's it gives a—to me—tremendously interesting and moving self-portrait of the man and artist. (Dr. Demény tells me that a second volume of letters is in preparation).

Time and again the puritanical simplicity and modesty of his life-pattern shows up. While composing his Divertimento for Strings (August, 1939) commissioned by Paul Sacher, the Basle conductor, he writes to his son from the chalet which the Sachers have placed at his disposal: "The caretaker cooks and cleans for me; she is a decent, nice woman, my every wish is like a command to her. The Sachers have even ordered a piano for me from Berne."

"Somehow I feel like an ancient musician whom his Maecenas

has invited! Work is progressing well; fortunately, I was able to finish the work of 25 minutes duration in fifteen days." And this significant aside: "Since 1934 I have been composing almost exclusively on a commission basis." With how little he seemed to be content! Being able, at long last, to work only on commission (from his 53rd year on!) is a fact he proudly notes as an achievement. And he also notes that "Casals is playing my Rhapsody everywhere in Europe" (the Rhapsody No. 1 dedicated to me and .ater transcribed by him him for 'cello). He took nothing for granted. He gravely mentions in 1922 that both *The Times*, the *Daily Telegraph* and *Daily Mail* wrote about him "favourably", that his London manager will bear the "risks" of his London concert, that he is receiving ten to fifteen pounds per concert!

The forty-one-year-old master writes to his mother from London like a novice (March 22nd, 1922): "It is quite a sensation that the papers write at such length about my first private concert. *The Times* wrote about it even for a second time. I am enclosing it, try and take it over to A—, perhaps someone will translate it for you. It is a great thing that the papers treat my coming here as if it were some extraordinary event. I would never have hoped for such a thing."

And from Malvern Wells on May 4th, 1923: "Just think, in England one can concertise even in such a beautiful, village-like place; I am playing here to-day at a girls' school!!"

In a letter to his mother (July 13th, 1931) there is this description:

There was a dinner party too, at the ——— minister's; only for me and for X, *chargé d'affaires*, with his wife (detestable female). The minister's wife is American, she only speaks "American" but made a great to-do about all things Hungarian.

The dinner consisted of such elaborately intricate delicacies that I can barely remember ever having eaten the like of such. There were five to six wine glasses by the side of each *convert*, all of expensive Venetian glass, with delphin bases, this kind and that kind. Before dinner an indefinably marvellous concoction: a cocktail (a sort of Schnapps) at the end of the meal—Tokay (naturally)! But the dinner was not pleasant in spite of all this, even apart from Madame X's ugly screechings; these smooth, slippery diplomats—they are such an artificial different sort, completely different from the artist-kind. The hotel is good, a quiet simple family affair, a sort of boarding-house, not too expensive.

It is the modesty of his material objectives which strikes the reader of these letters as so poignant! When in need of scientific materials for folklore research he calls his requirements of 600 blank phonograph cylinders per year at a pre-1914 price of 3 francs each (then about the equivalent of half-a-crown) an "unattainable budgetary goal" for the Hungarian State (in 1919)!

One is tempted to go on quoting, trying to pass on to others glimpses of the man! How revealing, for instance, this reply to a question whether it be true that Bartók intended leaving Hungary for good. On June 3rd, 1939, he writes from Budapest to the composer Veress in London: "If someone stays on here, when he could leave, he can thereby be said to *acquiesce tacitly* (italics mine) in everything that is happening here." And further on, in the same letter: "Did you hear about that interdiction of one of the Philharmonic concerts? They say the minister of 'a foreign country' (I wonder *which* country!) forced them to do this! Under such circumstances one can no longer undertake public appearances."

We know the rest of the story. He went to America and died there. Voluntary exile was his alternative to "tacit acquiescence".

INDEX

ACKNOWLEDGMENTS

The American Record Guide and its editor, Peter Hugh Reed, for permission to reprint an article of mine;

Sir Thomas Beecham and G. P. Putnam & Co., for permission to quote from *A Mingled Chime*;

John Murray & Co., for permission to quote from Walter F. Starkie's *Raggle-Taggle*;

Carl Fischer, Inc., for permission to quote from *The Art of Violin Playing, Book Two,* "Artistic Realization and Instruction" by Carl Flesch;

Jarrolds & Co., for permission to quote from James Agate's *Playgoing*, a part of "The Pleasure of Life" series;

Harper and Brothers for permission to quote from Albert Jay Nock's *Memoirs of a Superfluous Man*;

Alfred A. Knopf, Inc., for permission to quote from Thomas Mann's *The Magic Mountain*;

Rudolf Kolisch and G. Schirmer, Inc., for permission to quote from Mr. Kolisch's article, "Tempo and Character in Beethoven's Music," originally published in *The Music Quarterly*;

Listen, and its editor, Kurt List, for permission to reprint two articles of mine that appeared in that magazine;

Longmans, Green & Co., Inc., for permission to quote from Bernard Shore's *The Orchestra Speaks*;

W. W. Norton and Co., Inc., for permission to quote from Nicholas Slonimsky's *Music Since 1900*;

Hugues Panassié for permission to quote from *Hot Jazz*, published by M. Witmark & Sons; Hugues Panassié and Smith and Durrell, Inc., for permission to quote from *The Real Jazz*;

Princeton University Press for permission to quote from Artur Schnabel's *Music and the Line of Most Resistance*;

Simon & Schuster, Inc., for permission to quote from *Stravinsky: an Autobiography*;

The Viking Press, Inc., for permission to quote from Sam Franko's *Chords and Discords*.